THE CYCLADES IN THE BRONZE AGE

The Cyclades
in the Bronze Age

R.L.N. BARBER

Duckworth

First published in 1987 by
Gerald Duckworth & Co. Ltd.
The Old Piano Factory
43 Gloucester Crescent, London NW1

First translation on p. vii: reprinted from *The Axion Esti*
by Odysseus Elytis, trans. E. Keeley & G. Savidis,
by permission of the University of Pittsburgh Press.
© 1974 by E. Keeley & G. Savidis

ISBN 0 7156 2160 2

British Library Cataloguing in Publication Data

Barber, R.L.N.
   The Cyclades in the Bronze Age.
   1. Cyclades—History
   I. Title
   939′.15   DF901.C9

ISBN 0-7156-2160-2

Photoset in North Wales by
Derek Doyle & Associates, Mold, Clwyd
and printed in Great Britain by
Ebenezer Baylis & Son Limited, Worcester

To Olga

Τότε εἶπε καὶ γεννήθηκεν ἡ θάλασσα
Καὶ εἶδα καὶ θαύμασα
Καὶ στὴ μέση της ἔσπειρε κόσμους μικροὺς κατ᾽ εἰκόνα καὶ ὁμοίωσή μου:
Ἵπποι πέτρινοι μὲ τὴ χαίτη ὀρθὴ
καὶ γαλήνιοι ἀμφορεῖς
καὶ λοξὲς δελφινιῶν ράχες
ἡ Ἴος ἡ Σίκινος ἡ Σέριφος ἡ Μῆλος
"Κάθε λέξη κι ἀπό 'να χελιδόνι
γιὰ νὰ σοῦ φέρνει τὴν ἄνοιξη μέσα στὸ θέρος,, εἶπε
Καὶ πολλὰ τὰ λιόδεντρα
ποὺ νὰ κρησάρουν στὰ χέρια τους τὸ φῶς
κι ἐλαφρὸ ν᾽ ἁπλώνεται στὸν ὕπνο σου
καὶ πολλὰ τὰ τζιτζίκια
ποὺ νὰ μὴν τὰ νιώθεις
ὅπως δὲ νιώθεις τὸ σφυγμὸ στὸ χέρι σου
ἀλλὰ λίγο τὸ νερὸ
γιὰ νὰ τό 'χεις Θεὸ καὶ νὰ κατέχεις τί σημαίνει ὁ λόγος του
καὶ τὸ δέντρο μονάχο του
χωρὶς κοπάδι
γιὰ νὰ τὸ κάνεις φίλο σου
καὶ νὰ γνωρίζεις τ᾽ ἀκριβό του τ᾽ ὄνομα
φτενὸ στὰ πόδια σου τὸ χῶμα
γιὰ νὰ μὴν ἔχεις ποῦ ν᾽ ἁπλώσεις ρίζα
καὶ νὰ τραβᾶς τοῦ βάθους ὁλοένα
καὶ πλατὺς ἐπάνου ὁ οὐρανὸς
γιὰ νὰ διαβάζεις μόνος σου τὴν ἀπεραντοσύνη

ΑΥΤΟΣ
ὁ κόσμος ὁ μικρός, ὁ μέγας!
(from O. Elytes, *To axion esti*)

*

τὰ καλοκαίρια χανόμασταν μέσα στὴν ἀγωνία τῆς μέρας
ποὺ δὲν μποροῦσε νὰ ξεψυχήσει.

Φέραμε πίσω
αὐτὰ τ᾽ ἀνάγλυφα μιᾶς τέχνης ταπεινῆς.
(from G. Seferes, 'Mythistorema')

Then he spoke and the sea was born
And I gazed upon it and marvelled
In its centre he sowed little worlds in my image and likeness:
Horses of stone with manes erect
and tranquil amphorae
and slanting backs of dolphins
Ios, Sikinos, Serifos, Milos
"Each word a swallow
to bring you spring in the midst of summer," he said
And ample the olive trees
to sift the light through their fingers
that it may spread gently over your sleep
and ample the cicadas
which you will feel no more
than you feel the pulse inside your wrist
but scarce the water
so that you hold it a God and understand the meaning of its voice
and the tree alone
no flock beneath it
so that you take it for a friend
and know its precious name
sparse the earth beneath your feet
so that you have no room to spread your roots
and keep reaching down in depth
and broad the sky above
so that you read the infinite on your own
THIS WORLD
this small world the great!

(tr. Edmund Keeley and George Savvides)

*

On winter nights the strong wind from the east maddened us,
in the summers we were lost in the agony of the day which could not die

We brought back
these carved reliefs of a humble art.

(tr. Edmund Keeley and Philip Sherrard)

Contents

Illustrations

Preface

The contributions of others to an undertaking whose origins reach back nearly twenty years are many and sometimes profound. My parents cannot now share the satisfaction of a project completed but, without their unstinting support, it would never even have been begun. My research supervisor, Hector Catling, was a source of inspiration, not least in his humane attitude to the interpretation of archaeological evidence, so rare these days. To the late Jack Caskey, I feel a similar debt. At a practical level, the help of many colleagues and friends, especially in the Greek Archaeological Service, is gratefully, if not always individually, acknowledged.

Perversely, I have sought little comment and criticism and the defects of this work are thus peculiarly my own. Kerin Hope read drafts of the first few chapters and gave me good advice, though the final result is very different from what either of us anticipated. The anonymous reader of the Iowa University Press, whose identity I suspect but remains concealed in the bibliography, was generous and offered corrections and suggestions which have mostly been incorporated with thanks.

Olga Filaniotou made me believe that I had done something worthwhile and to her I dedicate this book.

R.L.N.B.

Acknowledgments

I am indebted to Mrs Seferiades for permission to quote from G. Seferes' poem *Mythistorema* and to Mr Elytes for the passage from his *Axion Esti*. My thanks are due to Messrs Keeley, Savvides and Sherrard for allowing me to use their translations of these passages. I was very pleased to learn that the lines chosen were ones for which Mr Elytes and Professor Keeley have special affection.

Mr K. Zachos has kindly allowed me to mention some unpublished finds from his excavations on Naxos and, likewise, the Cycladic Ephorate (Mrs Hadjianastasiou, Mrs Zapheiropoulou) some results of our joint work at Mikre Vigla on the same island.

Preparation and acquisition of illustrations is a large task and I am obliged to several people for help. I am particularly grateful to Angela Wardell who, with Derrick Gannon, made virtually all the drawings, to Joe Rock and Sheila Lithgow who processed photographs and copy-proofs, and to Tucker Blackburn who must have put herself to considerable inconvenience to supply what I wanted with such speed and efficiency.

In this context I thank too the American School of Classical Studies at Athens, Keith Branigan, the British School at Athens, Ann Brown, John Cherry, Brian Cook, Jim Coulton, Katy Demakopoulou-Papantoniou, Christos Doumas, Lesley Fitton, Noel Gale, Pat Getz-Preziosi, The Goulandris Museum of Cycladic Art, the Greek Archaeological Society, Olga Hadjianastasiou, Euan McKie, Nanno Marinatos, Marisa Marthari, Clairy Palyvou, Colin Renfrew, Chris Scarre, Dimitri Schilardi, Elizabeth Schofield, Ann Thomas, Robin Torrence, the University of Cincinnati, Martha Wiencke, Michael Vickers and Carol Zerner.

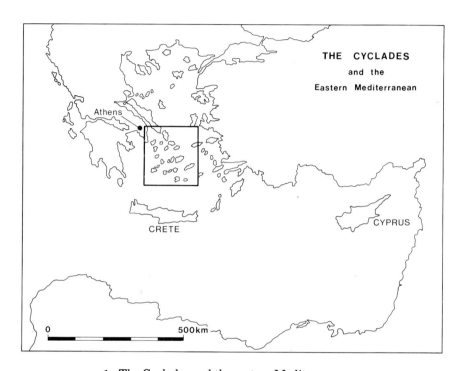

1. The Cyclades and the eastern Mediterranean.

1

The Cyclades: Ancient and Modern

Ancient writers explain the name Cyclades as inspired by the circular pattern formed by the islands round the sacred centre of Delos (Fig. 2). Spreading out south-eastwards from mainland Greece into the Aegean, they are in fact the peaks of submerged mountain ridges, whose westerly limits are the island of Euboea and the peninsulas of Attica and Methana. They stand on a relatively shallow submarine platform, which is separated by deeper channels from the islands to the east (Ikaria, Samos) and south (the Dodecanese, Crete) and, in this sense at least, are a distinct group.

Seen from the sea or air beneath the hot summer sun, the Cyclades present a dry, barren but none the less enchanting face to the visitor. In the poem quoted above, Odysseus Elytes has captured, more effectively than any prose analysis, the essential qualities of the landscape and life of the islands. He sees them scattered on the sea like seeds, their mountain spines arching upwards – like the manes of stone horses or the slanting backs of dolphins. Flat land is scarce. At closer hand, water is short, trees rare, the soil thin and stony. But nature provides some compensations too. The shade of an olive tree protects one's summer rest from the sun – and the hardy tree itself is peculiarly suited to the rugged background of the Cyclades.[1] This patchwork of impressions elegantly evokes not only their austere but compelling natural beauty but also some of those elemental influences which, unchanged since remote antiquity, have shaped local culture and the way of life. Such influences are visible still in the architecture of island villages and where traditional customs survive as originally shaped by the environment.

There has however been much change in the Cyclades in recent times – especially in the last thirty years, during which the population[2] has fallen from a level only a few per cent below its late-nineteenth-century peak by a further 30 per cent. The causes and symptoms of the exodus are many; some obvious, some less so, and most beyond the scope of this book. But two aspects stand out, as vital now as in prehistoric times – communications and agriculture.

The sea and air communications which now facilitate the departure of people also encourage the importation of food; so less is produced locally

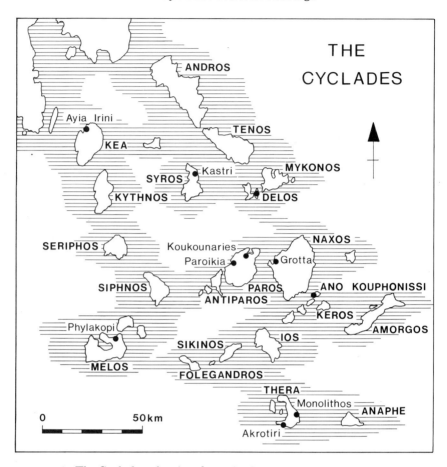

2. The Cyclades, showing the main sites mentioned in the text.

and less manpower is needed. The lack of manpower, whether because of literal absence or disinclination, leaves visible marks in the countryside – in neglected fields certainly, but more particularly in the decay of the terraces, so unfamiliar a sight in western Europe, so essential a feature of the Greek landscape, where they retain earth on substantial areas of sloping hillside which would otherwise lose their soil and become uncultivable. The terraced cliffside below the Chora on Folegandros (Fig. 3) is a remarkable instance of the extent to which sheer and unpromising areas of land can be reclaimed for agriculture in this way.

Terrain, agriculture and farming

The agricultural potential[3] of the Cyclades is closely related to their

3. Folegandros, terracing below the Chora.

climate and physical character. The latter differs a good deal from island to island, adding greatly to their appeal, as any visitor soon finds. In size, they range from Delos (not quite the smallest) with an area of $2\frac{1}{4}$ square miles, to Naxos (170 square miles). Even within individual islands there are extreme contrasts both in steepness of terrain and quality of vegetation. Northern Syros (Fig. 32) is bleak, high and harbourless, while the south is much flatter, easier to farm and with readier access to the sea. There is a somewhat similar contrast between northern and southern Andros, though the Chora valley itself is much the richest area there. Coasts are often high and steep. The cliffs of south-east Amorgos or of Folegandros are forbidding. On the other hand there are some fine deep and sheltered harbours – on Kea, Paros, Ios and Amorgos (Fig. 4), for example. These are particularly attractive to modern shipping, though small and protected beaches (as those with which the unexcavated Bronze Age settlement at Mikre Vigla on Naxos is provided: Fig. 5) would have been equally satisfactory for the slighter craft of prehistoric times.

In spite of the miles of high and rocky coastline, there are some sizable stretches of coastal plain – especially in south-west Naxos (Fig. 6) and reaching back behind the larger bays in other islands. There the land is often flat and fertile. Inland, the Cyclades are always mountainous but they vary in the extent to which the barren heights are alleviated by zones of flat land. This aspect is also related to size. Thus Naxos has quite extensive areas of inland plain (the Tragaia: Fig. 7); Paros has a

4. The bay of Katapola, Amorgos.

5. Beach to the south of Mikre Vigla, Naxos.

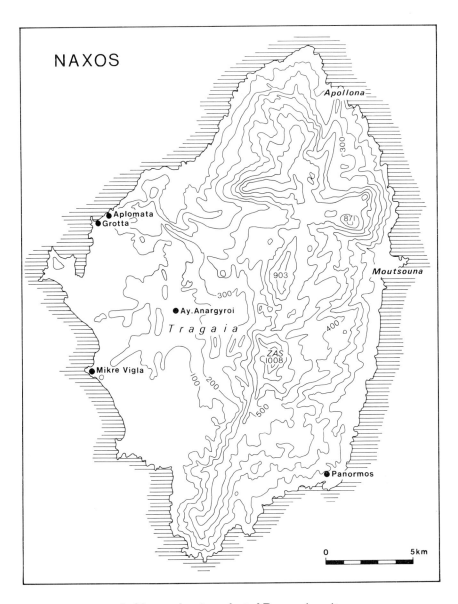

NAXOS

Apollona

Aplomata
Grotta

Moutsouna

Ay.Anargyroi

T r a g a i a

Mikre Vigla

ZAS
1008

Panormos

0   5 km

6. Naxos, showing selected Bronze Age sites.

steep mountain spine, but lower-lying land at its periphery; Seriphos a
good plain behind its port Livadhi, but no other flat or substantial tracts
of farmland. All the islands, to a greater or lesser extent, are terraced to
permit the cultivation of land other than that in the level and readily
workable areas. The crucial role of this feature in island agriculture has
already been pointed out and can profitably be re-emphasised. In the

7. The Tragaia, Naxos, looking west.

modern context, however, we need to bear in mind that the use of fertilisers has to some extent compensated for the loss of fields by allowing greater yields from those that remain under cultivation.

In the sheltered inland parts of the larger islands, like Naxos, Andros and Tenos, there are some wooded areas. Elsewhere trees are not thickly spread, except in specially protected spots – though olives are hardy, if unobtrusive, and tamarisks sometimes line the waterfront, as at Adhamata on Melos. It is not entirely clear how accurately the present state of tree cover reflects the situation in the Bronze Age.[4] Certainly the clearance of wooded areas for cultivation which had begun in the Neolithic period continued, and the depredations went on into later times. Wood was used too for building houses and ships, also for fuel, and felled timber was not replanted. Goats as well are particularly destructive of vegetation. It is however possible that the exposed Cycladic slopes never supported extensive tree cover, though the more thickly wooded islands in the northern Aegean, like Skiathos and Skopelos, Thassos and Samothrace, suggest the possibility of quite extensive forests, at least on islands where there was a reasonable rainfall.

Although regular large-scale importation of food into the Cyclades has brought about a radical decline in the intensity of agricultural activity and mechanisation has, to some extent, changed its style, age-old practices still continue[5] and can be a fascinating and informative guide to the past. Indeed the limited scale of many agricultural operations and the hard terrain often prevent the introduction of modern machinery and methods.

The main grain crop in the Bronze Age, as now, was barley. Pulses were cultivated and grapes and olives were also important. Since basic agricultural activities are largely conditioned by climate and geography, it is unlikely that they have changed radically, though it is impossible to deduce the extent to which methods like crop-rotation and fallow may have been employed in the past.

Cycladic summers are long, hot and dry; the winters short, mild and quite wet, and the present climate does not appear to be significantly different from prehistoric times.[6] Such conditions encourage a system of 'dry-farming' where land has to be ploughed frequently in order to reduce moisture-loss from the soil. This treatment is applied in various ways. Fallow land is given several ploughings during the time it is not sown. Land to be planted with a crop that will not mature until late in the summer is given repeated ploughings earlier in the year to ensure a supply of moisture, even in high summer. A form of ploughing or furrowing may take place between olive trees, for the same reason. Even land which is treated in more ordinary fashion will receive one main ploughing and a second to accompany the sowing. The main grain crop is sown late in the year, when ploughing has followed the autumn rains, and is harvested in early to mid-summer. It is possible also to sow in spring for a second crop, though the conditions are obviously less favourable then.

Pulse crops require an approximately similar regime. Olives and vines, once established, need mainly care and maintenance; the grapes being harvested in August/September and the olives later in the autumn.

Simple ploughs were probably available in Bronze Age times, or other digging tools (Fig. 8, no. 2) could have been used. Both these kinds of equipment are still in use. Crops were reaped with sickles: there are some ancient examples in bronze (Fig. 8, no. 3), while others may have been formed of obsidian blades set in a wooden handle (Fig. 8, no. 1). Threshing floors must have existed in some form, almost certainly the same circular paved shapes that remain a prominent feature of the Greek landscape (Fig. 9), since animals can thus be readily employed to beat a path round the central pole. Winnowing needs only a wooden fork (and some wind). Granaries for storage may be represented in some Bronze Age models.

The harvesting of other crops – vegetables, grapes or olives – does not require the use of specialised equipment, and the subsequent treatment, storage and use[7] of many agricultural commodities involves simple artefacts and processes which are to be seen in peasant households the world over.

Grain mills for grinding grain to produce flour are commonly found, as are spindlewhorls and loomweights for the preparation and weaving of yarn. From other areas of the Aegean, Bronze Age presses for the production of olive oil and wine are known. Examples have not yet been

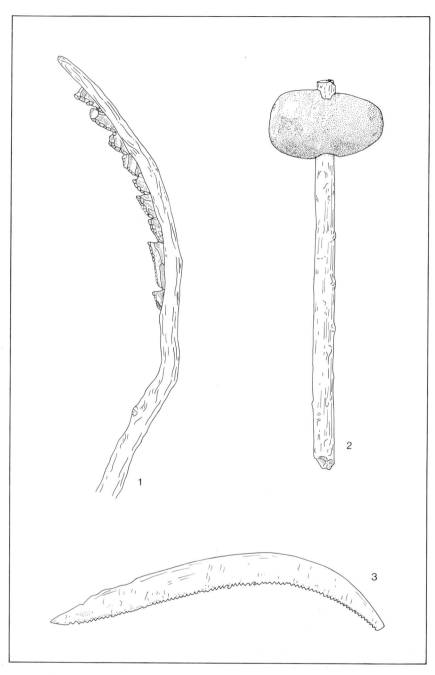

8. Prehistoric agricultural implements: 1. Sickle – modern reconstruction with stone (including obsidian) blades set in a wooden handle; 2. Axe-head with modern haft; 3. Sickle blade (bronze). (1, 2. After Theochares 1973 figs. 120, 246b; 3. After Marinatos 1968-76, IV, pl. 89b.)

9. Threshing floor on Melos.

found in the Cyclades, but no doubt they existed. Modern peasants can still be seen treading their grapes in permanent stone tanks in the corners of the fields – surrounded by wasps and with the raw juice trickling out into an earthenware jar.

Other items do not survive (the ovens for baking, the looms (Fig. 10) to which the weights belonged); and others again (containers for the various commodities) are not specifically recognisable among the numerous varieties of pottery. Wooden vessels and baskets (Fig. 11), both commonly used today, are only preserved from prehistory in exceptional conditions.

All the produce mentioned is simple and the various uses are mostly evident, but one – olive oil – has many more applications than we might immediately recognise. It can be used as a food, in place of butter, for cooking, as soap, as a body ointment or as fuel for lamps.

Animals[8] are the farmer's other chief preoccupation – for meat, milk, wool, skins and traction and transport. Cattle have always been relatively rare in the islands and goats and sheep most common, with a few pigs. Oxen were probably used mainly for traction (for drawing ploughs or carts: Fig. 12) as they still sometimes are. Recent research on Melos[9] has shown a superficially rather surprising increase in the numbers of cattle at the time (Middle Bronze Age) when settlement on the island had become concentrated in one main centre rather than being

10. Loom on an Attic black-figure vase of the sixth century BC. (British Museum).

11. Basket, restored in plaster, from Akrotiri, Thera. (C. Doumas).

12. Ploughing with oxen on an Attic black-figure vase of the sixth century BC. (British Museum).

dispersed in a number of smaller ones, as previously. This is thought to be the result of a greater need for transport, with farmers now having to travel some distance from the town to work the fields. Donkeys are known elsewhere in Greece by this time and were on Melos at least by the beginning of the Late Bronze Age.

In general, it seems likely that, from the Middle Bronze Age, much agricultural activity was organised in this way and, once again, contemporary parallels are illuminating. Farmers today often work their lands from a village base, though they frequently maintain small steadings in the fields as stores for equipment or for occasional accommodation. Such buildings can be seen scattered over island landscapes. Evidence for Bronze Age farmsteads is rare, but two on Thera, one of which included a byre for animals, are discussed in Chapter 4.

At the fifth millennium (Neolithic) settlement on Saliagos, near Antiparos, bone finds showed that fishing[10] was an important element in the economy. Fishhooks and some scenes of fish and fishermen on Bronze Age vases and frescoes (Fig. 13) show that it was important then too, though finds from Phylakopi suggest that this was not true of that important coastal town.

13. The Fishermen Vase from Phylakopi, Melos. (Atkinson *et al.* 1904 pl. XXII).

Non-agricultural resources[11]

Building stone is one commodity in which the Cyclades abound, and the
varying petrological characters of the different islands are reflected in the
construction of their buildings (Figs. 14-16). Flat schist slabs in neat
courses make up the walls of the houses on Kea, rounded sea boulders
with mortar and small wedging stones in the interstices the buildings on
Melos, and blocks of volcanic rock some of the settlement at Akrotiri.

In fact the geology of the islands is quite varied. The rocks are mainly
ancient and crystalline, but those of the southern arc (Melos,
Folegandros, Sikinos, Thera) are volcanic.

Several islands have marble sources. These were not used for building
but the best material (from Naxos and Paros) was employed for the
manufacture of the fine stone vases and figurines of the EC I-II periods
(e.g. Figs. 70-73, 94-96). Marble does not appear to have been much, if at
all, used thereafter until the Archaic period (seventh-sixth centuries
BC). Emery, which was used as an abrasive in the working of marble,
and for tools as well, is found on Naxos and Sikinos.

Melos is the main Aegean source of obsidian (Figs. 88-92) – the hard
volcanic glass which was of great importance as a basic material for the
production of tools and weapons. It was of particular significance in the
Early Bronze Age, when metal was still relatively rare, and is common in

14. Early Bronze Age buildings at Ayia Irini, Kea. (University of Cincinnati).

15. Late Cycladic fortification wall at Phylakopi, Melos. (C. Renfrew).

16. Ashlar construction at Akrotiri, Thera.

later Bronze Age contexts too. Obsidian was widely exported in the Bronze Age and control of the prime source was a key factor in the history of Melos and its main settlement, Phylakopi, as well as of the island group as a whole.

There is a good deal of evidence for the existence of metalliferous ores in the Cyclades. This comes from ancient, though post-prehistoric, literary sources, modern workings and analysis of archaeologically recovered artefacts. The deposits include lead, silver, copper and gold (as well as iron, which was not used until the very end of the Bronze Age). Signs of prehistoric mining activity have so far been found only on Siphnos (silver), Kythnos (copper) and possibly Seriphos (copper), but it seems very likely that other sources of copper, now worked out, were exploited, particularly in the Early Bronze Age when the Cyclades were prominent in metallurgical developments.

Other local resources include the salt of Melos and Naxos and the millstone rock of Melos.

Communications

The question of land communications has already been touched on in relation to the need for transport of equipment and produce to and from distant fields. Footpaths or plain levelled trackways leave no trace or continue in use without any sign of their ancient origin, and there is as

17. Mycenaean roadway, Grotta,   18. Calderimi on Seriphos.
Naxos. (Courtesy O. Hadjianastasiou).

yet no evidence of built country roads in the Cycladic Bronze Age. That such could have existed is suggested not only by the paved streets at Mycenaean Grotta (Naxos: Fig. 17) and the substantial remains of roads of this period elsewhere in the Aegean, but also by the fine built tracks (calderimia) of the Ottoman period which honeycomb every island (Fig. 18), though many are now either in decay or replaced by modern roads.

More important, however, were sea-borne contacts. Boats could have been used for local communications, as well as more distant trips to other islands or still further afield. Even today, transport between two points on the same island can be easier by sea than land. Steamers call at both Katapola and Aiyiali on Amorgos and smaller boats ply the same route.

There is no lack of evidence for Bronze Age shipping[12] in the Aegean. Melian obsidian must have been transported by sea to the Franchthi cave in the north-eastern Peloponnese, where it probably occurs as early as the eleventh millennium, and certainly by 7000 BC. Later on, more obsidian and other Cycladic artefacts abroad and foreign objects in the islands provide more abundant proof. For the ships themselves, there are models and drawings of oar-powered vessels and steering oars from the Early Bronze Age (Fig. 19). By the beginning of the Late Bronze Age, the Thera frescoes[13] show ships (Fig. 126) which are sophisticated in both construction and finish. They have decks with cabins, both rowers and sails, and elaborate adornment.

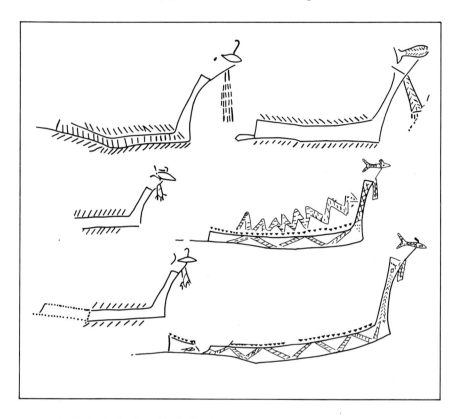

19. Ships incised on Early Cycladic vases. (After Tsountas 1899, 90).

We have already given some consideration to island harbours. There were a good many places suitable for beaching boats, even if the number of deep sheltered bays is limited. Although the latter are most suitable for modern shipping and would have been attractive to prehistoric sailors, they were by no means essential. In some cases the extra time needed to sail into a deep gulf may have been a positive disincentive to establishing a port there, unless there were other advantages as well. The main site on Melos, Phylakopi, is a good example. The island is almost cut in two by a fine deep gulf (used as a naval base in the First World War: Fig. 20) but Phylakopi itself is on the relatively exposed north coast. In fact, the coastline has changed considerably since the Bronze Age[14] when the site would have been on a short promontory, itself sheltering a small but perfectly adequate harbour on the landward side (Fig. 21). Here there was ready access to the open sea, whereas a harbour on the inner gulf would have added up to an hour's extra sailing time onto every journey.

Ancient navigation, when we have documentary evidence, seems to

20. The gulf of Melos from the south.

21. Phylakopi, Melos, from the south. The lighter area shows the site of the original harbour. (C. Renfrew).

have been a seasonal affair, with a close season lasting approximately from October to May. In the fairer months, when sudden squalls can still make travelling dangerous, sailing cannot have been too different from today. It is necessary always to keep in sight of land and suitable shelter. For this reason the islands were crucial links in the chain of communications between the Greek Mainland, Crete and more distant lands.

Both the prevailing winds of the sailing season and the general direction of Aegean currents (north-south) make southerly journeys much faster and easier than those to the north. There were probably fixed routes and calling places, which we may eventually be able to trace. One such route has already been tentatively identified[15] in the period at the beginning of the Late Bronze Age, when the islands were dominated by Crete. The main pattern of Cretan influence may be reflected in a sailing/trade route which was directed from Crete, first through Thera, and then up the western Cyclades (Melos, Kea) to Mainland Greece. A route to the Argolid (Mycenae, Tiryns etc.) from central rather than western Crete, would also have passed through some of these islands. A Chania (western Crete)-Peloponnese route is suggested by Cretan finds from the island of Kythera, and from Messenia and Lakonia.

Seamanship is endemic in island life (the original inhabitants must themselves have arrived by sea) and shipping is likely to have been a major factor in the prosperity of the Cyclades. In the Early Bronze Age they were probably more advanced in this respect than any other part of the Aegean – the export of Cycladic products and the establishment of Cycladic settlers on both Crete and the Mainland bear witness to this. With the later development of contacts between those two areas, their superior skills remained in demand and they must have prospered as carriers and middlemen. A very attractive theory, proposed some years ago[16] (Ovenden) set the naming of the constellations on the island of Astypalaia (south east of Amorgos) in the Bronze Age. This theory is not susceptible of absolute proof but is based partly on local place names which might conceivably have survived since the Bronze Age; also on the argument that the constellation names are much more appropriate to the shapes which would have been seen by an observer in the Aegean in the Bronze Age than at any other place and period. The idea fits neatly with the concept of a shipping service dominated by islanders.

Conclusion

Evidence for those basic aspects of Cycladic life which have been surveyed in this chapter is still incomplete. In time we should learn more about the character of the prehistoric landscape, the nature and treatment of animal and vegetable products, and the use of other natural resources. The precise character and intensity of land and sea communications is another topic for investigation.

But Cycladic life is shaped by the physical character of the islands, their climate and native resources – factors which remain essentially unchanged since the Bronze Age. Thus traditional practices, which were developed in response to just these conditions, still survive to some degree. Here we have a valuable source of extra information, although care is needed in its use for the introduction of modern elements can easily distort the picture. Peasants still employing traditional methods of cultivation may ride to their fields on motorcycles, saving a very high proportion of normal travelling time. Fertilisers alter the yield or the very feasibility of a crop. The internal combustion engine entirely changes the range and flexibility of quite small craft, whose dynamics, in any case, should have been much improved by the application of millennia of research!

Nevertheless, the assessment of the essential qualities of the Bronze Age environment of the Cyclades as not radically different from today's seems secure. We must therefore not neglect the contemporary landscape and the way of life of its inhabitants, though they have to be viewed with both the archaeological evidence and the limitations of a pre-industrial society in mind. We can return again to the words of Elytes, not primarily as beguiling reflections of the poet's art, but as leading us directly to the unchanging heart of Cycladic life.

2

The Bronze Age Sequence in the Cyclades[1]

Introduction

This chapter contains an outline of the Bronze Age sequence in the Cyclades and the archaeological evidence on which it is based. The finds and other aspects of Cycladic culture, as well as a more detailed consideration of historical events and developments, will be found in subsequent chapters.

In archaeological discussion, the term 'Cycladic' is reserved for the Bronze Age culture of the Cyclades. A historical framework (Fig. 22) is provided by a basic subdivision into Early, Middle and Late phases which are themselves further subdivided, where appropriate.

The Cyclades in the Bronze Age were part of a larger Aegean cultural family with which they had relations of varying intensity throughout the period. Some appreciation of the civilisations of Crete (Minoan) and Mainland Greece (Helladic, with the term Mycenaean as a synonym for Late Helladic) is essential for understanding the culture and history of the islands, since each of them in turn exerted considerable influence on the Cyclades.

In the Early Bronze Age (Early Minoan and Early Helladic periods) both Crete and the Mainland had essentially village-based societies. At the end of the Early Bronze Age in Crete, developments began which led to the establishment of the Minoan palaces and the palace-based society of the Middle Minoan and early Late Minoan periods. The Cretan palaces were all destroyed by the early fourteenth century BC (LM IIIA) and Minoan culture then continued in a still sophisticated but no longer palace-centred form.

The Mainland maintained a relatively simple standard of living in the Middle Bronze Age (Middle Helladic) until increasing contacts with Crete induced spectacular progress, culminating in the rise of Mycenaean palace civilisation after 1600 BC (Late Helladic or Mycenaean). Mycenaean power supplanted Minoan in the Aegean in the

B.C. (approx)	Cycladic Period		Settlement Phases	External Contacts	
				Mainland	Crete
3000	LNII		Kephala Ayia Irini I (?)		
	ECI		Phylakopi Pre-City (A1)	EHI	EMI
2600	ECI/II		Kampos Ano Kouphonissi		EMIIA
	ECII		Phylakopi I-i (A2) Ayia Irini II	EHII	EMIIB
2300					
	ECIIIA		Ayia Irini III Mt. Kynthos B Kastri Christiana	EHIII	EMIII
	ECIIIB	early	Phylakopi I-ii	early	MMIA
			Paroikia		MMIB
1800		late	Phylakopi I-iii	middle	
	MC	early	Phylakopi II-ii Ayia Irini IV	MH	MMIIA
					MMIIB
		late	Phylakopi II-iii Ayia Irini V	late	MMIII
1550					
	LCI		Akrotiri – early destn. Phylakopi III-i Ayia Irini VI Akrotiri – final destn.	LHI	LMIA
1500					
	LCII		Phylakopi III-ii Ayia Irini VII	LHIIA	LMIB
1450				LHIIB	LMII
	LCIII	early	Phylakopi III-iii early Ayia Irini VIII early Grotta	LHIIIA	LMIII
1250				LHIIIB1	
		middle	Ayios Andreas Koukounaries occ.	2	
				early tower	
			Koukounaries destn. Phylakopi shrine coll.	developed	
1100		late	Koukounaries reocc. Aplomata Kamini	LHIIIC	advanced
		final	Ayia Irini shrine-latest	final	

22. The Cycladic Bronze Age, site phases and relative chronology.

AYIA IRINI, KEA

Period (Ceramic Phase)	Select Archaeological Features	Cycladic Period
I (A)		LN II / EC I?
II (B)	Buildings	EC II
III (C)	'Anatolian' pottery Temporary abandonment	EC IIIA
IV (D)	Reoccupation Construction of fortifications	(EC IIIB?) MC early
V (F)	New fortifications	MC late
VI (G)	LC 'Houses'	LC I
VII (H)	Earthquake destruction	LC II
VIII (J, K, L, M)	Partial reconstruction Last use of shrine Desertion of site	LC III – early – middle – late – final

23. Ayia Irini, Kea, main features of the archaeological sequence.

later fifteenth century BC, but the Mycenaean palaces were themselves destroyed by unknown agency about 1200 BC. After this there was a brief revival of Mycenaean culture ('post-palatial'), until it faded away in the earlier eleventh century.

Our detailed understanding of developments in the Cyclades depends essentially on long occupation sequences at the two most fully investigated sites – Phylakopi on Melos (excavated 1896-9, 1911, 1974-7) and Ayia Irini on Kea (excavated 1960-71; publication in progress). Other sites which are less well known can be related to these. The spectacular settlement at Akrotiri on Thera is now of crucial significance for an appreciation of Bronze Age life in the Cyclades and, although at present providing information chiefly about the first phase of the Late Bronze Age, can be expected in due course to produce further important information about the earlier periods as well.

The major features of the sequences at Ayia Irini and Phylakopi are illustrated in summary form in Figs. 23 and 24.

PHYLAKOPI, MELOS

City	Select Archaeological Features	EC Period
Pre – City (AI)		EC I
I – i (A2)		EC II
– ii (B)		EC IIIA (?) / B
– iii	Destruction of settlement	EC IIIB
II – ii (C)	Rebuilding. First fortifications (?)	MC – early
– iii	Destruction of settlement	MC – late
III – i (D)	Rebuilding – Mansion; Fortifications	LC I
– ii	Partial destruction (burning)	LC II
– iii (E)	Megaron Shrine; Fortifications Shrine destruction Desertion of site	LC III – early – middle – late – ?

24. Phylakopi, Melos, main features of the archaeological sequence.

Chronology, relative and absolute[2]

Throughout most of the Cycladic Bronze Age it is possible to establish the relationship of the Cycladic sequence to those of Crete and Mainland Greece by observing the points at which distinctive artefacts (especially pottery types) imported from one area are found in another. Thus the Cycladic periods can be reasonably well dated in relative terms.

Absolute dates can be established either by similar contacts when they occur with civilisations which have written historical records or by modern scientific techniques, such as Carbon 14 dating.

The Cyclades have almost no direct contacts of the first kind, though dates so calculated for Cretan and Mainland periods on the basis of Egyptian connections can be applied to the Cyclades at one remove.

A similar situation obtains in the case of C 14 dating. Very few dates are so far available for the Cycladic Bronze Age, though Cretan and Mainland dates can be applied relatively.

The C 14 system is in fact of limited interest for the absolute chronology of the Aegean Bronze Age since the dates it produces have a wide margin of error, whereas the Egyptian links provide good historical dates from the mid-second millennium, and reasonable indications even before that time.

Terminology[3]

The terminology in which the archaeology of the prehistoric Cyclades has been traditionally described – and the terminology to which this book subscribes – is based on the view that Cycladic culture, at least in the Early and Middle Bronze Age, has a distinct, unified and localised character within which certain chronological stages are discernible, as well as on the broader assumption that the objectives of the archaeologist should be primarily historical. Hence the use of the descriptive term 'Cycladic' and the basic chronological periods Early, Middle and Late, with further divisions (I, II, III) and subdivisions (A, B) as required.

In recent years, a number of new terms (Fig. 25) have been introduced, which particularly affect discussion of the Early Cycladic period and render the existing body of literature very confusing to those approaching it for the first time.

The principal alternative system offers a scheme in which the archaeological material is divided into 'cultures' (in a much narrower sense than that used in the preceding paragraph), which are themselves to some extent subdivided into groups. The 'cultures' are named after sites or areas which have supposedly produced typical material, although in fact these names are often very misleading. They are then placed chronologically in a very broad framework ('Early Bronze' I, II, III etc.) which is supposed to apply to the Aegean area as a whole. Behind this proposal are apparently the demands of archaeological theory that the terms used to describe material culture and those used for chronological designation should always be kept strictly separate and that material should be considered from the point of view of the academic archaeologist rather than the cultural historian. This artificial distinction has arisen from attempts by modern archaeologists to fabricate for themselves an independent discipline from a hotch-potch of materials and methods which are much more constructively employed within the individual fields of study to which they more properly belong (the History of Art, Science or Religion, Geography, etc.).

Much of the disagreement on this question thus stems from radically different views of the most constructive way of assessing archaeological material. It is no accident that the new system concentrates on an extremely narrow archaeological definition of 'culture', while allowing the overall chronological framework to become meaninglessly vague. It is in fact quite impossible to apply the same Early, Middle and Late Bronze Age divisions over the whole Aegean region in any precise

EC Period	Cultures	Groups
I	Pelos – Lakkoudes or Grotta – Pelos	Lakkoudes Pelos Plastiras Kampos
II	Keros – Syros	Syros
IIIA		Kastri
IIIB	Phylakopi I	Amorgos

25. The Cycladic Bronze Age, alternative terminological systems.

chronological way. It is however entirely possible, as Fig. 22 shows, to produce a reasonably detailed chronological breakdown of Cycladic culture in the Bronze Age which makes discussion of all aspects of the archaeology of that area and period historically illuminating.

Quite apart from the loss of historical precision and orientation, the new system is not even required by its own standards. Early Cycladic culture, at least in its major phases of development, is demonstrably a unity and it is difficult to see what significant meaning the new 'cultures' can have.

Another method of classifying the Early Cycladic material is into a series of local 'groups'. Provided that these are then placed within the overall chronological framework, this is useful, since it allows the distinction of local aspects within a broadly similar Cycladic picture.

At a more general level, it has been the view of many archaeological authorities that the most constructive attitude to terminology is a conservative one and that terms should not be altered without good cause. This is partly because the introduction of new terms immediately renders all earlier literature, which refers to the same material in different language, more difficult to use; partly because, although the ever-increasing body of archaeological material inevitably involves adjustments to terminology, a continuously evolving system of this type has a natural logic, which may be completely contradicted by the introduction of a fundamentally different system.

While one must allow that different views of the best use of archaeological material undoubtedly exist, the introduction of the 'culture' framework seems to the present writer to have brought no benefits whatsoever to the field of Cycladic archaeology beyond the greater attention which the subsequent controversy has certainly encouraged.

We now turn to the evidence for the Cycladic sequence.

Earliest settlement: the Cycladic Neolithic[4]

The Cyclades seem to have been first inhabited in the Late Neolithic period (c. 5000 BC). Well before this, obsidian from Melos is found, certainly in Mesolithic levels (c. 7000 BC) and probably earlier (eleventh millennium), in the Franchthi cave in the north-east Peloponnese. There is however so far no sign of human occupation on Melos so early and the obsidian was probably discovered and exploited by transient sailors.

The Cycladic Neolithic is known from two excavated sites and a number of surface finds. Saliagos near Antiparos belongs to LN I, and Kephala on Kea to LN II (also called Final Neolithic), although there is no close relationship between them.

The earlier sites (Saliagos and others unexcavated) are of interest primarily as marking the beginnings of settlement in the islands, probably by immigrants from the Greek Mainland. There is usually thought to be no material connection between them and Bronze Age material, though this question may need reinvestigation. Kephala however is directly relevant to Early Cycladic culture, since a number of features there[5] are clearly related to Early Cycladic developments. These are the use of stone-built cist graves; and terracotta figurine heads and stone vases which are similar to Early Cycladic stone forms. There are none the less difficulties over this connection, since the pottery from Kephala is not like that of EC I and the figurine type which the terracotta heads resemble is not normally thought to have developed until well after the beginning of the Early Cycladic period.

These uncertainties stem from our inadequate knowledge of settlements of the latest Neolithic and EC I periods and the absence at present of any excavated site spanning the transition. Such a site may well be found in due course. It is also possible that Kephala was contemporary with the development of EC I characteristics elsewhere, while itself essentially representing an older tradition. In any case, it is clear that some important elements of the subsequent Early Cycladic culture were established in the Cyclades at the time Kephala was occupied.

The single C 14 figure for the Kephala settlement indicates a calendar date of about 3600 BC. Comparison with the fuller series of dates from a related site, the Kitsos cave near Lavrion on the east coast of Attica (Mainland Greece), has led the excavator (J. E. Coleman) to suggest that the sample may have been contaminated and the correct date may be some three hundred years earlier.

Early Cycladic I[6]

Although there is no stratigraphic evidence for the transition from Late Neolithic to EC I, EC I material is itself found in stratigraphic relationship to that of subsequent phases, most notably at Phylakopi on Melos,[7] where it is termed 'Pre-City' in the original excavation report and 'Phase A 1' in preliminary notices of recent work. At the same site, it is in turn succeeded by EC II material (City I-i = Phase A 2). The finds consist mainly of pottery and there are scant traces of architecture. This is certainly partly due to the inaccessibility of these early deposits beneath later buildings, but it is also possible that the first structures on the site were mainly of perishable materials.

Most of our information about EC I comes from cemeteries and there is insufficient stratigraphic evidence to document the sequence of change within the period itself. Since however we do at least know in general terms what precedes EC I (viz. Late Neolithic Kephala) and what succeeds it (EC II), it is possible to suggest a chronological sequence of the cemeteries by assessing the balance of earlier and later material in each case. This has been done by C. Doumas,[8] who isolated four groups (Fig. 25) each named after a representative site. In chronological order, they are the Lakkoudes, Pelos, Plastiras and Kampos groups. Some caution is necessary here for, as already explained, the significance of the groups is partly that they represent different local characteristics within the Cyclades, though the chronological succession seems essentially correct.

The Kampos group[9] has many features which are characteristic of EC II and is often regarded as more properly belonging to that phase. Nevertheless the connections with EC I originally observed are not in doubt and it is perhaps best considered as transitional between the two main periods.

EC I pottery[10] (see Chapter 5 (ii): Figs. 58, 59) is reasonably well known, the most common fabric being fairly coarse but with surfaces highly, if somewhat crudely, burnished. The range of shapes found in settlements differs somewhat from that in the tombs, where incised decoration is also more common. All EC I decoration is in the form of incised patterns which are mostly simple and rectilinear, though more complex in the Kampos group.

EC I sees the development of other characteristic features of Early Cycladic culture – increased settlement, the use of cist graves and the manufacture of marble objects, though the latter are not yet known from the earliest Early Cycladic group (Lakkoudes). This early absence of marble finds appears to contradict the connections with LN II material suggested by the finds from Kephala (above).

There is virtually no exchange of objects between the Cyclades and the rest of the Aegean in EC I, but more generalised parallels between aspects of material culture suggest that it is to be correlated with the end of the Neolithic and earlier EH I on the Mainland and EM I in Crete.

Early Cycladic II[11]

The position of EC II within the sequence is best shown at Phylakopi (Fig. 24) where the material is from City I-i (Phase A 2) and stratified between EC I and EC IIIB. Ayia Irini (Fig. 23) was now properly settled for the first time (Period II, Ceramic Phase B) and there are substantial remains, including well-built houses, of this period, which precedes EC IIIA in the local sequence.

In the pottery (see Chapter 5 (ii): Figs. 58, 61-63) there are clear connections with EC I, in the continued use and development of certain shapes and motifs and the coarse burnished fabric and incised decoration. New in EC II are painted decoration and the fine light-coloured fabric on which it is found (Patterned ware). Also new is another fine light fabric with a darker semi-lustrous coat called 'Urfirnis' (German for 'early glaze'). Shapes include the sauceboat and the so-called saucer (actually a small bowl), both of which are better known on Mainland Greece and provide clear signs of contacts between that area and the Cyclades in EC II.

The settlement of Ayia Irini in EC II is symptomatic of contemporary developments in the islands, where there was a marked growth in the number of occupied sites. The general increase in activity is demonstrated by the much greater variety and quantity of artefacts produced in bronze and marble, as well as pottery, and the wide-ranging contacts of the Cyclades, both within the Aegean and beyond.

Imported and exported objects, as well as cross-influences such as those in pottery mentioned above, show that EC II was generally contemporary with EH II on Mainland Greece and EM II in Crete. It is probable however that the Cycladic period began before the end of EH I on the Mainland and possible that it continued after the start of EM III in Crete (see Chapter 5 (vi)).

Early Cycladic IIIA[12]

The only site which has provided clear stratigraphic evidence for the transition from EC II to EC IIIA is Ayia Irini (Period III, Ceramic Phase C), though this can be supplemented by finds from Lefkandi in Euboea, where similar material is found in the first stratum of a long sequence. Kastri on Syros has an important group of finds but appears to have been occupied only in this period. At Mount Kynthos on Delos it has proved possible to distinguish EC IIIA material from that of EC II by careful comparative analysis of finds from earlier excavations. The remote Cave of Zas on Naxos now promises important new information.

Although at first found in company with material of the preceding period, the diagnostic pottery of EC IIIA[13] is very distinctive. A new slipped and highly burnished fabric is introduced, together with a range of completely new shapes (see Chapter 5 (ii): Figs. 58, 64) whose origin lies in Anatolia.

The sudden appearance of these new forms is only one of a number of highly significant changes at this time. Some settlements were abandoned, others built with fortifications and in defensive positions. Cist-tomb burial went out of fashion. The manufacture of marble objects ceased or at least sharply declined. Together with the pottery, new metal types were introduced and possibly the apsidal house form, both of which have Anatolian parallels.[14] It even seems possible that the ore smelted at Kastri came from an Anatolian source. The conclusion that these changes represent the arrival of immigrants from Asia Minor seems inescapable, especially when we know that there were serious disturbances there at about the same time. There are no foreign imports in the Cyclades at this period or identifiably Cycladic material abroad, a situation entirely consistent with the unsettled conditions of the time.

EC IIIA is contemporary with late EH II and EH III on the Greek Mainland and EM III (possibly even very early MM IA) in Crete.[15]

Early Cycladic IIIB[16]

Early Cycladic IIIB is best represented at Phylakopi (City I-ii/iii, Phase B) where it falls between the EC II and Middle Cycladic strata. Paroikia on Paros has also produced a considerable body of EC IIIB material. On the basis of the Phylakopi stratigraphy, supported by the evidence of the pottery (see below), it is possible to subdivide the period into earlier and later stages.

The relationship of EC IIIB to EC IIIA is not yet clearly shown in the stratigraphy of any Cycladic site, but the soundness of the chronological succession is demonstrated both by the derivation of some EC IIIB pottery features from those of the earlier repertoire and by the occurrence of material related to each of the Cycladic periods in successive strata of other sites (e.g. the Heraion on Samos).

The pottery of EC IIIB has elements both old and new but is again distinctive. The more traditional class, only found in the earlier phase, has a dark surface (see Chapter 5 (ii): Figs. 58, 65) often with incised patterns. It has clear connections in shape and decoration with EC IIIA. Entirely new and found in both early and late phases is the 'Geometric' or 'Rectilinear' class (see Chapter 5 (ii): Figs. 58, 66-69), which has a distinctive fabric and, as the name implies, is characterised by Geometric designs. This class has close links with the pottery of the early Middle Helladic period on Mainland Greece (Middle Helladic matt-painted ware), but no earlier history.

The difficulty of documenting the change from EC IIIA to EC IIIB is not surprising in view of the turmoil which appears to have engulfed the Cyclades at the end of EC II. But EC IIIB sees the re-emergence and consolidation of Cycladic culture, especially in the foundation of more substantial towns, which seem to have absorbed the population of the smaller and more scattered villages of earlier times. New burial practices – urn burials and chamber tombs – begin in this period and suggest changed attitudes, but aspects of material culture other than the pottery are not well known.

One problem (see further Chapter 6) is the relationship of the sequence at Ayia Irini to that at Phylakopi just described. The Kea site was deserted after EC IIIA but probably re-occupied before the end of EC IIIB, since there are one or two imports of Melian EC IIIB types and pottery which parallels early Middle Helladic matt-painted, even if it is not particularly close to the Geometric class found on Melos and Paros. Most of the finds from this stage at Ayia Irini (Period IV) are however more closely linked to those from Phylakopi City II (Middle Cycladic); and material which is only found in EC IIIB contexts at Phylakopi (urn burials, incised decoration) occurs with clearly Middle Cycladic associations at Ayia Irini. There is as yet no adequate explanation of these inconsistencies.[17]

Although EC IIIB is Early Bronze Age in Cycladic terms, its external links are with the early Middle Bronze Age of the Mainland (Middle Helladic) and Crete (MM IA).

Middle Cycladic – Early Phase[18]

A major stratigraphic break in the form of a total destruction of the site, probably by an earthquake, marks the division between the First and Second Cities at Phylakopi, and this is the basis of the distinction between the Early and Middle Cycladic periods. At Ayia Irini, the early Middle Cycladic phase (Period IV, Ceramic Phase D) follows EC IIIA, but after a break in the occupation of the site. The earliest part of Period IV probably belongs to EC IIIB (see above) but that period is not clearly distinguishable on Kea.

In the report of the original excavations at Phylakopi, the Middle Cycladic period (Second City = Phase C of the recent excavations) was divided into three sub-periods. The first of these (II-i), to which was attributed a continuation of the Geometric pottery of EC IIIB, had no clear stratigraphic character and recent research[19] has suggested that the phase was not a genuine one and that Geometric pottery was rarely, if at all, found in the Second City. The 'early Middle Cycladic' phase here employed is thus equivalent to II-ii of original system.

The characteristic classes of pottery are now Dark Burnished and Cycladic White (Chapter 6: Figs. 103-111). The former is no doubt descended from the heavier burnished pottery of the Early Cycladic period, but its technical level is much higher and the slip and burnish often of excellent quality. The range of shapes is also different. Cycladic White is a new fabric, very fine, if soft, and decorated with patterns in matt black paint. These patterns are occasionally combined with burnished red elements in an attractive 'Black-and-Red' style (Chapter 6: Fig. 108) which is however more common in late Middle Cycladic. There is a broad correspondence of styles between the two major sites which permits a confident definition of Middle Cycladic pottery, but there were also localised features pointing to the existence of considerable individuality in the different island centres.

Once again our knowledge of the material culture is mainly dependent on the pottery. There seems to have been a decline in the use of bronze, and marble objects are still absent. Some recent Middle Cycladic finds from Thera (Ftellos)[20] may be datable to this phase. The spread of settlement was still restricted and single major centres on most islands remained the rule.

The external contacts of the period are with mature Middle Helladic and MM IB-II (possibly also late MM IA).

Middle Cycladic – Late Phase

A later stage of Middle Cycladic culture has been identified at both Phylakopi and Ayia Irini. At Phylakopi the material comes from the latest floors of the Second City (II-iii); at Ayia Irini from a phase associated with the laying-out of a new fortification system (Period V, Ceramic Phase F). At Akrotiri too, there is late Middle Cycladic material in strata underlying the LC I town, where it is mixed with early LC I in destruction levels of the beginning of the Late Bronze Age. Little pure Middle Cycladic material from the site has yet been published.

On Melos the period ends with another massive earthquake destruction. On Kea, the fate of the Middle Cycladic town is less clear. There was extensive rebuilding and rearrangement of the site at the beginning of the following period but it was not consequent on any general disaster and there was overall continuity of material culture.

The main Middle Cycladic pottery types continue, though Dark Burnished becomes markedly less common. Cycladic White acquires a more ambitious range of motifs, involving naturalistic patterns, often derived from Crete. Coarser varieties of the fabric are more in evidence. The Black-and-Red style becomes more common. Cretan influence in general is on the increase and there are indications of the development of the local style so heavily dependent on Cretan inspiration which becomes prominent in the following period.

Relationships are mainly with late Middle Helladic on the Mainland and MM III in Crete, though the discovery of a few LM IA potsherds in the late Middle Cycladic levels of recent excavations at Phylakopi suggest that we should put the end of the Middle Cycladic just after the beginning of the Cretan period.

Late Cycladic I[21]

After the destruction which brought an end to the life of the Middle Cycladic town, Phylakopi was rebuilt and fortified (or re-fortified). The first phase of this Third City (III-i = Phase D) marks the beginning of the Late Cycladic period. Major replanning and reconstruction also took place at Ayia Irini (Period VI, Ceramic Phase G), though the reason for it is not immediately evident. The most spectacular and productive site of the period is that at Akrotiri on Thera, marvellously preserved by its covering of volcanic debris. The main town reached its final form after an early LC I earthquake, though earlier buildings were repaired and/or modified and thus the origins of many of the house plans and much of the town layout must be assigned to the Middle Cycladic period.[22]

At all sites the most significant ceramic feature is the importation and extensive local copying of Cretan LM IA pottery (see Chapter 7: e.g. Figs. 118-120 and cf. 123 (import)). Local initiative in pottery manufacture and decoration, which had been conspicuous in the Middle Cycladic period, was now much reduced, although some of the LC I pottery from Thera shows a fresh and more original approach and local stylistic elements can be defined.

The very strong influence of Cretan over Cycladic culture at this time is confirmed by its appearance in material other than pottery. The most striking proof of this trend is to be found in the architecture and frescoes of Akrotiri (Chapter 8) but there are many objects too – stone vases and bronzes for example. Fragments of a tablet inscribed with a Cretan bureaucratic script (Linear A) found at Phylakopi show that the administration of the site may have been conducted on a Cretan model. In spite of this, contacts with the Mainland were also important.

The period came to an end with the volcanic cataclysm on Thera, which buried the Akrotiri settlement but does not seem to have affected the other islands in any tangible way, unless some evidence of destruction (probably by fire and earthquake) within Ayia Irini Period VI can be connected with the seismic disturbances.

Pottery imports and a few exports show that LC I was contemporary with LM IA in Crete and LH I on the Mainland.

Late Cycladic II[23]

At Phylakopi, the following phase (III-ii) is defined by later floors which belonged to houses destroyed by fire at a time when imported LM IB pottery (see Chapter 7: Fig. 114) was in use. At Ayia Irini this stage (Period VII, Ceramic Phase H) is marked by similar changes in the character of the imports. There the period ends with a massive earthquake destruction which laid waste the prosperous town.

At both sites this stage is essentially a continuation of the preceding one, with Cretan influence still strongly evident. Ayia Irini reached the acme of its prosperity now, and seems to have had relations with the Mainland at least as close as those with Crete.

It was during LM IB that many sites in Crete, including all the palaces except Knossos, were destroyed, probably by Mycenaean invaders, and it is likely that the damage at Phylakopi had a similar cause, in view of the signs of Mycenaean presence in the following period. The destruction of Ayia Irini however must have been due to natural causes.

As stated already, ceramic relations are with LM IB/LH IIA.

Late Cycladic III – Early Phase[24]

Following the destructions at the end of LC II, reconstruction took place at both main sites. At Phylakopi the town as a whole was rebuilt (III-iii = Phase E), even though only a part of the site seems to have been destroyed. At Ayia Irini the devastation had been more severe. The town was partly repaired after the earthquake (Period VIII early, Ceramic Phase J) but the size of the population and the standard of living probably both declined, though the site may have been more prosperous than has so far been apparent.

The pottery is still heavily dominated by foreign influence but with the difference that this is now from the Mycenaean culture of the Mainland (see Chapter 9) whence there are numerous imports. Cretan styles which had been so prominent earlier are now virtually non-existent.

The changed cultural orientation is reflected also in other ways. The rebuilding of Phylakopi included a 'megaron' or palace unit of unmistakably Mycenaean type (see Chapter 9: Figs. 154, 155) showing that the Mycenaeans had taken control of Melos in the course of their expansion into the southern Aegean. A recently discovered shrine complex at Phylakopi also contained many objects of Mycenaean type (see Chapter 9: Figs. 161-164).

Some new sites appear to have been settled about this time, perhaps as a result of the stability now brought to the area by Mycenaean authority and the Mycenaeans' interest in foreign trade routes which passed through the islands.

In terms of the Mycenaean pottery sequence, which is well known, this Cycladic stage relates to LH IIIA-B1.

Late Cycladic III – Middle Phase

This period is defined by the construction of major new fortifications at Phylakopi (Phase F) and probably by the occupation of other defensive sites in the islands, particularly those newly excavated at Ayios Andreas on Siphnos and Koukounaries on Paros, though their foundation is not yet accurately dated. It ends with the abandonment of Ayios Andreas.

The pottery and general material culture continue thoroughly Mycenaean in character. Imports however decline very sharply and this is obviously a result of the unsettled conditions of the time which are reflected in the fortifications and the defensive sites and are probably connected with the destructions of the Mycenaean palaces at the end of LH IIIB.

The limited imports are of LH IIIB2 and early LH IIIC date.

Late Cycladic III – Late Phase

This period of revival in the Cyclades can be stratigraphically defined by the main period at Koukounaries, and recently excavated finds from the Phylakopi shrine (Shrine Phases 2b-3a). There is important material too from Naxos – the Grotta settlement and tombs at Aplomata and Kamini.

Although the pottery is still essentially Mycenaean and there are other Mycenaean objects from the Naxos tombs (Chapter 9: Fig. 159) the picture becomes much more complicated. Mycenaean pottery is no longer the standardised product of earlier LC III and the Cyclades were influenced now by the Dodecanese and Crete as well as the Greek Mainland (chiefly the eastern part) and, even further afield, Cyprus. Indeed they now form part of a new grouping with those areas which is yet to be fully understood but must be the result of the disappearance of the Mycenaean palaces and the general realignment of Aegean centres which followed.

The related Mycenaean pottery phases are LH IIIC 'developed' and 'advanced'.

Late Cycladic III – Final[25]

The dates of the final desertion of most Cycladic Bronze Age sites are not known with certainty. Several were perhaps abandoned at the end of LC III-Late. But the latest pottery from Ayia Irini (Ceramic Phase M), allied to the stratigraphic evidence from Lefkandi in Euboea, shows that, at least in places, there was a period of occupation following that described above, when pottery of a simpler character (White ware) was in use and the population of the site was probably very small. Parallel material from other islands has not so far been recognised with certainty.

The reasons for the final decline of Mycenaean civilisation have been much discussed but are still unclear and further investigation of the Cycladic evidence may help to answer some of the outstanding questions. This is the time of the Ionian migrations reported by later writers, and the archaeological material which follows that of the latest Bronze Age in the Cyclades, namely Protogeometric, is also found on the coast of Asia Minor. This must represent the movement of peoples from Greece across the Aegean to Ionia in the troubled and changing times of the Dark Ages.

3

The Exploration of the Cycladic Bronze Age[1]

The built cist tombs of the Cycladic Bronze Age (Fig. 54) often lie only just below the ground surface and peasant farmers can easily stumble on them in the course of cultivating their fields. Indeed it was the objects from such graves, especially the fine marble vases and figures, seen in the hands of local islanders, which first drew the attention of travellers and scholars to the existence of a pre-classical civilisation in the Cyclades.

One of the first to discuss Cycladic antiquities from a scholarly viewpoint was a German, Ludwig Ross. Ross travelled in the islands in the later 1830s and recorded his impressions, with descriptions of ancient sites, in three volumes published in Stuttgart between 1840 and 1845.

The first serious field investigation took place some thirty years later. This was conducted by F. Fouqué, a French geologist who was prosecuting research into the vulcanology of Thera. At that time, the Suez Canal Company began seriously to exploit the volcanic deposits of the island because the ash provided a high grade constituent for cement which was required for the construction of the harbour and buildings at Port Said.

The ash layers of Thera are extremely thick (up to 60m in places) and the ancient remains which lie below them would be unreachable in normal circumstances. The first place where prehistoric buildings were uncovered by mining operations was not on Thera itself but on Therasia, an islet in the bay which had been part of the main island until the Late Bronze Age catastrophe.[2] Excavation at the site was begun by the landowner Alafousos and a local doctor, Nomikos, and in 1867 continued by Fouqué, who subsequently worked on other sites on Thera itself.

In 1879 Fouqué's book, *Santorin et ses éruptions*, was published. As the title suggests, it was primarily concerned with the volcanic history of Thera, but an entire chapter was devoted to the antiquities and their interpretation. In fact Fouqué's description and discussion of the finds was full and accurate and is still very valuable. He was also the first person to use a form of clay analysis (visual, in his case) to determine whether vases were made locally or imported. Other French scholars,

26. J.T. Bent. (British Museum).   27. Christos Tsountas. (Ekdotike Athenon).

including Gorceix and Mamet, whose work was reported by Fouqué, took an interest in Theran antiquities and some of their finds, as well as those of Fouqué, form the small collection which is still kept in the French School in Athens.

Another key figure working at this time was an Englishman from Yorkshire, James Theodore Bent (Fig. 26) who travelled with his wife in the islands and, in 1885, published the charmingly titled *The Cyclades, or Life among the Insular Greeks*. As the subtitle suggests, this was more a work of social anthropology than archaeology, but the author was deeply interested in the local antiquities and in fact excavated a cemetery on Antiparos, publishing his findings in the *Journal of Hellenic Studies* for 1885. Bent opened about forty graves and described them and their contents, which included pottery, marble, obsidian and metal objects, in considerable detail.

The last decade of the nineteenth century saw crucial developments. Christos Tsountas (Fig. 27), of the Greek Archaeological Service, investigated numerous sites in the islands, mainly cemeteries, and added enormously to the amount of published material available for study in two articles, still fundamental, in the Greek journal, *Archaiologike Ephemeris* (1898 and 1899). A fine selection of the finds made by Tsountas (and others) is on display in the Cycladic room of the National Archaeological Museum in Athens.

The other event of importance at this time was the excavation, by the British School of Archaeology at Athens, of the Bronze Age settlement of Phylakopi on Melos. The British archaeologists had originally gone to

28. Duncan Mackenzie. (Ashmolean Museum).

Melos to work on the Classical capital of the island but the results were disappointing, and in 1896 excavations were started at Phylakopi, which had already been recognised as a site of great importance from surface finds. It remains today the most extensively excavated settlement of the Cycladic Bronze Age and will figure prominently in the following pages.

The excavations at Phylakopi are particularly well documented. Duncan Mackenzie (Fig. 28), a Scot from near Inverness, who went on to act as field supervisor for Sir Arthur Evans at Knossos, was in day-to-day charge of the site and kept detailed records of the work. His daybooks are in many ways a model of archaeological recording at a time when a systematic approach was rare.

The early reports of the Melos excavations contain some fascinating insights into conditions at the time, including the information that, at the beginning of one season, the boat from Athens to the island took a week to complete the journey because of adverse conditions. Steamers today take an average of about nine hours and can do it in six.

The work at Phylakopi was published in an impressive monograph in 1904.

The prehistoric cemetery of Pelos, on the same island, was also investigated by the British team and is important for its characteristic range of finds of the earlier phase of the Cycladic Bronze Age (EC I).

The second half of the nineteenth century thus saw the beginning of intensive excavation. In the early years of the twentieth, Greek archaeologists continued to work in the islands and the British team returned to Phylakopi for a single season in 1911. This period also saw German work on Paros, where a prehistoric site was uncovered beneath later remains at Paroikia, the main port on the island. The site occupies a most attractive position on the gulf of Paros and readily catches the eye of the visitor today as he approaches by sea. Among the white houses of the town, the little mound is topped by the blue-domed church of Ayios Konstandinos, below which a cascade of greenery reaches down to the shore-side road. Because of the overlying buildings, both ancient and modern, only part of the prehistoric remains could be reached but the site was certainly occupied for most of the Bronze Age, though the majority of the finds belong to the EC IIIB period. The excavator, O. Rubensohn, published his discoveries in the *Mitteilungen* of the German Archaeological Institute in Athens for 1917.

From 1873, the French School in Athens had been active in uncovering the antiquities of the island of Delos, most noted for its classical remains. In 1913, work was begun on Mount Kynthos (A. Plassart), the most prominent hill on the island, and in 1916 a prehistoric settlement (now known to be of EC II and IIIA date) was uncovered beneath later material. The site was published in the series of the Delos exploration reports (Volume 9, 1928) and the material has been restudied recently.

By this time, enough material was available for scholars to try and establish an overall view of the Bronze Age culture of the Cyclades and of its relationship to that of other areas of the Aegean.[3]

For the next twenty years there were comparatively few developments until, in 1949, Professor Nikolaos Kondoleon of the University of Athens began work in the prehistoric settlement of Grotta, beside and largely beneath the modern town of Naxos. Kondoleon's excavations, which continued intermittently until his death in 1974 (and have since been carried on by his successor at the University, V. Lambrinoudakis), uncovered parts of an extensive town dating mainly to the Late Bronze Age, though with traces of earlier habitation as well. The site has proved very difficult to work because it lies below sea level due to local changes since antiquity, and the trenches rapidly become inundated. On the coastal slopes of Aplomata, close to Grotta, Kondoleon also found Early Cycladic cist graves and rock-cut chambered tombs of the Late Bronze Age. Two of the latter have been fully published by C. Kardara.

Kondoleon's work inaugurated a new era of activity in the study of the Cycladic Bronze Age and was of great importance in itself as revealing substantial remains of the 'Mycenaean' (= LC III) period in the islands, and raising the possibility of some émigré mainlanders on Naxos in the later years of the Bronze Age. Apart from Grotta, Aplomata (and the neighbouring cemetery of Kamini, excavated in 1960 by Dr. N. Zapheiropoulos), the island of Naxos, so large, rich and fertile and so prominent in the Early Bronze Age, has been little explored for evidence

29. J.L. Caskey. (University of
Cincinnati).

of the later periods.

In the 1950s and 1960s, successive members of the Cycladic Ephorate
of the Greek Archaeological Service carried out numerous excavations,
often in response either to the kind of illicit digging whose history reaches
back to the beginnings of Cycladic archaeology, or else in areas where
construction work was intended in the vicinity of archaeological remains.
A great deal of work was also done in the reorganisation and
rearrangement of Museum collections (at Apeiranthos and Naxos on the
island of Naxos, on Tenos, Mykonos, Syros, Paros and Thera).

Inevitably much of the excavation was on cemetery sites and a major
contribution to our understanding of the Early Cycladic period came
with C. Doumas' publication (1977a) and analysis of finds from
excavations conducted by him at this time.

The bias towards cemetery finds was further redressed, partly by
Doumas himself with work in the small Early Cycladic fortress at
Panormos on Naxos and partly by Professor E.-M. Bossert's
re-excavation (1962) of an important EC IIIA settlement at Kastri on
Syros (first investigated by Tsountas), but most of all by the work at Ayia
Irini on Kea of Professor John L. Caskey (Fig. 29) of the University of
Cincinnati. Charmingly situated on a promontory in the bay of Ayios
Nikolaos, Ayia Irini was occupied almost continuously from EC II until
the end of the Bronze Age. In addition to its long stratified
sequence, the wide range of non-ceramic finds has given us a much

30. Akrotiri, Thera. Layers of pumice (lower) and ash (upper, eroded) overlying prehistoric buildings.

broader view of the character of island life at the time. Situated at the other end of the Cycladic group from Phylakopi, Ayia Irini is well placed for comparison with the Melian site, thus allowing us to explore the extent of variations in the material culture of different islands within the group. In addition to the settlement, a number of tombs have been excavated in the immediate vicinity.

The Kea excavations began in 1960. Fieldwork has now been completed and the first volumes of the final publication have appeared (Keos II Part 1, III, IV, V). The LN II settlement of Kephala, not far from Ayia Irini, on the same island, was excavated as part of the Kea project by Professor John E. Coleman and has already been published (Keos I, 1977).

The other outstanding event of the 1960s was the start, in 1967, of work at Akrotiri on Thera by Professor Spyridon Marinatos. Marinatos continued working there until his death in 1974, since when the excavation has been supervised by Professor Christos Doumas of Athens University. Akrotiri is a unique site for the Aegean Bronze Age, buried as it is beneath volcanic debris (Fig. 30) with its buildings and other finds (including splendid wall paintings) spectacularly preserved. Akrotiri brings a much needed breath of immediacy to our view of daily life in that distant age.

Because of the continuous commercial exploitation of the Thera deposits since the time of Fouqué and further archaeological work in the intervening period, the prehistory of the island is surprisingly well known, in spite of the inaccessibility of the remains. One or two small farmsteads, such as are rarely discovered in the Aegean, have been located, the most recent being that at Ftellos (1972), where remains of a roofed animal byre and small farmhouse were found by Doumas.

In the 1970s, renewed work at Phylakopi by the British School at Athens (Professor A.C. Renfrew) brought some additions to our knowledge of the site and its occupation sequence and uncovered an important shrine[4] of the Mycenaean (LC III) period, with figurines and other interesting and unusual finds. A broader field study of the island's resources and historical remains investigated relationships between the environment and historical developments.

Two important refuge settlements of the late thirteenth century BC have been excavated in recent years (1970s and continuing) and have emphasised the instability of conditions in the islands at that time. One is the acropolis of Ayios Andreas on Siphnos, first discovered by Tsountas and now being further investigated by Dr. Barbara Philippaki, formerly Ephor of the National Archaeological Museum in Athens. The second, which has impressive fortifications, numerous finds and exciting evidence of a final destruction by fire with local inhabitants crowded inside for refuge, is at Koukounaries on the bay of Naoussa in northern Paros. Dr. D. Schilardi of the Greek Archaeological Service is responsible for work here, which began in 1976.

Finally, a small but very important site was discovered in 1979 at Ayia Thekla near Panormos on the island of Tenos and excavated by Professor G. Despinis of Thessaloniki University. This was a tholos (beehive) tomb of fairly rough construction but characteristically mainland Mycenaean type (c. 1300 BC) and the only one of its kind known in the Cyclades. (Another was apparently discovered early this century by Stephanos at Khosti on Naxos but its whereabouts are unknown.)

Finds outside the Cyclades themselves, though inevitably of less immediate interest, have also contributed significantly to Cycladic studies and new efforts have been made to understand the connections of the islands with other areas of the Aegean. The settlement and cemetery at Ayios Kosmas in Attica (published by Professor G. E. Mylonas in 1959), the cemetery at Marathon (Marinatos, 1970 onwards), as well as excavations at Iassos on the Aegean coast of Turkey (Italian School at Athens, Professor D. Levi, Dr. C. Laviosa, 1960 onwards) have all produced finds of Early Cycladic character. The same is true of sites in Crete – at Archanes (Dr. J. Sakellarakis, 1966 onwards) and Ayia Fotia near Siteia (Dr. C. Davaras, 1972). This list is far from exhaustive and could easily be extended to include, for example, such material as the Cycladic objects from the famous Shaft Graves at Mycenae, especially Grave Circle B (excavated by Dr J. Papademetriou from 1951 onwards and published, after his death, by Mylonas in 1972-3).

Such are the efforts that have been expended on the study of the Cycladic Bronze Age, over more than a century, by what John Caskey once referred to as 'a goodly company of philhellenic scholars from many lands'.

All these finds ultimately come to our notice through publication in one form or another, whether in the preliminary and fairly prompt notices[5] in the annual periodicals of the Greek Archaeological Service and Archaeological Society and of the various foreign schools which are permitted to operate in Greece, or in the final excavation reports which take much longer to prepare.

The latter, of unimaginable and sometimes quite unnecessary tedium, are none the less essential as permanent records of the details of excavation, finds and find-spots so vital to present study and future re-assessments of the culture and history of the Cycladic Bronze Age.

4

The Settlements

The settlements will take first place in our review of life in the prehistoric Cyclades for they provide not only its essential setting but also, in a real sense, the connecting link between the landscape and the civilisation that grew there. Local conditions of geology and climate imposed certain characteristics on the location and architectural character of the buildings: but there was also an element of choice, and in the operation of this are revealed the needs or preferences of the islanders at different periods. Such preferences are often re-emphasised in architectural features of the settlement as, for example, when the protection of a naturally defensible site is completed by the addition of suitable fortifications.

The layout of settlements and houses, their architectural character and the amenities with which they are provided, are all part of the picture of the civilisation of the prehistoric Cyclades. They reflect the attitudes and requirements of their inhabitants and, like any cultural features, sometimes betray outside influences. They tell us too something about social habits and structure, in terms of the design of settlements and of the organisation needed to build them. Finally they provide information about the various crafts involved in construction and furnishing.

Choice of site[1]

The location and architectural style of Cycladic settlements in the Bronze Age were influenced by a number of factors, some permanent, some transient – whose relative importance varied from time to time, in accordance with changing social, economic and political conditions.

Unchanging needs are for shelter from wind or sun and drainage of the fierce winter storms. Sloping hillside sites are good for drainage and, to some extent, for wind-protection. When the summer 'meltemi' is blowing from the north in the Cyclades, you can be almost swept off your feet on a hilltop or exposed slope, while the sheltered side is virtually windless. Summer sun and winter cold can both be countered by thick walls and small windows; the former also by whitewash or whitened plaster.

Broader considerations are access to fresh water, fishing grounds, agricultural land and perhaps other resources (e.g. minerals). Important too were the existence of suitable harbour or beaching facilities and defensive potential.

In the Cyclades today, many islands are dependent on a single fresh-water source, supplemented by rainwater collected in cisterns during the winter. The local availability of water may have been roughly similar in prehistoric times but consumption was probably not so high and it is difficult to gauge how closely the present number and situation of sources reflect the prehistoric. Phylakopi is today situated close by the only fresh-water source on Melos, though it is not within the perimeter of the ancient site. At Ayia Irini, there was a spring on the promontory. In the Late Bronze Age, this was approached by a specially built passage and chamber incorporated in the fortification system.

As for collection in cisterns or other receptacles, it seems very likely that this method was used but evidence for it is scarce.[2] There is a rock-cut cistern at Ayios Andreas, a possible cistern (or tomb!) at Phylakopi, and some remains of terracotta pipes and possible water-spouts. The latter are not necessarily to be associated with cisterns, since several sites had drainage conduits and lavatory systems. Large earthenware pithoi may have been used for the catchment of water channelled from the roofs, and for storage.

Proximity to agricultural land or other resources such as metal ores, obsidian or marble, which underlay the economies of certain settlements, seem likely to have been important influences on general location. At times (EC I, II) when settlements were small and scattered, this was probably the case, but later, with the growth of larger and fewer settlements, such factors may not have been so important, at least to the major centres. On Melos, Phylakopi is not particularly well situated to exploit fully either the best agricultural land on the island or the obsidian quarries. In modern times too, the inhabitants of the Cyclades often live in centralised village communities and travel quite long distances to cultivate their fields. Today a family's fields may be very scattered because of the system of inheritance and dowry, but of course this is no indication of the pattern of land-ownership in prehistoric times.

A coastal situation was good for maritime trade and communication, even locally, and obviously also for fishing. All these activities require the use of boats, and thus suitable harbours or beaching facilities. Some sites (Ayia Irini, Paroikia, Ios – Fig. 31) were in deep, sheltered gulfs where the care of vessels was not a great problem. Phylakopi (Fig. 21) was in an exposed coastal situation but had a small harbour protected by the projecting promontory. Mikre Vigla (Fig. 5) on the west coast of Naxos had wide sandy beaches on either side of the promontory where boats could easily be drawn up.

Fishing from boats is of course possible from any harbour, though the distances to the best locations will vary. There are Bronze Age pictures

31. The bay of Ios.

32. Kastri, Syros, from the south-west. (J.A. Macgillivray).

(Fig. 13) of fishermen and finds of fishhooks (Fig. 76) and fish bones. The latter suggest that some sites (Neolithic Saliagos) depended heavily on fish, while others (Bronze Age Phylakopi), although coastal, did not. Tunny fishing[3] may have played an important role in the Bronze Age economy of the islands and in the location of some sites. At the appropriate season, lookouts would have been posted to warn of the approaching fish, which followed predictable runs. They could then be trawled or driven ashore.

The need for protection[4] was another influence on site location which varied in importance according to current circumstances. The defensive capacity of a site might be enhanced by artificial fortifications either at the time of its original construction or later. Protection could be achieved in various ways – by choosing a promontory which was nearly surrounded by sea and required additional fortification only across the neck (Ayia Irini: Fig. 46; also perhaps originally Phylakopi); or by building in a location difficult of access because remote and/or naturally hard to scale (Kastri on Syros (Fig. 32), Ayios Andreas on Siphnos, Koukounaries on Paros (Fig. 153)). Most hill or promontory sites were to some extent naturally defensible and could be further reinforced with fortifications in times of stress. Vryokastro on Tenos, a seaside acropolis, seems to have been walled at some time in its history.

Building materials and construction[5]

The style of construction at individual sites was much influenced by the character of locally available material – a circumstance which forbids ready generalisations. Although the passage of time sees the appearance of some instances of more sophisticated architecture, most notably at Late Cycladic Akrotiri, many features and practices remained virtually unchanged throughout the Bronze Age, and indeed into modern times – at least where stone is used rather than concrete. Thus the history of Cycladic architecture in the Bronze Age does not present a picture of regular and consistent development.

The lack of EC I house remains suggests that the structures were often made of perishable fabrics but it seems likely that stone, so often easily available close at hand, was always the preferred material for houses and walls in the prehistoric Cyclades. Reed and branch impressions preserved in plaster show that they too were used in building. Flat slabs of easily-split local schist (with mortar) formed the walls at Ayia Irini (Fig. 14) and the houses and graves at Late Neolithic Kephala, not far away: rounded boulders from the sea shore were often used at Phylakopi (Fig. 15), with mortar and smaller stones filling the interstices to give stability. There is a little evidence for the use of brick in Early and Middle Cycladic Kea and, later, at Akrotiri. By the Late Cycladic period, at least, organised quarrying was undertaken, since some of the 'villas' at Akrotiri were built of stone which all came from the same source (Fig. 16). By this time we may guess that it was quarried by some means such as that employed in the Archaic period (sixth century BC), when a channel was drilled and cut round the stone to be removed, and then wooden wedges were hammered underneath and drenched with water so that they swelled and thus detached the material from its bed. Where regular blocks were required, bronze saws and chisels were available. Transport to the site would have been on animal-drawn carts or sledges. The blocks may have been put into place by being dragged up earthen ramps raised against the walls as they were built.

None of these methods of quarrying or lifting were necessary for most Bronze Age construction where the stones could have been collected, broken, carried and set in place by hand.

In the Early Bronze Age walls are of fairly small stones, sometimes irregular and set in clay (Grotta), sometimes very neatly laid, with mud or clay mortar (Ayia Irini, where there is also some use of brick). Walls are sometimes founded on a bedding course of small stones, sometimes directly on the rock. The rock face is occasionally used as all or part of a wall. During the Middle Bronze Age, there was some limited use of roughly squared (ashlar) blocks, perhaps copying those seen by Cycladic visitors to the Cretan palaces, where such masonry was standard. In house building, for instance at Middle Cycladic Phylakopi, the quoins were often of ashlar and the rest of the walls built of smaller stones. The same was true of those earlier buildings at Akrotiri (Fig. 33) which survived within the 'Minoan' rebuilding of LC I. There was also some crude coursed ashlar, as in the fortifications at Ayia Irini (Fig. 34).

Ashlar masonry is common in the new LC I town at Akrotiri, and entire buildings were constructed in this style (Fig. 16). But the habit did not spread to other sites, except for some of the fortification systems (Ayios Andreas, Koukounaries: Fig. 50), where large, roughly squared blocks were used. The standard of Late Cycladic construction at Phylakopi was very variable and sometimes less sophisticated than in the preceding period. The people of Ayia Irini continued to build in the neat flat-slab style dictated by the local schist.

At Akrotiri, a wooden framework was often inserted into the walls (Fig. 35) in accordance with the well-known Minoan practice, the intention being to allow some flexibility in the case of earthquake. This method is not so evident at other sites. House floors, at their simplest, were of beaten earth, sometimes with a stone underlay. Others were made of pebbles packed in clay and, later, quite often of flagstones. At Akrotiri at least, even the upper stories were flagged, the stones laid on wooden joists.

Roofs were almost certainly flat, as usually in the Cyclades today, and were probably of a type still common – layers of branches with packed earth and clay superimposed. On smaller units the roofs could have been of stone, either using large slabs, like the cist tombs, or else corbelled. Columns or pillars (usually of wood) were sometimes used as roof supports, again a practice regularly noticeable in rural building today.

Doors and windows had stone jambs and thresholds, and stone or wooden lintels and sills (Fig. 36). The doors, at least, sometimes had a wooden post which fitted into the stone jamb, and some of the windows at Akrotiri were subdivided by wooden transoms. Stair treads and supports might be of either wood or stone (Fig. 37) and wooden ladders were used for access to basements.

Interior walls were plastered more frequently as time went on, initially as a form of extra insulation. In the Middle Bronze Age the plaster was sometimes painted monochrome or with very simple patterns. By the

33. Ashlar quoins in a building at Akrotiri, Thera.

34. Rough ashlar masonry in the fortifications at Ayia Irini, Kea. (University of Cincinnati).

35. Slots left by the decay of a wooden framework inset in walls at Akrotiri, Thera.

36. Window (reconstructed) at Akrotiri, Thera

37. Stairway in a building at Ayia
Irini, Kea. (University of Cincinnati).

Late Bronze Age, complex figured scenes are found (Chapters 7, 8). Some
of them are of course on internal dividing walls which had become
common by the Late Bronze Age. These were considerably less
substantial than the main outside walls and might be built of smaller
stones and/or light wood or stakes daubed with clay, sometimes of brick.

It is not entirely clear whether houses were plastered on the outside as
well. White painted plaster is a good protection against the summer sun
and there is a little evidence for the practice in Late Bronze Age Crete.

Use of rooms

Within the buildings, there are sometimes indications of the ways in
which the rooms were used. In Early Cycladic settlements, families
probably had to cook, eat, sleep, even work in the same room, perhaps
also making use of the flat roof-space for everyday activities or for
sleeping in fine weather. There is evidence for some such use of roofs from
rural settlements in modern Turkey[6] but no absolute proof of similar
practices in the ancient Cyclades, where their feasibility would have
been dependent in part on the solidity of the roof. In the Late Bronze
Age, the elaborate decoration of the upper storeys (Chapters 7, 8) shows
that these were living quarters, sometimes also the location of quieter

38. Storage basement with pithoi built
into a bench at Akrotiri, Thera. (C.
Doumas).

and cleaner crafts such as weaving. Many of the frescoes are thought to
have ritual significance and to indicate the presence of such activity in
the rooms where they are found. Bathrooms are also found upstairs. The
downstairs rooms and basements were used for storage (e.g. those with
large pithoi: Fig. 38) or more robust activities such as the milling of grain
(Fig. 148), perhaps also as shops. Obsidian tools were made within the
settlement at Phylakopi, stone vases at Ayia Irini.

There are a few very distinctive buildings with highly specialised uses
(the Temple at Ayia Irini, the shrine and megaron at Phylakopi), which
are described more fully below.

Dirtier and potentially dangerous activities, like pottery manufacture
and the smelting or working of metals, were probably located outside the
confines of the settlements. Indications of this may be seen in the
discovery of an Early Cycladic pottery kiln some distance outside the
town at Ayia Irini and the evidence for smelting at the mines of Ayios
Sostis on Siphnos. The metalworking activities within the fort at Kastri
on Syros may be the exception to prove the rule since, in those dangerous
times, weapon production would have been all-important and the
process itself needed to be safeguarded.

Similarly Koukounaries on Paros – a citadel under siege – is the only
site where there is clear evidence of animals kept within the settlement.

39. Stone bench in Xeste 3, Akrotiri, Thera.

It seems unlikely that there was enough space for this except *in extremis* and, at least on Late Cycladic Thera, livestock was kept in farmsteads away from the main sites.

Within the rooms, there are sometimes built hearths of stone or clay, and stone benches (Fig. 39) which could have been used as beds, seats, tables, or a combination of the three. They could also support installations like the millstone at Akrotiri or the series of built-in storage pithoi at the same site. Closets or cupboards could be let into the walls.

Lavatories and bathrooms are among the more sophisticated (Fig. 150) conveniences of life in the Late Bronze Age. The lavatories have a seat, a drainpipe with an outlet to the main street drain and a large jar to hold water for flushing close at hand.

The extensive drainage systems which ran beneath the streets of the Late Cycladic settlements presumably served for both household effluent and rainwater. There are one or two instances of connections from individual houses to the system, either from lavatories or washing areas. (The question of water catchment and storage has been discussed earlier in this chapter).

All our knowledge of wooden furnishings, whether fixed or mobile, comes from Akrotiri. There was some wooden shelving, and wooden beds, tables, stools and baskets (Figs. 11, 149) have been recovered by making plaster casts from holes left in the pumice fill by the decay of the wood. Such objects were probably common at other sites too. Unfortunately we cannot recover more intimate details of furnishing like textiles, trinkets or devotional objects. Food vessels and tools were also kept in the home.

The settlements[7]

Early Cycladic period

Building remains of EC I are scanty, the structures perhaps being often of wood or other perishable materials. This picture however is undoubtedly due, at least in part, to the small number of excavated sites and the inaccessibility of earlier remains below later strata. The use of stone for the buildings and graves at Late Neolithic Kephala, which in any case has some cultural links with EC I, shows that stone construction was standard there before the beginning of the Bronze Age.

The Kephala settlement consisted of houses scattered on a hillside by the sea. The individual units were small but often of more than one room. The houses were probably constructed entirely of stone but incorporated natural features (ledges, scarps) as floors or walls where convenient. The total population was about fifty. The cemetery was close by.

Sites of EC I are much more common than those of the Late Neolithic period but settlements are very much less well known than the cemeteries. Settlements were usually located on sloping ground near the sea, with a cemetery close at hand. Occasionally they were inland. The existence of a cemetery can be taken to imply a settlement nearby but, since the cemeteries are small, there might have been more than one per settlement. It is perhaps more probable that the dwelling sites were also small, like Kephala.

There are some fairly substantial remains from Naxos (Grotta) which belong to late EC I. The houses are not so different from those of Late Neolithic Kephala, being small (one or two rooms), essentially rectangular, and scattered. The walls were carefully constructed of small to medium-sized stones, often slabs, either in a dry-stone technique or embedded in clay. They were sometimes set on a levelling course of small stones, sometimes laid directly onto bedrock.

There is further evidence of EC I architecture in the cemeteries in the form of the retaining walls and platforms, as well as the graves. At Ayioi Anargyroi on Naxos (late EC I: Fig. 53), a large platform included a flight of steps and there are platforms in earlier cemeteries too.

The rapid development and increasing prosperity of the islands in EC II are reflected in more substantial architectural remains. In general the locations of the settlements are similar to those of EC I. Fine EC II houses are preserved on part of the site at Ayia Irini (Figs. 40, 14). A single large complex of buildings (at least 15 x 30m) is laid out on a consistent axis and constructed of neatly laid slabs. The preserved height of some of the walls strongly suggests that they were constructed of stone throughout. Some of the rooms were certainly basements since they had no doors and must have been entered from above. The buildings may have been entirely roofed in stone or else with branches, earth and clay.

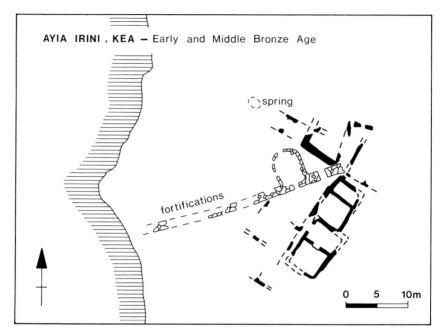

40. Early Cycladic (black) in relation to Middle Cycladic (outline) structures at
Ayia Irini, Kea. (After Caskey 1971a, 370).

Floors were usually of earth or packed clay or a mixture of the two; there
are some roughly flagged floors at Ayia Irini. The doorways have stone
threshold blocks, door jambs and pivot slots for the doors. The doors
probably had wooden frames. Pan hearths, a stone-ringed fireplace and a
storage-bin made of large slabs were also found.

The difference in constructional technique between Ayia Irini and
Grotta is worth noting since it is clearly the result of differences in local
stone. The area round Ayia Irini is full of outcropping schist which can be
easily split into neat flat slabs, whereas such material is not available in
the vicinity of Grotta.

Several EC IIIA settlements are known but since Kastri on Syros (Figs.
41, 32) was actually founded in this period and has well-preserved
remains, it may conveniently be taken as the exemplar. Its remote
situation, fortification and house plans are all indicative of the uncertain
nature of the times. In marked contrast to the low-lying villages of EC I
and II, Kastri is situated on a hilltop high above the sea and can be
reached only by a precipitous ascent. In spite of this inaccessible
location, the site was strongly fortified with a circuit wall with projecting
semicircular bastions. Beyond this there was an outwork with a defended
gate, though it is not clear whether this extended round the whole site.
Within the walls are crowded groups of tiny houses, divided by
passageways. These often had curving walls which, in general, seem

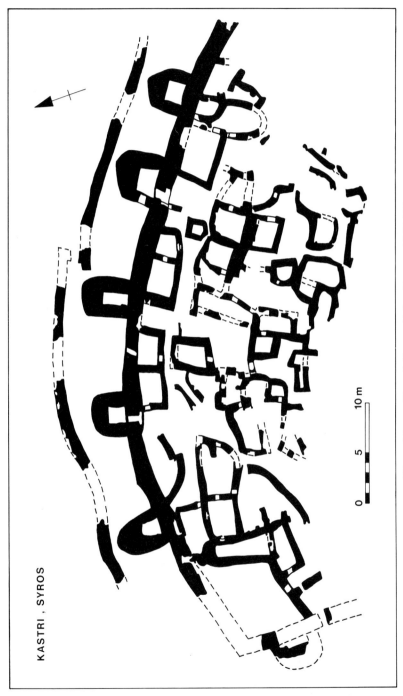

KASTRI , SYROS

0   5   10 m

41. Plan of fort at Kastri, Syros. (After Bossert 1967, 56).

42. Naxos, view of the Chora.

characteristic of this period. They may simply be the result of compressing dwellings into the irregularly shaped hilltop area, but a more convincing explanation is that they represent the inherited preference of immigrant settlers from Anatolia, whose presence or influence is indicated by the new EC IIIA pottery types and other features of material culture.[8]

Other fortified EC IIIA sites are at Panormos on Naxos and Mount Kynthos on Delos. At Panormos the circuit wall of the tiny fort was built to a plan which automatically provided bastions similar to those at Kastri, but they were not actual additions to the wall as at the Syros site. These fortifications are quite similar to those at Lerna on the Greek Mainland. Mount Kynthos may have had defences too, provided by the thickening of the house walls at the edge of the plateau. This method of allowing the outer walls of houses at the edge of the settlement to provide a defensive circuit was also used in the mediaeval villages (Fig. 42 – Naxos) of the Cyclades.

Since Mount Kynthos was probably also occupied in EC II, and Panormos may have been, it is not absolutely certain that their fortifications belong to EC IIIA, though the historical circumstances make this most probable. The Cave of Zas on Naxos is not actually fortified but its situation is so remote that artificial defences would have been superfluous.

Against this background, the EC IIIA settlement at Ayia Irini seems exceptional. It was apparently undefended. At the time of the appearance of the new elements of material culture, the buildings originally constructed in EC II continued in use. Some were altered and repaired, but in the same style as before. In one area, where EC IIIA houses were abandoned and covered over, another building was erected within the same period. The reason for this is not known. Most known settlements of EC IIIA were abandoned, at least temporarily, at the end of the period.

Apart from the use of curved walls, there are no striking architectural developments, though it may be noted that the small houses of the Kynthos settlement may have had corbelled roofs.

The character of EC IIIB settlements is known from building remains at Phylakopi and Paroikia, and it is probable that the essentially Middle Cycladic town at Ayia Irini (Period IV) was also built about this time.

It is usually thought that these settlements were larger and more carefully laid out and built than those of earlier times, though this is partly based on the fact that fewer sites are now known, and evidence for such trends is actually stronger in the next phase (Middle Cycladic).

Houses were small and rectangular. Those at Phylakopi were thought by their excavators to have been scattered, though only a relatively small area could be investigated. Paroikia had a more unified overall plan, though again only part of the site was uncovered. One of the houses there was apsidal in form – probably a relation of the EC IIIA buildings with curved walls.

Middle Cycladic period

By the Middle Cycladic period it seems clear that the populations of all but the larger islands were concentrated on a single main centre which was consequently more extensive and carefully organised than those of earlier times, although we have already seen signs of the closer juxtaposition of buildings and more coherent overall planning in EC II and III. No doubt this centralisation of population was partly due to a desire for more effective protection, to which the fortifications of some sites also bear witness. But there was probably too an appreciation that the more efficient social organisation which the settlements themselves reflect was itself best served by a concentration of human resources.

Middle Cycladic settlements are represented by Phylakopi City II, Ayia Irini and Akrotiri. At neither of the latter two sites is the overall character of the Middle Cycladic layout yet clear but, at Phylakopi, a substantial area was excavated. The town was now laid out in blocks of small houses (Fig. 43) built on a grid of streets orientated to the points of the compass. The streets were about 1.5m wide and probably had steps to negotiate changes of level. The houses, usually of two to four rooms (Fig. 44), though it is often difficult to identify the limits of the individual houses within the block, were larger and more complex than their Early Cycladic predecessors and there was limited use of crude coursed ashlar masonry.

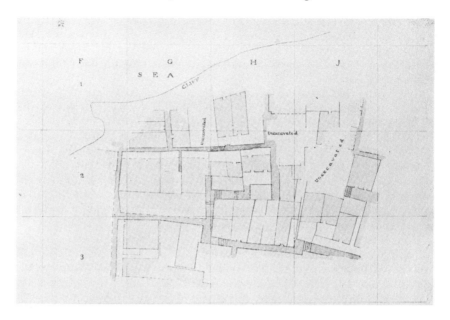

43. Phylakopi, Melos. Block plan of City II (Middle Cycladic), with drainage system dotted. (Atkinson *et al.* 1904, 39).

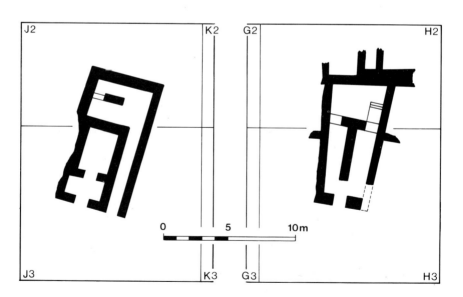

44. Phylakopi, Melos. Plans of Middle Cycladic houses. (After Atkinson *et al.* 1904, 44, 45).

At Ayia Irini there was a separate shrine building in the Middle Cycladic town, though our knowledge of it derives mainly from the following period (see below).

There is some uncertainty about the extent to which Middle Cycladic sites were fortified.[9] Ayia Irini had a fortification wall with semicircular towers (Fig. 40) from the beginning of Period IV (late EC IIIB or early Middle Cycladic). The Second City at Phylakopi was said by its original excavators to have been fortified. Recent excavations have shown that parts of the fortifications at the site are much later (LC I and III), but it remains quite likely that a smaller system existed in the Middle Bronze Age – perhaps simply a wall across the neck of the promontory. Other unexcavated Middle Cycladic sites (Vryokastro on Tenos, Kastro on Siphnos, Kastri on Amorgos, Mikre Vigla on Naxos) are in good defensive positions and Vryokastro has walling which might be Middle Cycladic.

Late Cycladic period

With the Late Cycladic phases at the major sites, at last we get a truly comprehensive picture of the character of the settlements and a fuller understanding of life within them. Much of this is due to the recent (and continuing) excavations at Akrotiri on Thera whose remains, remarkably preserved under the volcanic debris, are more fully described in Chapter 8. The towns at Phylakopi (City III) and Ayia Irini are also well known and other sites contribute too. For the first time we know of minor settlements in the form of simple rural farmsteads. Now too we see the first unmistakable signs of outside influence on the architecture, to begin with in LC I-II, Minoan: later in LC III, Mycenaean.

The towns

The general layout of blocks of houses separated by narrow lanes which we have seen at Middle Cycladic Phylakopi became the standard for Late Cycladic town sites, though they are by no means of uniform character. Phylakopi (City III: Fig. 45) and Ayia Irini (Fig. 46) (Periods VI and following) were extensively reconstructed at the beginning of LC I.

Drains ran below the streets and were regularly relaid. There may have been small open squares and courts. Both sites had defence walls. The layout of Ayia Irini was much less regular than that of Phylakopi, probably because of the more uneven character of the site.

The third major site of early Late Cycladic times, Akrotiri on Thera (Fig. 144; see Chapter 8), which is the most important because of its excellent state of preservation, is at the same time probably exceptional, at least in its final form. The most recent studies suggest that, at the beginning of LC I, Akrotiri may not have been so different from the other two sites, with buildings in a fairly modest style. After the rebuilding in

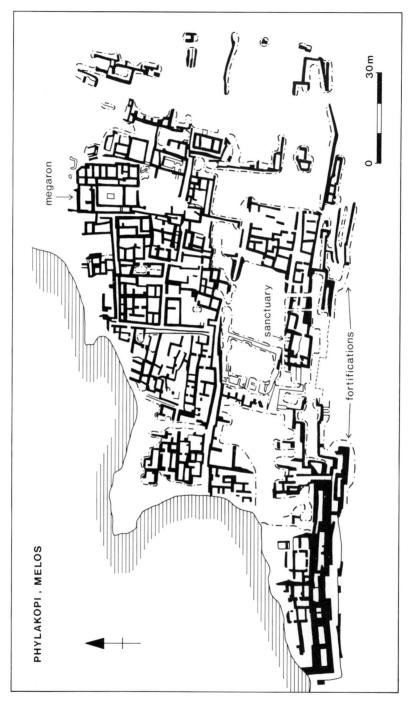

45. Phylakopi, Melos. Plan of City III (Late Cycladic). (After Renfrew and Wagstaff 1982, 42).

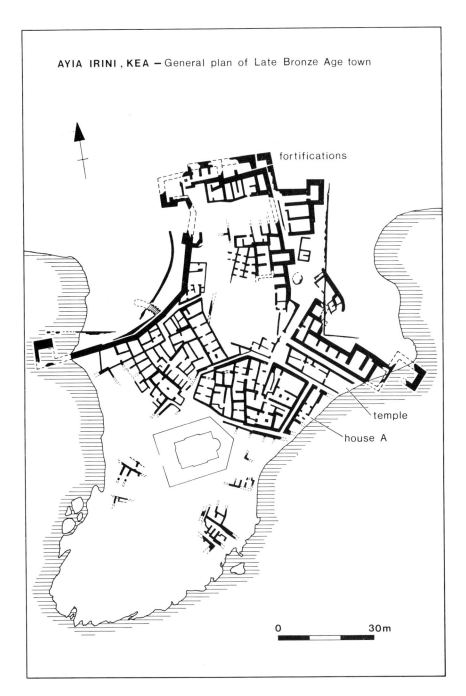

AYIA IRINI, KEA – General plan of Late Bronze Age town

fortifications

temple

house A

0   30m

46. Ayia Irini, Kea. Plan of the site in the Late Cycladic period. (After Cummer and Schofield 1984, pl. III).

the early part of LC I, the site was still laid out on an irregular block plan but, as well as relatively wide lanes and sizable open spaces, the blocks are mingled in the overall layout with independent 'villas' of essentially Minoan type, such as are not found at either Phylakopi or Ayia Irini. The use of fine ashlar masonry, sometimes for entire buildings, of certain distinctively Minoan units such as the pier-and-door partition and the lustral basin (Fig. 146) and of Minoan constructional techniques such as the insertion of wooden frameworks into the stone walls, not to mention the strongly Minoan character of many of the finds, all indicate a uniquely close connection with Crete. At the other sites this connection is evident in the finds but not in the architecture – a contrast which may have something to do with the greater availability of stone suitable for cutting on Thera, but is likely none the less to have a more profound ·significance.

Apart from the villas of Akrotiri, richly decorated with wall paintings, as well as architecturally sophisticated, there are other buildings of special character in the LC I-II settlements. At Phylakopi there was a large 'mansion'[10] (Fig. 117) in LC I which was probably the administrative centre of the site. At Ayia Irini the structure of the Temple[11] (Figs. 134, 135), which had existed since the Middle Cycladic period, is now clear. It is the only independent building on the site, long and sub-rectangular, and stands by the main entrance to the town. It was divided into three rooms and a passage, with a hearth, benches and other structures, some designed to hold the large terracotta figures found there.

Akrotiri, of course, no longer existed after LC I. Ayia Irini was destroyed by an earthquake at the end of LC II and subsequent building activity was confined to repair and reconstruction rather than redesign. At Phylakopi the entire site was rebuilt at the beginning of LC III following a limited destruction at the end of the preceding period. The rebuilding included a 'megaron' or palace[12] (Fig. 154) of distinctively mainland Mycenaean type, which incorporated part of the earlier mansion. The later unit consists of a porch or anteroom with a threshold of two large blocks and an inner chamber, passages to either side and smaller rooms to the east. A simple comparison of the Phylakopi megaron plan with that of Pylos (Fig. 155) or any other Mainland palace makes the relationship clear immediately, though the unit at Phylakopi is somewhat simpler. No details of the interior arrangments were preserved but there was a rectangular gap in the centre of the coarse plaster floor of the main room where the ceremonial hearth had presumably stood. This is one of the very rare instances where architectural remains point unambiguously to a real political event – the imposition of Mycenaean authority on Phylakopi.

In early LC III, not long after the megaron, a large shrine building[13] (Figs. 156, 157) was constructed at Phylakopi. Many, though not all, of its contents are of characteristically Mycenaean type. The identification of the building as a shrine is made certain by the existence of altars, platforms and ritual objects. It had a complicated history lasting through most of LC III. The West shrine was the first element, but an additional unit (the East shrine) was added about a hundred years later. The West shrine had one large room (6 x 6.6m) with altars, and a smaller room adjoining where cult equipment was kept. The two were connected by narrow hatches as well as a door. The space outside the entrances to the two shrines was paved and had a stone bench and a large shaped stone or 'baetyl' which must have had some ceremonial use. Like the Kea temple, the Phylakopi shrine stood close to the city limits as well as to the middle LC III fortification wall.

Two other sites have important remains of this period. An extensive building complex on Delos[14], whose history may go back to LC I, has been planned from disjointed walls located beneath the extensive remains of the later sanctuary. This has been thought a palace but the characteristic megaron unit is not evident. Grotta on Naxos was certainly an important settlement in LC III, and perhaps even earlier. The limited house plans recovered and the evidence of aerial photography from a balloon suggest that its layout may not have been dissimilar from that of Phylakopi III, namely regular blocks of houses divided by streets. A fortification/sea wall on the seaward side can also be seen on the aerial photograph.

LC I-III early saw the acme of the Late Cycladic towns from the point of view of size and probably architectural refinement though, in the case of Phylakopi, the excavators were not as impressed with the building of the Third City as with that of the Second (Middle Cycladic). Late Cycladic Thera was certainly the most sophisticated settlement of the Aegean Bronze Age.

Later, in middle LC III, political troubles began to leave their mark on island settlements. The Phylakopi fortifications were strengthened during the early thirteenth century and new settlements (e.g. Ayios Andreas on Siphnos, Koukounaries on Paros) were established, where defence was obviously the prime consideration. There seems no tangible change in architectural style at these sites nor decline in constructional standards, though the buildings were compressed within fortified circuits.

The most important Late Cycladic towns appear to have escaped or warded off the troubles that brought about the destruction of Koukounaries and the abandonment of Ayios Andreas and entered, architecturally unchanged, on a new era of prosperity. This is especially true of Grotta and its associated cemeteries of Aplomata and Kamini.

The final stage of the Late Cycladic period is something of a mystery, both from a historical and from an architectural point of view. This may be due, at least in part, to the fact that the latest levels of sites like Phylakopi are seriously eroded and accordingly difficult to interpret. There is nothing to tell us how the site came to an end or what it was like in its last years. We want to know whether the life of the town was somehow cut off in the midst of prosperity, or whether it suffered a slow decline. The evidence from Ayia Irini hints at the latter, at least on Kea.

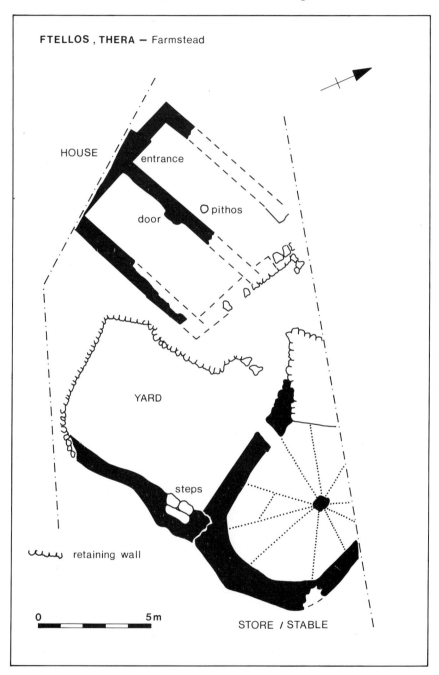

47. Ftellos, Thera. Plan of farmstead. (After Doumas 1973, 162).

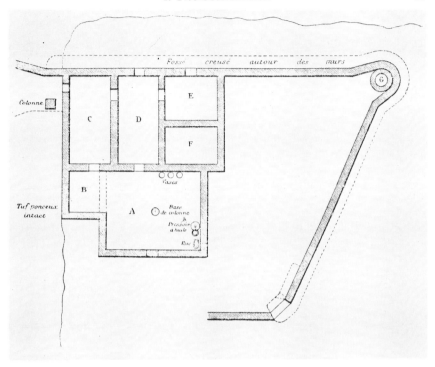

48. Therasia, plan of farmstead. (Fouqué 1879, 96).

The pottery of the final prehistoric phase is poor in contrast to what went before and the sad little shrine, built over a corner of the formerly splendid Temple, indicates a period of decline, when buildings gradually went out of use and the population dwindled. This may have been the case on other islands too. Continuity of occupation into later periods is hard to prove anywhere and seems probable only on Naxos (at Grotta). This was a 'dark' period in more senses than one, though new discoveries may slowly illuminate it.

Farmsteads[15]

Three LC I sites on Thera – at Balos, Ftellos (Fig. 47) and on the islet of Therasia (Fig. 48), part of the main island before the volcanic catastrophe – provide unique information about the character of Bronze Age farmsteads. It is quite surprising that such sites have been found on Thera, since the deep overlay of volcanic debris makes ancient remains particularly difficult to locate there. Usually it is impossible to get any clear idea of the real nature of smaller sites on the basis of surface finds alone.

Proof of the existence of minor farmsteads is clearly very important for our understanding of the overall settlement structure of prehistoric communities in the islands. Although there is no direct evidence, it seems that such small and relatively isolated establishments are more likely to have existed in periods of stability, such as that provided by the Minoan 'thalassocracy' of LC I.

The buildings at the three sites are of decidedly cruder construction than those of Akrotiri – the major settlement of the island in LC I – and the finds also lack the sophistication of the metropolis. At Balos, the complex included a yard enclosed by a wall, which was probably used for stabling, since a thick layer of straw and sheep and goat bones were found there. The finds included large storage vessels and some tools and other implements. At Ftellos, a two-roomed building had an attached byre with a wooden roof made of branches radiating from a central column. The Therasia unit again included an enclosed yard. There was a good deal of evidence of agricultural and domestic activity – grinding mills and carbonized grain, much animal bone, an oil press, loomweights and various other weights and tools.

The only other site comparable to these is at Karvounolakkoi on Naxos. This was reported as a farmstead and dated to LH IIIC by its excavator, but details have not been published.

Fortifications[16]

Mention has already been made of the fortification systems which have been found at some Cycladic sites from EC IIIA to Late Cycladic times. Such systems may have been in use even earlier but we have as yet no evidence from EC I, and possible EC II defences are only found at sites which also have EC IIIA occupation. Since the EC IIIA period was so unsettled and there are defensive works certainly of that date – from Kastri (Fig. 41) and perhaps Panormos and Mount Kynthos, it seems not unreasonable, for the present, to see the origin of Cycladic fortifications in that period.

The earliest fortified areas are relatively small (Panormos 500m², Kastri 3,750m²), at least as compared with Middle Cycladic Phylakopi (18,000m²). Small houses are huddled within the cramped circuits, often built up against the fortifications which may thus provide the back walls of a number of houses. Such dual-purpose building can be seen also in Cycladic villages of much later but also unsettled times (Fig. 42). There are small entrances and semicircular projecting towers. The Kastri towers resemble those at EH II Lerna on the Greek Mainland, from which they may perhaps be derived. The construction is clearly similar to that of contemporary houses – locally acquired stones of various sizes, sometimes set dry, sometimes in clay. There could conceivably have been upper works of brick but stone would have been stronger and plenty was available in the vicinity of most sites.

49. Phylakopi, Melos. West end of fortifications. (C. Renfrew).

The kind of attacks which these defences had to withstand were probably not very sophisticated – but there is not much to go on. We know of obsidian and metal arrowheads and other weapons which could have been shot, thrown or used in hand-to-hand fighting. Stones were also probably used as missiles (at Koukounaries, they were piled up inside the wall: Fig. 50). Occasional outworks (Kastri) may represent attempts to keep enemy 'artillery' at a distance. We do not know however about armour or about means of breaking through defences such as scaling ladders, rams or tunnelling.

Middle Cycladic fortifications are known from Ayia Irini (Fig. 40) and perhaps also from Phylakopi. At Phylakopi there is uncertainty about the date of the western sector of the main wall. The original excavators were themselves uncertain but thought that it was of Middle Cycladic origin, altered in later times. Recent investigations have dated a section of the wall further east to LH IIIB and it is tempting to apply this date to the whole of the main structure. But this may not be correct. The westernmost section seems differently constructed from that further east, making use of roughly squared masonry (Fig. 49) in marked contrast to the predominantly beach-boulder construction of the line further east (Fig. 15). The site of Phylakopi was originally on a promontory with a harbour, now silted up, on the inland side (Fig. 21). The silting process began in prehistoric times and may have advanced considerably by the Late Bronze Age. The western part of the fortifications is set so as to defend the site from the hinterland by blocking the neck of the promontory, precisely as at Ayia Irini in the Middle Cycladic period. From a historical point of view, it thus seems possible that the earliest system (Middle Cycladic?) was simply a wall across the neck of the promontory and that other parts were only built after silting of the harbour made other areas of the site vulnerable for the first time, in the Late Bronze Age. The western section of the Phylakopi wall (Fig. 49) has survived in parts to a height of about 4m and was originally even higher. It consisted of two walls, each 2m thick and 2m apart, with cross walls between – the intervening spaces being filled with rubble, or sometimes used as rooms. It had indentations, projecting bastions and probably a protected gateway, though apparently no regular system of towers.

It should be added here, for clarity's sake, that there is some further evidence for fortifications at Phylakopi. In the original excavations were found traces of an outwork (Fig. 45), undated but presumably contemporary with the larger wall, some 2.5m outside the main line; more recently, a line of wall (Fig. 15) has been discovered, perhaps the same as the outwork though the section located was further east, which belongs to a separate system built early in the Late Cycladic period. The middle LC III works are considered below.

The first fortifications at Ayia Irini (Fig. 40) belong to an early if not the earliest Middle Cycladic phase. The stretch of wall excavated is made of flat slabs of irregular size but well laid in a dry-stone technique. A rounded projecting bastion guarded a narrow entrance. In the later Middle Cycladic period the site was enlarged and a completely new fortification system built. This had fine ashlar fabric but a crude inner face. This system was subsequently altered and extended (Fig. 46), the circuit now including a number of square or rectangular towers, one of which protected the entrance into the town.

In the Late Cycladic period, the fortifications at Ayia Irini continued in use and were repaired in early LC III, after the earthquake which so devastated the site at the end of LC II. We have already considered the wall of roughly squared masonry which was built at Phylakopi in LC I, though its full extent and character are not yet known. If there was no Middle Cycladic wall, this will have been the first at the site. New sections of wall (Figs. 15, 156) were certainly built in the thirteenth century using large rounded boulders from the sea shore. As stated above, it is possible that the whole of the main system was built at this time.

Roughly contemporary with the new section of wall at Phylakopi were the occupation and fortification of Ayios Andreas and Koukounaries. The wall at the former site was reconstructed and reused in the Geometric period. In the thirteenth century the defences, which ran round the edge of the plateau, consisted of an outer wall about 1.20m thick, with insets, and a much more substantial inner wall (about 3.50m thick) which had eight projecting rectangular towers. The walls are well built of dry-stone blocks, relatively large though somewhat variable in size. There were narrow gateways. Behind two of the towers were inset spaces and stairs to the rampart. In addition to its fortifications the site was remote and on a hilltop and thus exceptionally well protected.

At Koukounaries the wall (Fig. 50) which blocked the main entrance to

50. Koukounaries, Paros. Inner face of fortification/terrace wall at top of ascent. Stone missiles are piled against the wall. (Courtesy D. Schilardi).

the site also served as a retaining wall for the terrace above, on which the building complex stood, and the buildings nearest the wall used it as an element in their construction. The technique is not dissimilar from that at Ayios Andreas. There are two built walls with a rubble filling. Many of the blocks are large and roughly squared and the construction has been described as 'Cyclopean'. Fortifications, as yet not investigated in detail, also existed on the lower terraces of the site. At some point an attempt was made to block the ascent to the upper citadel by dropping an enormous boulder across the steep, narrow path.

Koukounaries was destroyed and Ayios Andreas abandoned in middle LC III, in spite of their defences. At Phylakopi, the fortifications presumably remained in use until the site was abandoned in late LC III, and the same may be true of Ayia Irini.

These Cycladic defence systems point to the uncertainties of island life throughout much of the Bronze Age, even in times of considerable material prosperity and apparent stability. Whether they were to give protection against neighbours from the same or other islands (pirates have often been a problem in the history of the Aegean), or intruders from further afield, it is difficult to tell, though they can sometimes be plausibly associated with events attested by other archaeological evidence, such as the EC IIIA invasions. Whatever else, they represent the results of a coherent and planned attitude to defence and required a high degree of organisation of manpower in terms of the quarrying and/or collection of stone, its transport and construction.

Settlement patterns and history[17]

Some fundamental influences on the choice of places for settlements have already been considered. But, in spite of these, there remained a substantial element of choice which was partly dependent on contemporary historical circumstances. As well as influencing the location of settlements, these circumstances also affected their size, number and character. It is therefore useful to conclude this chapter with a look at the changing patterns of settlement during the Cycladic Bronze Age and the information that we can derive from them.

It is clear that there was a marked increase in the number of sites in the Cyclades between the Neolithic period and EC I-II. In EC I-II it appears that defence was not a primary consideration since the sites are relatively numerous (Fig. 51), unfortified and the buildings probably scattered. Within the Early Cycladic period, we have tended to assume that, since it was in EC II that the islands achieved their highest level of material prosperity, this must also have been the time when settlements were most numerous. Although this may still prove to be true, at present the evidence points the other way.

EC I sites are in fact more in number, though this does not necessarily mean that the EC I population of the islands was larger or more sophisticated than in the following period, and the difficulty of dating from surface finds alone means that a large number of sites can only be assigned rather generally to Early Cycladic.

EC I settlements were small and not highly organised. A recent survey[18] suggests that many of them had populations no bigger than about 28 persons. EC II villages were probably larger and better planned, at least if we may judge by the buildings at Ayia Irini, and this view seems in accordance with the generally higher level of material culture which required and encouraged more effective social organisation.

Against this background, the drop in number of known settlement sites between EC II and IIIA by about 75 per cent is staggering but nevertheless comprehensible in the context of the incursions into the Cyclades by people from Anatolia, which are suggested by other archaeological evidence. The changed character of the sites, which are almost all either older settlements newly fortified (Mount Kynthos), newly built fortified eyries (Kastri) or remote natural refuges (Cave of Zas), also fits into this historical picture – though one should remember that Ayia Irini remained undefended. We cannot tell who occupied these sites – islanders seeking refuge or invaders consolidating their foothold. The mixed pottery finds – traditional Cycladic and newly intrusive Anatolian – suggest at least that locals had had time to be absorbed or to acquire some of the new foreign elements, or vice versa.

EC IIIB sites are no more numerous than those of EC IIIA, and perhaps even fewer. The little that we know of the settlements (Phylakopi and

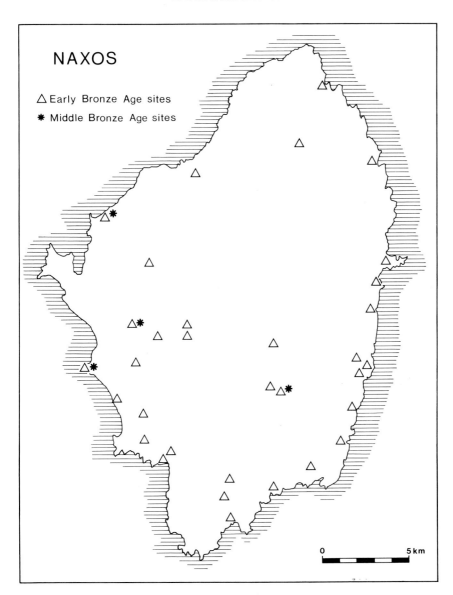

51. Distribution of Early and Middle Cycladic sites on Naxos. (After Fotou 1983, 17).

Paroikia) suggests that they retained the greater degree of cohesion developed in EC IIIA but were in more accessible positions and unfortified. Since however fortifications appear to be characteristic of both the preceding (EC IIIA) and succeeding (Middle Cycladic) periods they may well eventually prove to have been usual also in EC IIIB.

Middle Cycladic sites are more numerous than in EC IIIB. They also seem to be larger and more complex, probably because each acted as the main centre for a considerable area, often the whole island. Attention was paid to defensive potential and there were sometimes, perhaps usually, fortifications. It seems likely that the centralisation of population which had been desirable in EC IIIA for mutual protection, was subsequently found to have other advantages – organisational and economic. The consequent development of these more sophisticated centres formed the basis for Middle and Late Cycladic developments.

Little change in the pattern is discernible in the early Late Cycladic period (LC I-II), although the three small farmsteads on Thera (Fig. 115), remote from the main centre at Akrotiri, perhaps suggest a greater degree of stability. It will be interesting to see if this partial reversion to a scattered settlement pattern, though without weakening the status of the metropolis, proves to be characteristic of the Cyclades as a whole. At this time the material culture of the islands is dominated by Cretan influence – probably the archaeological foundation of the later belief that Minos, the legendary king of Crete, had once had a thalassocracy (sea empire).

In spite of these indications of relative stability, fortifications were still found necessary. Either the islanders did not submit willingly to Cretan control or else they were not at peace among themselves.

One aspect of the early Late Cycladic settlements which has provoked comment is the apparently uneven intensity of Minoan influence. Akrotiri, Ayia Irini and Phylakopi have seemed to display such influence to a far greater degree than other sites and the reason suggested[19] is that these islands were regular stops on a Minoan trading route to Mainland Greece, whereas others were not. The lack of Minoan material on the important islands of Naxos and Paros, in particular, has seemed to demand some such explanation. However, it will not have escaped the reader's notice that the three sites mentioned as especially 'Minoanised' (though not all to the same extent) are the three which have been most intensively excavated. Recent discoveries of early Late Cycladic (including imported Minoan) material on Naxos (Grotta, Mikre Vigla), where it was previously barely known, show that the previous 'absence' of such evidence was simply due to the accidental nature of archaeological discovery, and the concept of trading routes must be rethought.

There is little sign of change between LC I-II and early LC III, although we know this to have been the point when the Mycenaeans drove the Minoans from the islands. Only the site of Monolithos on Thera – the first known occupation of the island since the great eruption – gives a hint that Mycenaean involvement in the Cyclades may have brought about an expansion of settlement and that some of the sites where Mycenaean pottery has been found may have been first settled at this time. Again we may note that fortifications continued in use at the major sites.

Middle LC III sees significant changes. At least two important new fortified sites were founded (Ayios Andreas and Koukounaries), both in highly defensive locations and strongly protected with substantial walls. Other sites as yet unexcavated (Ayios Spyridon on Melos) may also belong to this period. New fortifications had been built at Phylakopi a little earlier and other unexcavated sites may be part of this pattern. Some unprotected settlements might have been abandoned now but there is as yet no proof of this. These new foundations are a clear indication of firm action against new and threatening circumstances in the islands, but their ultimate failure is demonstrated by the sacking of Koukounaries and the abandonment of Ayios Andreas at the end of the phase. It is tempting to associate these events with the destruction of the Mainland palaces at about the same time, but there is so far little positive evidence of this.

In late LC III some islands entered on a period of new and apparently unhindered prosperity and had wide-ranging contacts. The number of sites where this transformation occurred is not large – Grotta with associated cemeteries at Aplomata and Kamini, Phylakopi and some hints from elsewhere including, rather improbably, Kimolos. There do not appear to have been any new sites founded now and it may simply be that some islands benefited from the presence of Mycenaean refugees from the Mainland troubles, who already had established foreign contacts and who brought their personal wealth and skills with them.

Only a few sites – all previously occupied – remained in use in the final phase of the Bronze Age. These must have been gradually deserted and there may have been a brief period of virtual depopulation of the islands before the Iron Age revival began.

5

The Early Cycladic Period

We have now considered the physical character of the Cyclades, the archaeological sequence, the history of exploration, and the settlements of the Cycladic Bronze Age, and it is time to look more carefully at specific aspects of material culture for which there is archaeological evidence and at the changing historical picture which can be built up on the basis of an overall view of the different classes of finds.

(i) Settlements, cemeteries and burial customs

The sites of the Early Cycladic period were discussed in Chapter 4. In very general terms, they show a slow development in size and sophistication, and regular overall planning is evident in EC II and IIIB. The earlier sites (EC I and II) are usually coastal and undefended; in EC IIIA some sites are more remote, situated primarily with defence and security in mind, and provided with fortifications. The EC IIIB towns are coastal and unfortified, but apparently larger and more substantial than their predecessors.

Early Cycladic I-II cemeteries and tombs[1]

Finds from graves comprise a very large part of the known material culture of the Early Cycladic period. The solid stonework of the tombs is easily recognisable, in contrast to the more scattered and fragmentary evidence of settlement, and the possibility that they might contain fine objects (not, in fact, a *probability*) in the shape of marble vases or figurines or metal objects, has made them the target of thieves, especially in recent years.

The general character of Cycladic tombs has long been known.[2] Many were excavated in the nineteenth century, especially by Tsountas, who published his findings and comments on tomb types and burial practices.[3] More recently the work of Tsountas has been extended and updated by Professor Christos Doumas, who has excavated several cemeteries, clarified many issues with the aid of more advanced

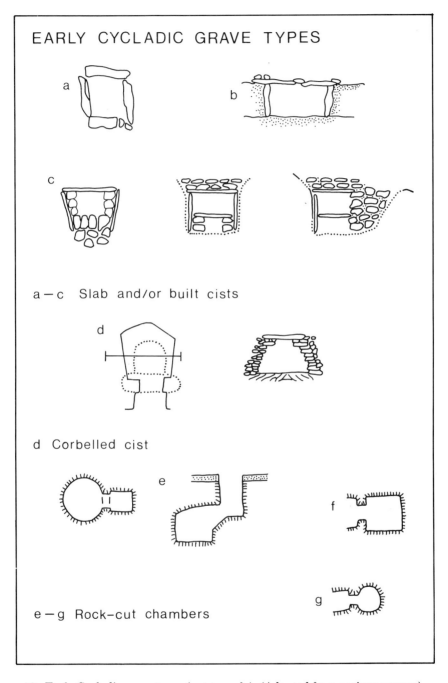

EARLY CYCLADIC GRAVE TYPES

a

b

c

a — c Slab and/or built cists

d

d Corbelled cist

e

f

g

e — g Rock–cut chambers

52. Early Cycladic grave types (not to scale). (Adapted from various sources).

techniques, and published a comprehensive review of Early Cycladic burial customs.[4]

Throughout the Early Cycladic period, graves were grouped in cemeteries close to the settlements, though grave types (Fig. 52) vary both in detail and in overall form. In EC I and II, various forms of the cist – a subterranean built box – were used for inhumation burials. On Syros, in EC II, there was also an unusual type of cist with corbelled roof and false entrance for show rather than use. In EC IIIA, some cists are still found and it is likely that rock-cut chambers were introduced. Both of these continued in use in EC IIIB, when the practice of burying children in urns within the settlements also began. Although a wide range of grave goods has been recovered from Cycladic tombs (pottery, marble vessels, weapons, bronze tools, obsidian, bone and stone jewellery, silver vessels, lead models and figurines), well furnished graves are in fact quite rare and burials accompanied by one or two clay pots or by nothing at all are common, especially in the earlier part of the period, when marble objects are entirely lacking.

The goods buried with the dead seem to have been things that belonged to them in everyday life, the variation in quantity and quality presumably reflecting differences in wealth and status. It is therefore likely that the belief of their surviving relatives was that the dead would continue to exist in some form, and might be able to maintain a standard of living not inferior to that achieved in life. The special treatment accorded to the skulls of old burials, which were carefully set aside while the remainder of the skeleton was cleared away, suggests respect for the head as the core of a person's being and is a further indication of a belief in some kind of personal survival.

There is a little evidence for some form of ritual activity within the cemeteries. This involved the use of clay vases and was associated with platform structures.

Cemeteries

The normal setting for a cemetery was on sloping ground close to the settlement to which it belonged. The graves were dug into the slope with their entrances looking outwards, and their orientation was governed by this alone. In the earlier cemeteries especially, the graves were laid out in clusters which are likely to have contained the burials of a family group. Use was made of natural features, like outcrops of rock which conveniently divided up the cemetery area, both to keep the clusters separate and to prevent the erosion of the tombs.

In the course of time and with the increasing practice of multiple burial in two- or even three-storied cists, this habit declined except, significantly, on Syros, where single burials continued to be deposited. This change indicates that the larger tomb, containing a greater number of burials, took the place of the family cluster.

Some support for the interpretation of the clusters and multiple tombs as belonging to family groups can be found at Late Neolithic Kephala where cist tombs fairly similar to those of Early Cycladic times had preserved skeletal remains which proved that they contained men, women and children together.

A rather different form of clustering which seems based on social status is that of the larger, better built, richer and more widely-spaced in contrast to the smaller, cruder, poorer, more cramped, which was noticed by Doumas at the transitional EC I-II site of Ayioi Anargyroi on Naxos (Fig. 53).

Most cemeteries consisted of between 15 and 20 graves. Doumas collated the evidence for cemetery size and noted only eight sites where there were 50 graves or more. Of these, only three had 100 or more graves. By far the largest was that at Chalandriani on Syros, with more than 600 tombs of EC II and occasionally EC IIIA date. A few isolated graves are also known.

The larger cemeteries either belong to the mature phase of Early Cycladic culture (EC II) or have finds of more than one period.[5] Some sites show continuity of use from one Early Cycladic phase to another, while others are more restricted in date.

Although one or two cist-tomb cemeteries were still used in EC IIIA, there is no evidence of further uninterrupted use of specific sites into later times. The cist tomb-type itself is however still found at the beginning of the Late Bronze Age.

Tombs

The cist (Fig. 54) is basically a pit dug in the ground, stone-lined and covered with a large capstone or stones. The exact shape varies but the trapezoidal is the most common. Dimensions are also very various but the length may be in the region of 0.80m (not more than 1.20m), the width 0.30-0.80m, and the depth 0.30-0.60m.

Easily the most common type in EC I has each side built of a single large slab. The usual EC II form was not dissimilar, but the fourth side was constructed of dry-stone walling, perhaps to facilitate re-opening and later insertion of further burials. There is some overlap between these two types but no doubt that the former is essentially EC I and the latter EC II, when multiple burials also became very much more common.

Graves were often floored with pebbles set in clay and a long 'pillow' slab was quite frequently provided for the head of the deceased. Floors and pillow slabs again are much more commonly found in late EC I and EC II than in early EC I.

A further type of grave (Fig. 52d), not a true cist, belongs to EC II but is peculiar to Syros. This consists of a subterranean pit, stone-lined up to a point, then roofed with corbelled stonework (each course laid further inwards than the one below) and finally closed with a small capstone. The tomb has a formal doorway, usually about 0.50-0.60m by the same,

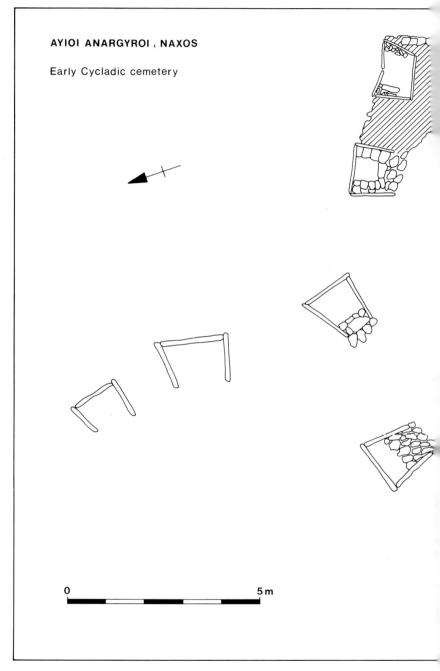

53. Plan of cemetery at Ayioi Anargyroi, Naxos. (After Doumas 1977a, fig. 17).

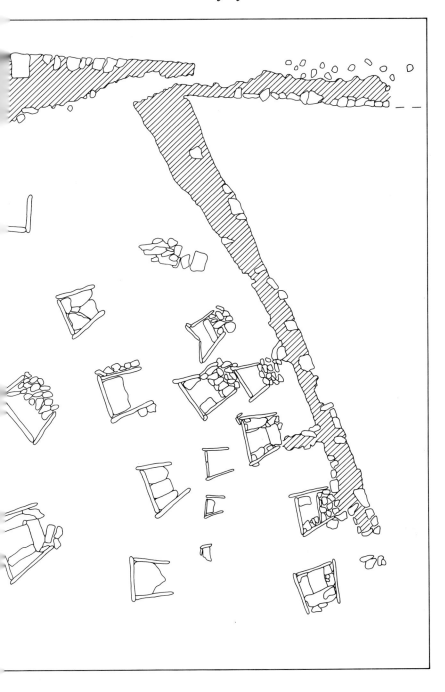

54. Early Cycladic cist tomb at Ayioi
Anargyroi, Naxos. (C. Doumas).

with jamb and lintel slabs over a stone threshold. In front of this there is
often a short entrance passage, always under 1m, and frequently less
than half that in length.

Burial

The dead person was always buried (inhumed): there are no instances of
cremation. The corpse was placed in the grave in a strongly flexed
(contracted) position, the knees drawn up under the chin – a posture
which must have been set soon after death and which may have been
maintained by some form of binding. The graves are rarely large enough
to have accommodated a body laid out at full length. The head might
rest on a 'pillow' and some of the grave goods be placed before it.
Sometimes stones were set on top of the body.

   When further burials were made in the same tomb, as they often were
in the case of single-storey graves, the skull of the incumbent was usually
left in position but the remainder of the skeleton was swept aside to make
room for the new occupant.

Multi-storey cists

When tombs were given an extra storey (Fig. 52c) – a practice most
common in late EC I and EC II – the original chamber was cleared to the
extent required for the building of internal wall-supports for a new floor
slab which would form the base of the upper chamber. After the upper

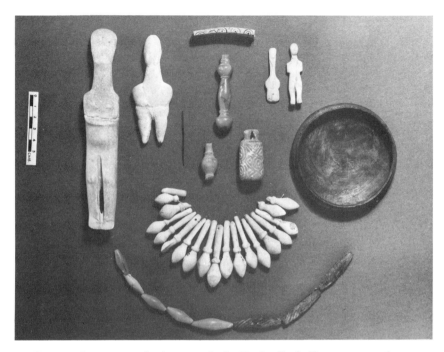

55. Group of grave goods from a single Early Cycladic grave on Amorgos. (Ashmolean Museum).

chamber was taken into use, the lower was used as an ossuary to contain the original burials that had been made in it, as well as any remains that were subsequently removed from the new chamber during its period of use. In the rare cases where a third storey was added, the lowest became disused, the middle the ossuary and the third the burial chamber. From the fact that multi-storey graves were sunk relatively deep into the ground, it is clear that they were designed as such from the start, even though the upper part was not built until required.

Burial practices and beliefs[6]

As already observed, there is great variation in the number and richness of the objects in different tombs. Some had nothing at all or merely a simple pottery vessel. A tomb on Keros, on the other hand, contained two marble figures of musicians as well as two folded-arm figures; one on Paros had fourteen schematic marble figures, a necklace of beads and sea-shells and a vase. Such differences in practice have some chronological significance since the earliest EC I burials have no marble vessels or figures, no obsidian blades or metal objects. Metal finds are extremely rare before EC II. Probably more important than the date, however, was the wealth or status of the occupant of the grave. This idea

– that those richer in life had more and finer grave goods (Fig. 55) buried with them – seems to be supported by the finer construction, larger size and more generous spacing of the richer graves at Ayioi Anargyroi.

Within the graves, the preferred position for grave goods seems to have been in front of the face of the deceased.

The fact that the dead were provided with objects from their earthly existence should mean that the ancient islanders hoped or expected to continue a similar existence in the next world. The poor could take little with them, or nothing, though they might perhaps have been buried with some perishable objects – wooden beads or figures, floral necklaces, for example – which have left no trace.

The marble figures of female form which accompany some burials are often thought to have had a specifically religious significance, to be figures of a deity or perhaps her worshippers. A number of them were repaired in ancient times, good evidence that they had been put to some use in their owners' lifetimes, conceivably in household shrines. They would then have been placed in the grave, as the particular possessions of the occupant which represented his or her devotion to the divinity and thus hope for happiness in the hereafter. Some further comments on the significance of the figures are offered in the relevant section below.

Other grave finds – lead boat models, obsidian tools – occasionally seem to hint at the occupation of the deceased and we may note a set of bronze carpenter's tools from a cist of later Bronze Age date at Aila on Naxos.

Weapons, tools and jewellery would have had obvious uses in life, as would pottery of which so many basic containers were made, including of course those for food and drink. Some of the vases found in the graves are uncommon on settlement sites and may have been made specially for grave use.[7]

Cemetery ritual

There is a little evidence for ritual associated with the built platforms (Fig. 56) which are found in some cemeteries. These platforms are of two types – small stone settings over the tops of individual graves; and larger structures built in or at the edge of the cemetery area. The platform has only been recognised relatively recently (by Professor Doumas) as an important element in the Early Cycladic cist cemetery, but there are indications in old excavation reports that such may have been found by earlier excavators who did not appreciate their importance.

For the question of ritual, it might be significant that vessels are occasionally, though not regularly, found on the capstones of tombs where they could have been left after use in some liquid-pouring ceremony. More important was the discovery, in the Ayioi Anargyroi cemetery, of a deposit of hat-like vases (Fig. 58, no. 8) in an area of the cemetery near a large platform, to which access was provided by a flight of steps. The number of graves, the fact that the shape is uncommon on

56. Platform over an Early Cycladic cist grave at Akrotiri, Naxos. (C. Doumas).

settlement sites, and their relationship to the platform, show that they must have been intimately connected with the use of the cemetery – probably for pouring libations or holding offerings of other kinds.

Early Cycladic III tombs and practices

There is virtually no evidence for burial ritual after EC II and the tomb types themselves are also less well known.

EC IIIA pottery is found in several cists, which must therefore at least have continued in use into that period. No rock-cut chamber tombs are known from the Cyclades at this time but EC IIIA-type pottery occurs in chamber tombs at Manika on Euboea (Fig. 52e), where some of the tomb plans have been compared to those at Phylakopi in EC IIIB. It is therefore not unlikely that the tomb type was introduced into the Cyclades in EC IIIA, though examples remain to be found.

EC IIIB chambers are known from the cemetery close by the settlement at Phylakopi, the unpublished site of Aspro Chorio in north-east Melos, and possibly from Cape Spathi (Fournakia), also on Melos, though there is no secure dating evidence for the latter site. The Phylakopi tombs (Fig. 52f, g) consist of round or sub-rectangular chambers, sometimes with hipped roofs (with short downward-sloping approach passages). Additional chambers sometimes opened off the central one. The tombs had been robbed in advance of the excavations

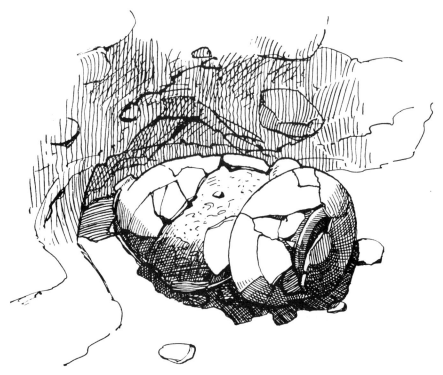

57. Pithos burial (EC IIIB), Phylakopi, Melos. (Dawkins and Droop 1911, 8).

and only fragments of pottery were recovered.

The other burial custom to make its appearance in EC IIIB is the practice of burying children within the settlements in jars, themselves covered with one or more bowls (Fig. 57). There are several examples from Phylakopi and one from Paroikia on Paros. These are dated to EC IIIB by the type of vessels in which they are found – i.e. Geometric painted, as well as coarser varieties. There are several instances also from Ayia Irini, but those are Middle Cycladic in date.

Origins and relationships of Early Cycladic tomb types

For the origins of the most common Early Cycladic grave type, the cist, it seems unnecessary to look outside the islands. Built stone tombs with superficial platforms, as well as slab-sided cists (and some examples of jar burial) are found at Late Neolithic Kephala. Other examples of similarities between Early Cycladic material culture and that of Kephala have already been mentioned.

Some areas of the Aegean coastline[8] and the island of Crete have yielded tombs and finds which are similar to those of EC I and/or EC II, but these do not antedate the Cycladic material. Their significance is discussed in (vi) below. The derivation of the EC III chamber tombs is uncertain. They may be a purely local development, worked out in localities where the rock could be easily excavated and the chamber left without further support. The object would have been to provide at the same time a more capacious and a more monumental burial chamber.

As for EC IIIB jar burials,[9] there are remote antecedents in Late Neolithic Kephala. It is perhaps also conceivable that they are connected with a similar practice known in Anatolia, since there are no instances from EC I or II and they appear in the Cyclades following the period of Anatolian intrusions, though not at the same time as its most obvious features.

Summary

Burial practices in the Early Cycladic period are thus dominated by the cemeteries of cist tombs. These held multiple inhumations, a tradition which, together with the cists, appears to go back to the later Neolithic period in the islands.

Grave goods were sometimes placed with the dead, occasionally in profusion. This practice may have been the norm if the offerings were frequently of perishable material and have not survived. Some form of ceremonies took place in the cemeteries, either at the time of burial or at anniversaries, or both.

EC III sees changes in this as in other spheres of material culture. A few cist burials are still found and the chamber tomb may have been first used. Chamber tombs are definitely attested in EC IIIB, when jar burials are also introduced, but no cists are at present known.

(ii) Pottery and stone vessels

Pottery[10]

It seems appropriate to begin a survey of Early Cycladic artefacts with the pottery, which is of fundamental importance both to the way of life of the Bronze Age islanders and to archaeological analysis.

The strictly archaeological uses of the corpus of Early Cycladic pottery are standard ones. Continuous scholarly investigation has established a sequence of development so that we know broadly what fabrics, shapes, decorative motifs and techniques are characteristic of each of the main chronological divisions of the period (Figs. 58, 59) and sometimes how they vary within it.

The establishment of such a sequence is inevitably a complex process, and not so clear-cut as the above remarks might suggest. The features mentioned do not of course change in unison so that, while a particular vase shape may be confined to a single period, the motifs that are used to

		SMALL BOWL SAUCER	SPHERICAL PYXIS	FRYING PAN	DUCK VASE
I	K A M P O S	4	1	5	
II		9 / 10	11	12	
IIIA		17	18		19
IIIB		23			24

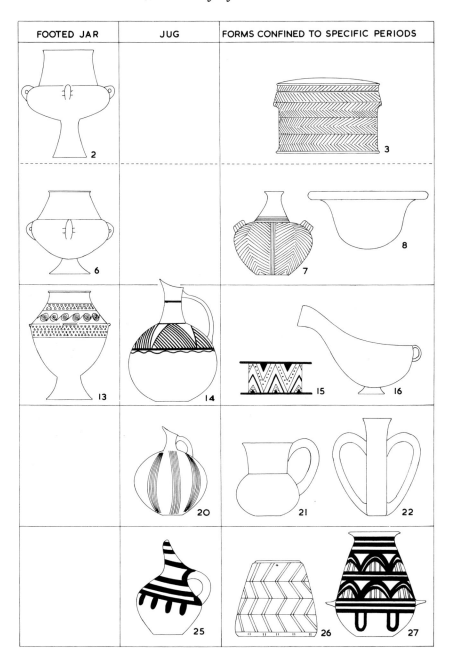

58. *left and above* Pottery forms of the Early Cycladic period. (Courtesy J.A. Macgillivray. For sources, see Barber and Macgillivray 1980, 142).

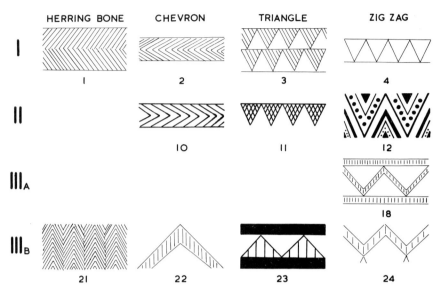

59. *above and right* Decorative motifs on Early Cycladic pottery. (Courtesy J.A. Macgillivray. Sources as for Fig. 58).

decorate it can be found earlier and/or later. So the dating of any group of pottery depends on a careful assessment of all the features represented and on exactly which are present or absent.

One special difficulty has confronted researchers in this field in the Cyclades, namely the very small number of excavated Early Cycladic settlement sites. Settlements, in contrast to tombs, can be expected to produce stratified (layered) deposits which give a reasonably clear picture of the sequence of change in the various ceramic features. The lack of such material has made analysis more speculative than it would otherwise have been.

Apart from use as a dating medium, where it is particularly valuable because so commonly found and in such large quantities, pottery may reflect influences either from or on other areas, thus providing information about the nature and extent of cultural contact between different sites and regions.

Pottery also illustrates other important aspects of Cycladic life. In itself it gives us some idea of contemporary attitudes to the aesthetics of shape and decoration and of the technical means developed to express them. In addition, it frequently illuminates the round of daily life, for clay vessels were used for a much wider range of functions than are likely to spring readily to the mind of a modern reader.[11] As well as for eating and drinking, mixing and cooking food, they would have been employed for carrying water and the collection, preparation and transport of other liquids (oil, wine). Storage of grain, fruit and other solids was also in ceramic vessels. Lidded vases ('pyxides') were probably used as boxes for

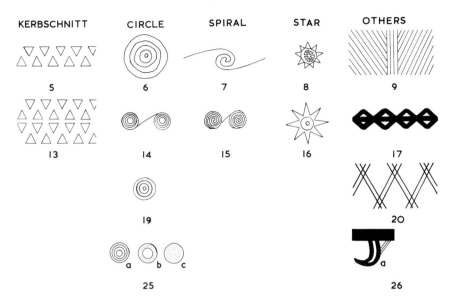

jewellery or other small objects. Lamps were often made of pottery and so, sometimes, were burial urns. Vases were regularly placed in graves, as we have seen, where they were probably intended to perform the same functions for the dead person in the next world as they had fulfilled in this one, though some forms which are only or mainly found in graves may have had special purposes.

Apart from one kiln at Ayia Irini, no evidence for the manufacturing techniques of Early Cycladic pottery has yet been discovered, other than that yielded by the vases themselves. Some quite sophisticated shapes were achieved, though normally without the use of the wheel, which was not used before EC IIIA, and then very rarely.

Early Cycladic I pottery

The basic fabric is usually heavy and gritty, though the surfaces are highly, if somewhat crudely, burnished to produce a dark (usually brown or black) lustrous finish. The only form of decoration consists of simple rectilinear patterns (Fig. 60) incised into the clay. The incisions were often filled with a white substance to make the patterns stand out. In the transitional EC I-II Kampos group a slightly different decorative technique – that of stamping designs onto the vase – is sometimes adopted. Curvilinear pattern elements are introduced at the same time.

The most common features in pottery from the settlements are the bowl shape which often has a thickened or 'rolled' rim and the use of a long tubular lug on the sides of the vessels.

60. Cylindrical pyxis (EC I) with incised and white-filled decoration. (Ashmolean Museum).

A wider range of shapes is known from the cemeteries, where fine fabric is more commonly found and the use of incised decoration is much more frequent. It is not yet certain whether these differences are a true reflection of EC I practices and that special vases were made exclusively for funerary use, or whether it is simply that the most common domestic vessels were not used as grave goods.

Among the best known cemetery shapes are pyxides (Figs. 60, 62) (lidded clay boxes) of both spherical and cylindrical form, the latter being characteristically EC I; footed collared jars (Fig. 70 – marble) with high, wide, conical necks, narrowing towards the top, lugs on the body, and often pedestals. Such jars without pedestals are found also in settlements.

In the Kampos phase, the frying pan (Fig. 61) (see EC II) is introduced and the hat vase, which seems to have been particularly associated with cemetery rituals (see above), is also found.

Early Cycladic II pottery

The most important developments of EC II are the introduction of new and finer fabrics, the first painted decoration, additions to the range of shapes, and some significant relationships with the pottery of Mainland Greece.

61. *right* Frying pan (EC II) with stamped decoration. (Ashmolean Museum).

62. *below* Painted cylindrical pyxis (EC II) from Syros. (National Archaeological Museum, Athens. Photo: T.A.P.).

63. Sauceboat (EC II) from Chalan-   64. Tankard (EC IIIA) from Ayia Irini,
driani, Syros. (British Museum).   Kea. (University of Cincinnati).

The most conservative EC II fabric is that decorated with incised or stamped patterns, whose heavy burnished character is similar to that found in EC I. The same is true of the decorative techniques. Several shapes (bowl, spherical pyxis, footed collared jar, frying pan) continue in use.

The simple painted decoration (Fig. 62), which now occurs for the first time, is found on a fine smooth light-coloured fabric (Patterned ware).

Another fine light fabric is treated with a darker surface coat: this is called 'Urfirnis' or Glazed ware.

Important and characteristic EC II shapes are the jug, which is introduced now, the 'saucer' (a small bowl with thin inturned rim and low foot) and the sauceboat (Fig. 63), whose form is indicated by its name but whose function is obscure. Lamp or drinking vessel are the most canvassed. The saucer and sauceboat are also standard on the Greek Mainland in EH II, though Cycladic potters might just as well have been responsible for their development.

Another new shape is the two-part cylindrical pyxis (Fig. 62). The earlier spherical pyxis continues in use, though the shape is now more squat. The function of the odd frying-pan form[12] has never been satisfactorily explained. The vessel is a shallow dish with vertical sides and a projecting two-pronged handle. The underside is often decorated (Figs. 58 no. 12, 61) with abstract or sometimes figurative scenes and frequently has a representation of the female vulva just above the handles (= legs?).

One interpretation is that these vessels were filled with water which, in conjunction with the shiny burnished surface of the clay, would have enabled them to be used as mirrors. It was thought at one time that they were an essentially funerary form, but they are in fact also known from settlements. The elaborate decoration and use of female genitalia in the

65. Duck vase (EC IIIB) with ridged decoration, from Amorgos. (Ashmolean Museum).

66. *above right* Barrel jar (EC IIIB) in the Geometric style, from Phylakopi. (National Archaeological Museum, Athens. Photo: T.A.P.).

67. *right* Melian bowl (EC IIIB), from Melos. (British Museum).

same way as on the marble figurines suggests that they had some special symbolic function which we do not yet understand.

A range of semifine to semicoarse domestic pottery, which should be added to the known EC II repertoire, has been found at Ayia Irini.[13] It has to be remembered that most published pottery, especially from older excavations, is in the finer or decorated fabrics and that coarser undecorated pottery has often been neglected. Although it is reasonable to expect coarse shapes to duplicate those of the finer wares in many instances, this is not inevitably the case, and an important aspect of the former class is that they are much more likely to throw light on everyday activities.

Early Cycladic IIIA pottery

This period is specially marked by the introduction of new and distinctive shapes. These include the tankard (Fig. 64), the depas amphikypellon (a tall narrow tubular vessel with two prominent handles), the bell cup and the straight-sided plate. Most of these are found in a fabric which was covered with a fine quality slip and then burnished to a

68. Kernos (EC IIIB) in the Geometric style. (Ashmolean Museum).

high glossy finish. The Anatolian origin of the forms has already been discussed.[14]

Incised (and white-filled) decoration is still found occasionally on vessels in this new fabric. There are a few rarer painted pieces – all pedestalled cups, a new shape but this time probably of local origin.

New too is a form which became much more common in EC IIIB – the duck vase, a closed globular vessel with a small handle on top and a narrow spout projecting upwards.

Other shapes – the saucer, spherical pyxis and jug – are inherited from EC II.

One or two examples of wheel-made vases have been noted but these are rare.

Early Cycladic IIIB pottery

The pottery of this period is related to that of EC IIIA through the continued use of incised, and often white-filled decoration on dark burnished surfaces (not so lustrous as in EC IIIA and conveniently called 'dark-faced') and the continuity of certain shapes, perhaps most notably

69. Beaked jug (EC IIIB) in the
Geometric style. (British Museum).

the duck vase (Fig. 65) and the beaked jug.

There are changes and developments as well. The dark-faced pottery includes some forms not found earlier and, in particular, there is a marked increase in painted decoration. This consists chiefly of geometric designs in dark paint on a thin white slip (Figs. 66-69). The slip was applied only over the area of the vase which was to be decorated. The fabric of this class of so-called 'Geometric' or 'Rectilinear' pottery is distinctive. It is much harder fired than was normal in Early Cycladic times and often had reddish surfaces and a grey core.

An important new shape is the barrel jar (Fig. 66). New too are various cup types and the spouted 'Melian' bowl (Fig. 67). The multiple 'kernos' (Fig. 68), which consists of a number of tiny vessels set on a stand, is a striking form which probably originated in EC II. The beaked jug (Fig. 69) is a characteristic shape, developed from forms found in EC II and IIIA. In broken fragments it can be seen that the handle was 'thrust' through the wall of the vase in the process of fitting and projects into the interior – an Anatolian feature.

At Phylakopi, the dark-faced incised ware ceased to be made in the latter part of EC IIIB. At the same time and perhaps as a replacement, there was some use of linear motifs in white paint on a dark ground. Curvilinear motifs were also introduced into the range of patterns.

Phylakopi is the only site which provides clear stratigraphic information for EC IIIB, and the features just mentioned seem to form the basis for a useful chronological distinction between earlier and later phases of the period. There are however some difficulties over this distinction,[15] because the evidence from Ayia Irini appears to conflict with that from Phylakopi. At the Melian site neither incised pottery nor the distinctive duck vase shape occur after EC IIIB, with the exception of two painted duck vases of eccentric shape which are still, in any case, probably EC III. On Kea, however, both are found in Middle Cycladic levels, the duck vase in typically Middle Cycladic fabric.

Apart from the fact that the Ayia Irini incised pottery may not be closely similar to that from Phylakopi, there is a possible explanation for this situation in the disturbed conditions of early EC III. Ayia Irini was abandoned at the end of EC IIIA and probably only reoccupied at the end of EC IIIB. Phylakopi was destroyed by earthquake at the end of a lengthy EC IIIB phase and entirely rebuilt soon afterwards. It therefore seems possible that some features of EC IIIB culture continued in use at Ayia Irini where there is no break between the end of EC IIIB and the Middle Cycladic, whereas the same features were lost in the serious break between the two periods at Phylakopi.

This is a speculative solution which will need to be reconsidered (especially as regards the introduction of such elements on Kea) in the light of further finds, but it does provide an apparently plausible answer to a difficult problem.

Decoration

In EC I the motifs employed are very basic and rectilinear until near the end of the period, when some curvilinear designs (circles, spirals) come in with the stamping technique.

The introduction of painted decoration in EC II inspired some experiment but the pattern elements remain very simple.

EC IIIA sees the continuation of a limited range of incised and stamped motifs and a very little painted decoration, but in EC IIIB very many vases are decorated and all the techniques so far mentioned are used. The incised patterns combine rectilinear and curvilinear motifs; painted designs are strictly rectilinear to begin with but curvilinear are introduced in the later part of the period.

Figured decoration (boats, people) is rare but does occur from EC II onwards – incised on EC II frying pans (Fig. 19), painted on one or two EC IIIB pieces.

Vessels of marble and other stone[16]

Although stone vases are more closely related to the figurines by material and technique, their nature and function is clearly nearer to that of the clay vessels and the two groups have many shapes in common.

There are a wide variety of stone (mostly marble) vases of EC I-II date but it is likely that they, together with the figurines, ceased to be made in the troubled period after EC II. It is certainly the case that none of the diagnostic EC IIIA pottery forms appear also in marble,[17] whereas quite the reverse is true of EC II.

Although often fairly simple in style, these vessels are very attractive and that quality, together with the additional problems of stone acquisition and manufacture, makes it *prima facie* likely that they were valued objects.

They are much more commonly found in graves than settlements, even though only a minority of graves contain such fine objects. The fragility of some vases and the weight of others have been taken as evidence that they were impractical for everyday use and might therefore have been acquired by wealthier citizens during their lifetimes, specifically to be placed in their graves at death to accompany them into the next world. In this respect, they may to some extent resemble the marble figures.

One or two shapes could have been created specially for grave use but this does not seem true of the majority which have identical forms in clay.

As with the figurines, the fine marble sources of Naxos and Paros make it likely that many of the vases were manufactured on those islands, though other islands too have marble. The manufacturing process[18] (see also below, p. 129) would have involved first the acquisition of stone by collection or simple quarrying, the rough shaping and hollowing out of the vessel and finally external shaping and polishing.

Rough shaping could be achieved simply by striking the original block and hollowing was done by the use of a hollow reed drill together with an abrasive such as sand or emery. The latter is found chiefly on Naxos. The drilled cores were then forcibly removed from the interior, the remaining protrusions chipped away and the surfaces smoothed inside and out. Final polishing would again have been done with an abrasive.

It is noticeable that, as with clay vases, the range and complexity of shapes increased markedly in EC II. This was no doubt partly due to greater prosperity, higher demand and the consequent stimulation of experiment amongst the craftsmen involved. But another major factor may have been the readier availability of metal tools (saws, chisels, perhaps drills) which enabled faster and more sophisticated work, including thinner vessel walls.

The majority of Early Cycladic stone vase forms are in marble, but a significant group are made of chlorite schist. This latter is softer and more easily worked and the range includes complex forms and decoration (often spiralform).

Early Cycladic I stone vessels

There are no stone vessels in the earliest stage of EC I. When they begin, basic shapes are the simple bowl, the collared jar (Fig. 70) or 'kandili' with or without a pedestal, the beaker and the palette. Some shapes have

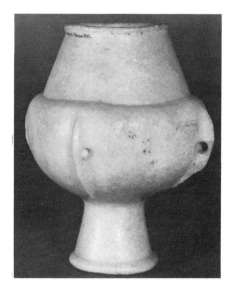

70. Marble footed collared jar or
'kandili' (EC I). (Ashmolean
Museum).

long pierced lugs attached.

The beaker and bowl are comparable to forms from Late Neolithic
Kephala and we should probably look there for their origin.

Traces of red or blue colouring matter are sometimes found in the
bowls and palettes, and stone pestles are occasionally associated with
those shapes. Such colouring may have been used in some way in funeral
ceremonies.

Early Cycladic II stone vessels

The range of shapes now increases to include spouted bowls, flaring cups,
the spherical, cylindrical (Fig. 71) and hut pyxides. The sauceboat,
frying pan and kernos are also represented but are not common. Many of
the vases have tall stems which terminate in a flaring 'trumpet' foot – a
feature characteristic of the period (Fig. 72). Lines in general are more
elegant than in EC I.

In both periods there are some unusual types. An EC I vessel is in the
form of a quadruped (Fig. 73) and another a headless figure which seems
comparable to the late EC I Plastiras type of figurine. Joined pairs of
identical vases are found in both periods but EC II sees the first multiple
vases (kernoi). A pyxis is capped by a bird, like some contemporary dress
pins.

The chlorite schist vessels include a group of 'hut-pyxides'. As the
names suggest, these are in the form of huts, with feet and detachable
roofs. One well-known example is more elaborate, having an entrance

71. Marble cylindrical pyxis (EC II).
(British Museum).

72. *right* Marble stemmed cup (EC
II). (Goulandris Museum).

porch with a gabled roof and, inside, seven circular compartments surrounding a central 'court'. It has been explained variously as a granary or a temple! Interpretation of such objects is inevitably both speculative and subjective. The storage of grain from contamination by damp or vermin is always a preoccupation of agricultural communities and thus likely to be reflected in their art. Religion too holds a prominent place in daily life but, while some of the hut-pyxides may represent temples, the peculiar form of the example under discussion seems to preclude that explanation here.

It also seems reasonable that the more ordinary huts were intended to represent the dwellings of individuals who then dedicated them in shrines to ensure divine protection for their homes.

The stone vases of the Early Cycladic period have a natural aesthetic appeal for us which stems not only from the innate attraction of the material but also from the simplicity and elegance of the forms. For Early Cycladic peoples, while they may have had some ritual significance, they were certainly also a material reflection of the gradually improving technical skills and quality of life.

(iii) Metallurgy and metal objects[19]

Developments in the production and use of metal objects during the Early Cycladic period both reflected and helped to promote important changes in many spheres of island life. New and more efficient tools became available for craftsmen, farmers and even housewives. New weapons made the islanders better able to defend themselves, and may have made them more belligerent at the same time! In a climate of greater prosperity, there was demand for non-essential articles in these valuable and attractive materials.

The finds do not merely indicate improvements in technology and the

73. Marble vase in the form of a ram, from Amorgos. (Ashmolean Museum).

general standard of living. Contacts with neighbouring areas, most obviously Crete and parts of Anatolia, are evident from the types and production methods, and there seem to have been some innovations for which the islanders themselves were responsible.

The metals in question are bronze (the largest category), lead, silver and, occasionally, gold. The history of the growth of metal technology in the Cyclades is interesting, if not yet entirely clear. Although a few copper objects, pieces of slag and fragments of crucibles or furnace linings from Kephala show that some copper was being worked in the islands at the end of the Neolithic period, the first stage of the Bronze Age (EC I) has yielded hardly any metal items.

From later Early Cycladic times, about 200 objects survive in the various metals, predominantly bronze.[20] The vast majority are from EC II or IIIA contexts. A number of new features[21] appeared about the time of the disturbances which marked the transition from EC II to IIIA. These are of Anatolian or East Mediterranean origin and must have been introduced by the intruders.

Metal objects[22]

The finds consist of weapons, tools, personal articles and some vessels and figurines (Figs. 74-7, 79-80). The *weapons* are spearheads and daggers, some of the latter being long and thin enough to be called swords.

Mainland Greece, Crete and north-west Anatolia, where the important site of Troy lies, have significant numbers of finds contemporary with those from the Cyclades and all these areas were engaged in local production. The localised concentration of the find-spots of certain types

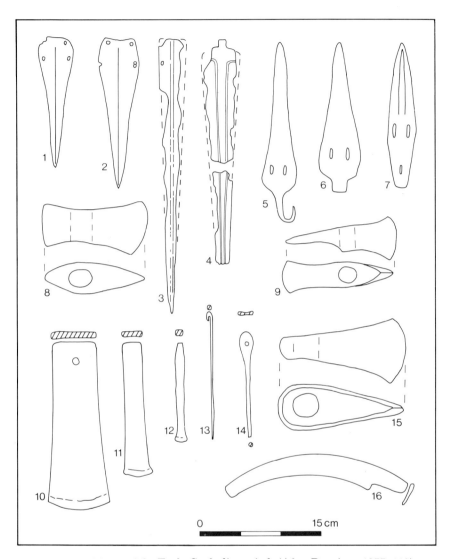

74. Metal objects of the Early Cycladic period. (After Branigan 1977, 119).

suggests that they were invented, produced and largely used in the areas where they are found.[23] In other cases, the wider distribution patterns indicate either trading between one area and another or the exchange of ideas which resulted in types native to one area being copied and produced in another. In the Early Bronze Age, both Anatolia and Crete have distinctive dagger forms, while another type (Fig. 74 nos. 1,2), tangless and with pronounced midrib, is thought to be Cycladic. Although found also in other parts of the Aegean, it does not occur in Anatolia.

75. Bronze dagger blade (*left*) and
spearhead (*right*) from Amorgos.
(Ashmolean Museum).

It seems likely that this dagger form represents a crucial stage in the
development of the Aegean sword,[24] since its prominent midrib is one
feature of a long, thinner weapon which may properly be called a sword
(Fig. 74 nos. 3,4). There are examples of this from Amorgos, though they
are not well-dated and could belong to the Middle Cycladic period.

One spearhead type (Figs. 74 nos. 6,7; 75 right) may have originated in
the Cyclades where it is quite common. It has a plain tang and elongated
slots for binding the head to the spear shaft. It presents a striking
contrast to the unslotted and 'rat-tailed' tanged type (Fig. 74 no. 5) which is
found in Anatolia and the East Mediterranean, but very rarely in the
Aegean.

Since the development of metal weapons in the Cyclades does not
appear to begin until EC II, whereas they have an earlier history in
Anatolia, it seems likely that Cycladic developments received some
stimulus from that source. This theory is made more plausible by the fact
that both tin and arsenic alloys are used simultaneously in both areas.

Tools are best known from two groups of finds – one of EC II date from
the island of Kythnos (Fig. 74 nos. 8-12), the other EC IIIA from Kastri on
Syros (Fig. 74 nos. 13-15). The nature of the tools points clearly to their
potential impact on contemporary crafts. Axes (the butts perforated to
accept firm wooden shafts), chisels, awls and saw-blades, in particular,
have possible applications to woodworking – from the initial point of
tree-felling to the creation of the final products, whether utensils,
household furniture or boats to sail the Aegean.

Some stone can also be cut with metal saws. Fishhooks (Fig. 76 nos. 7-8)

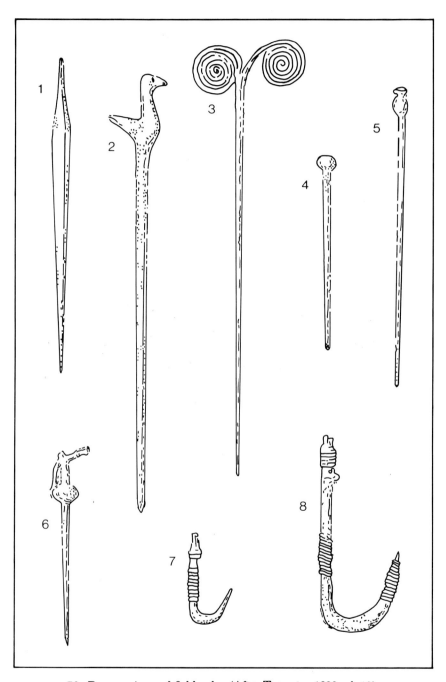

76. Bronze pins and fishhooks. (After Tsountas 1899, pl. 10).

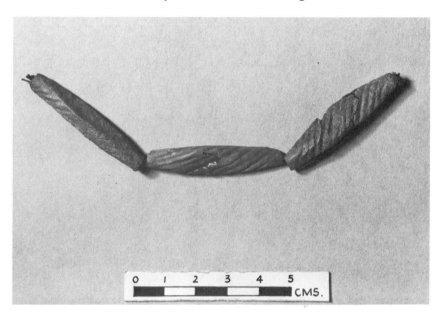

77. Beads of silver from an Early Cycladic grave on Amorgos. (Ashmolean Museum).

78. Beads of steatite from an Early Cycladic grave on Amorgos. (Ashmolean Museum).

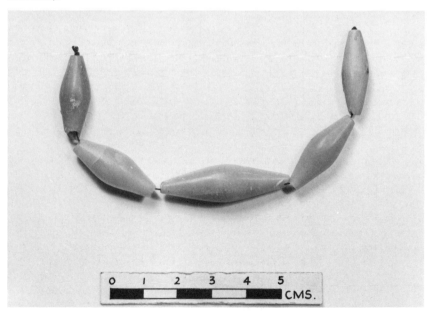

79. Silver bracelet (Early Cycladic) from Amorgos. (British Museum).

and sickles, possibly of Early Cycladic date, demonstrate the use of bronze in other spheres.

Objects of personal ornament are quite various and come in silver as well as bronze. Virtually all examples have been found in graves.

Dress pins (Fig. 76 nos. 1-6), mostly 9-12 cm in length and also made of bone, have heads either of simple geometric shapes or more elaborately ornamented – with double spirals, wreaths of twisted wire, even bird or animal forms, and once with a tiny jug.

Pierced beads (Fig. 77) were strung into necklaces and there are some simple pendants, though all these are more normally found in stone (Fig. 78 – steatite). There are flat, twisted or circular-sectioned bracelets of silver (Fig. 79), sometimes with simple ornamentation. There are a few diadems, simply shaped and decorated, though one piece had repoussée ornament with a complex array of animal and other motifs.

Toilet articles include tweezers, spatulae and razors.

Among the precious objects, a small number of silver vessels are outstanding. Two shallow bowls with plain but effective linear decoration, are said to have come from the island of Euboea but may well have been made in the Cyclades. The islands were clearly prominent in silver working (see below) and an undecorated vessel of identical shape was found on Amorgos (Fig 80).

Other objects of interest are one or two lead figurines of simple human form and three lead models of boats with square stems and high prows, quite similar to those which are occasionally represented on Early Cycladic vases. One of these models is said to be from Naxos. The method of lead isotope analysis[25] has proved that the material of all three is definitely from the same source and this source was, in all probability, Siphnos, which was evidently a centre of silver and lead production in the

80. Silver bowl (Early Cycladic) from Amorgos. (Ashmolean Museum).

Early Cycladic period.

Gold is represented by a solitary bead of thin sheet from Naxos.

Some of the forms mentioned find parallels elsewhere and may have been inspired by the products of other areas. There are headed pins from the north-east Aegean and Anatolia, and some diadems from Crete, for example. But the tweezer and spatula types most common in the Cyclades are distinctive and these, together with one or two of the weapon forms mentioned earlier, are probably local and thus evidence of local initiatives.

Metal sources and metal production[26]

The sources of the raw material required to produce the metals used in the Early Bronze Age Aegean have given rise to much speculation. One reason for this is that, even when a potential source of, say, copper ore can be identified, it is rarely possible to date the period of its exploitation. Another is that, until recently, there have been no scientific techniques which could aid this line of research.

Identification of these sources has more than simply an intrinsic interest within the study of the Aegean Early Bronze Age. Once the use of metals became known and their value appreciated, the acquisition of the raw materials would have been vital and certain to stimulate travel, trade, contact, even conflict. In the case of tin, for instance, which is the most desirable element for combination with copper to form a bronze alloy, there are no known sources in the Aegean and importation, from whatever source, would have been inevitable. Within the Cyclades, many workable deposits of copper and silver-lead ores have been located – and there are later literary references to the gold of Siphnos, though none has

81. Kapsalos, Siphnos. General view of the Frase mine. (N. Gale).

82. Bolioni, Siphnos. Ancient galleries exposed in modern mine. (N. Gale).

83. Ayios Sostis, Siphnos (mine 2). Ancient gallery with toolmarks. (N. Gale).

84. Casts of tool marks in the Frase mine at Kapsalos, Siphnos. (N. Gale).

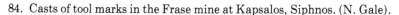

yet been discovered by modern investigators.

The only convincing signs of ancient mine-workings in the islands are also from Siphnos (Ayios Sostis).[27] From the primitive methods used and the discovery of obsidian tools (most prominent in prehistoric times) in the vicinity, use in the Bronze Age seems likely.

The galleries (Figs. 81-3) which are now largely below sea level and flooded, were reached from the surface by vertical shafts. Some of these were probably dug initially for prospecting; others added later for

85. Ancient stone hammers
from Ayios Sostis, Siphnos.
(N. Gale).

86. Wall of quarrying waste
in the Frase mine, Kapsalos,
Siphnos. (N. Gale).

ventilation and/or the removal of the ore. Fire setting (lighting bonfires against the rock surface, followed by dousing with water) was used to split and detach the stone. Tool marks are visible on the gallery walls (Fig. 83) and castings taken from pick-marks reveal the forms of tools that made them (Fig. 84). Crushing and sorting of the mineral ore took place below ground before the richer pieces, suitable for smelting, were taken to the surface. Special hard-stone hammers (Fig. 85) were imported from elsewhere for this purpose. Unusable waste remained in the mine and was built up to form walls (Fig. 86) in parts of it no longer being worked.

Smelting was probably done near the mine to avoid long-distance transport of heavy loads of ore. Circular depressions in the ground on the promontory of Ayios Sostis, near the mine and in an exposed position which would have ensured good draughts, may be the remains of ancient smelting furnaces.

Other evidence for the use of the mines at Ayios Sostis, though undatable, comes from the discovery of litharge (lead oxide, a by-product of silver refining) in another part of the island, which analysis shows to have originated from Ayios Sostis. We should remember also that an analysis of the Early Cycladic lead boats suggested a Siphnian origin.

The Siphnos evidence is new, unique, exciting, and worth careful attention because it begins to fill a large gap in our knowledge of Early Cycladic metallurgy.

Of the other raw materials required for Early Cycladic metal objects, copper ore was mined and smelted in basically the same way but, although sources are known in the Cyclades, none of them can be shown to have been exploited specifically in the Bronze Age. There were certainly sources on Kythnos, where very recent work has identified an EC II smelting site with the remains of furnaces.

One of the first results of the application of lead isotope analysis to the identification of copper sources has been to show that the metal objects from Kastri on Syros have a composition more closely related to Anatolian sources than to any others so far known. This is particularly interesting in view of the other strong Anatolian connections of the EC IIIA period to which the Kastri material is dated, though it is not necessarily a good pointer to the use of Anatolian copper sources in the Cyclades at other periods of the Early Bronze Age.

When bronze was made with an arsenic alloy, either copper ores naturally rich in arsenic were deliberately selected, or else arsenic was separately acquired and added. The sources of tin[28] for tin-bronze are quite obscure. Britain, Southern Europe and the East Mediterranean have all been proposed. For the Early Cycladic period, perhaps the most likely area is that of Troy (north-west Anatolia). There is an unconfirmed report of a tin deposit from the vicinity[29] and the early existence of arsenical beside tin bronzes in that area might indicate a supply of tin which was later worked out.

Gold may occur in native state and worked-out sources are

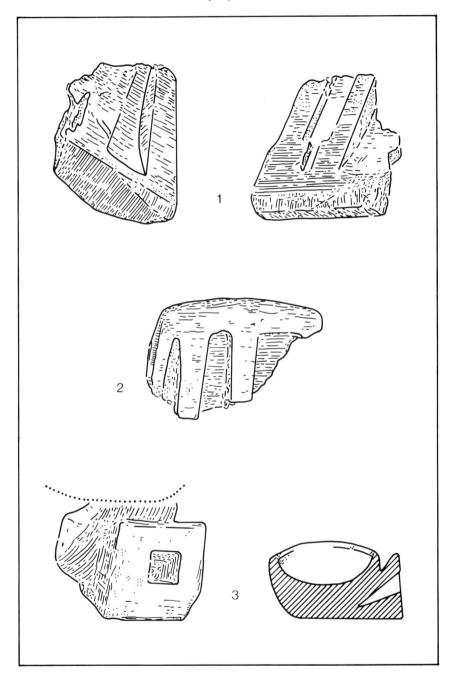

87. Moulds (1, 2) and crucible (3) from Kastri, Syros. (After Tsountas 1899, 125).

unidentifiable. Greece certainly had gold in later times – on Siphnos and in Thrace.

Metalworking

Fragments of crucibles or kiln linings and slag (the latter not certainly of Late Neolithic date) from Kephala show that the technical capacity for working copper existed in the Cyclades before the beginning of the Bronze Age.

The only site in the Cyclades which has produced direct evidence of metal-working is Kastri on Syros (EC IIIA). The finds, which came from Room 11, included a hearth with fragments of copper slag, crucibles (Fig. 87 no. 3) (one with traces of lead), two moulds (Fig. 87 nos. 1,2) (of clay and stone respectively) for casting axes and chisels. In addition, there was a hoard of tools, mostly of metal but some of obsidian.

There are crucibles and copper ingots from Phylakopi but these are probably all later than the Early Cycladic period. The persuasive evidence for the mining of lead-silver ore and the smelting of silver on Siphnos in EC II has already been mentioned.

There is therefore no doubt that the whole process of bronze- and silver-lead-working, from the mining of the ore to the production of finished objects, took place in the Cyclades from EC II and probably earlier. The existence of some distinctively Cycladic types (see above) is certainly in accord with this view. Although the mining and smelting of ore and the production of metal ingots probably took place near the mines,[30] production of artefacts may have been carried out in the settlements, where a specialist class of skilled metal-workers probably grew up. If this class was very restricted in size (to an exclusive family group perhaps), its members may have travelled from one site, or even island, to another to ply their craft. Such a practice would certainly have contributed to the interchange of types and the creation of specifically Cycladic forms.

Once the smelted metal is available in ingot form, the basic process is fairly straightforward, provided the necessary temperature can be achieved. Lead has a low melting point (327°C) and can be melted in a crucible on an open fire and then poured into a mould. Bronze requires a higher temperature (1005°C) and needs the heat generated by charcoal, preferably with a more sophisticated hearth and a strong draught.

The crucibles, which were of thick, coarse clay, were presumably removed from the fire by means of green, and thus initially non-inflammable, wooden shafts or tongs.

Hammering and subsequent decoration, if desired, took place when the object was cold.

Conclusions

The pretentious terminology ('industries', 'schools of metal-work') sometimes adopted in discussion of Bronze Age metallurgy tends to obscure understanding of the basic effects of such innovations on the lives of contemporary islanders. These were in fact quite straightforward. They had more effective tools and implements in domestic life and for the crafts of stone- and wood-working. More effective weapons – for attack, defence and hunting – became available; as did better implements for fishing and agriculture. Finer objects could be produced for personal possession and adornment and perhaps for ritual purposes too. Inter-island and international contact, peaceful or otherwise, was also stimulated.

We should remember too that, in spite of the undoubted significance of these innovations, the total number of objects known is not so very large, though there is, of course, no way of knowing what proportion this represents of the original total. It was thus not till a much later period that metal implements, vessels, weapons and tools would have been common sights in island households.

(iv) Obsidian[31]

Obsidian (Figs. 88, 89) is a glassy volcanic stone, dark blue to black in colour, which was used in prehistoric times to provide cutting edges for tools and weapons. Although its uses are similar to those of flint, it is sharper and thus more efficient.

Sources

Sources of obsidian are not very common[32] and those producing material suitable for the manufacture of artefacts even less so. Thus the extensive quarries on Melos were of exceptional importance for the whole Aegean area in the Bronze Age.

There are two main quarries on Melos (Fig. 90), at Sta Nychia on the gulf of Melos just above the modern port of Adhamata; and at Demenegaki, a high plateau on the east coast of the island. The other known Aegean source of any size, on the islet of Yiali, near Nisyros in the Dodecanese, was never very seriously exploited. It was not visited in the Early Bronze Age and, later, the distinctive white-spotted obsidian was chiefly used for making vases.

Obsidian objects and their uses

Obsidian was particularly important in the Neolithic and Early Bronze Age, before bronze artefacts were common. But even after the spread of bronze technology, obsidian implements continued to be widely used. This is shown, for example, by the recent excavations at Koukounaries on Paros,[33] a site which was occupied only in later LC III but has nevertheless produced numerous obsidian finds.

88. Obsidian parallel-sided blades (Early Cycladic). (R. Torrence).

89. Obsidian cores (Early Cycladic). (R. Torrence).

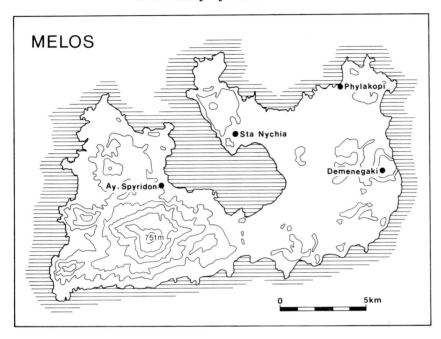

90. Melos, showing locations of obsidian sources and selected Bronze Age sites.

Although the precise functions[34] of individual implements are rarely certain – few forms are as explicit as the arrowhead (Fig. 91 nos. 3,4), for example – the general uses seem clear. These would have been for cutting, scraping and making perforations, in the gathering of various crops, preparation of food, dissection of meat and treatment of skins. Cutting tools included sickles (Fig. 8), made from a number of serrated blades set in a wooden haft. Saws of obsidian were probably employed to cut wood and sometimes stone. Spearheads are known, as well as the arrowheads, and there seems no reason why there should not have been daggers with obsidian blades.

Another agricultural use may have been for threshing sledges. Such sledges were in use until quite recently to separate grain from chaff. They consist of a flat board, with teeth on the underside, which is drawn round the threshing floor by animals, while the driver stands on top.

As for the blade forms which constitute such a large proportion of the surviving artefacts, work on distinguishing different types and their likely dates has advanced little until quite recently, when it has received fresh impetus with the work of Dr. Robin Torrence.[35] The most important basic fact to emerge is that there is a marked difference between blade types of the Neolithic and those of the Bronze Age. The former are mostly wider, thicker and irregular in shape; the latter long, narrow, predominantly parallel-sided and prismatic in section (Fig. 91 no. 2).

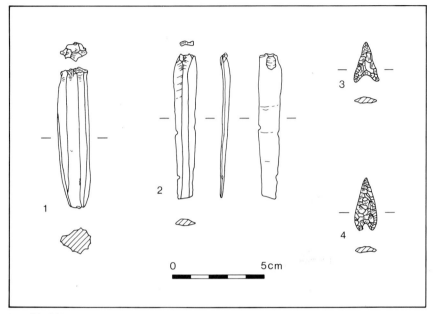

91. Obsidian core (1), parallel-sided blade (2) and arrowheads (3, 4) (Early Cycladic). (After Cherry and Torrence 1984, 16).

This change in type is connected with a change in manufacturing techniques (see below).

Quarrying and working

In its raw form, obsidian is easily removed from the quarries, where it often occurs on the surface, inset in lumps into the softer surrounding material. Waste flakes from the quarry areas (Fig. 92) show that these lumps were often partially worked on the spot, to provide suitable cores of material from which blades could then be struck off. A few finds of obsidian lumps from settlement sites however show that it was also occasionally taken away in entirely unworked form.

The principal methods of producing the blades themselves were either to strike them off the core with a sharp blow from another stone, or else to apply a more subtle form of pressure with, for example, a wooden point. The former method, which produces cruder and more irregular results, was more common in the Neolithic period; while the latter, which gives long, thin symmetrical blades with parallel sides (Figs. 88, 91 no. 2), is characteristic of the Bronze Age. One result of the second method is that the cores from which blades have been struck have a more regular appearance (Figs. 89, 91 no. 1). It was also much more economical of raw material because the standard blade form meant that more pieces could be got from each single core.

92. Obsidian quarry at Sta Nychia, Melos. (C. Renfrew).

From time to time in the process of blade production, cores were 'rejuvenated' – when the core shape became unsuitable for the production of blades of the required form, flakes were struck from it until a suitable shape was regained. Such waste flakes are always found in workshop debris.

The obsidian trade and its significance

By a combination of scientific (trace element) and visual analysis, it has proved possible to identify most of the obsidian found in the Aegean area in Neolithic and Early Bronze Age contexts as Melian. In the Bronze Age, the distribution of finds covers the Greek Mainland as far north as Thessaly, and the Aegean islands, including Crete.

Obsidian may have been exported in three forms – as unworked lumps, prepared cores or finished artefacts. All three, as well as waste material, have been found in workshop contexts outside the Cyclades – at the palaces of Knossos and Mallia in Crete, for example.[36] These contexts prove also that artefacts were manufactured outside the Cyclades, but they do not provide any evidence for or against the export of finished objects from Melos and it is difficult to see how this could be conclusively proved. On the site at Phylakopi there is the debris of an apparently large workshop, but it is impossible to tell whether this was producing artefacts for home use or export or both.

The transfer of obsidian from Melos began at least as early as the seventh (and probably by the eleventh) millennium BC, as is shown by finds of that date from the Franchthi cave in the north-east Peloponnese[37] and has a significance beyond the purely technological. In the first place it is closely connected with the development of communications, which the discovery of obsidian must certainly have stimulated. Secondly it draws attention to the possible political primacy of Melos – founded on the island's possession of this vital commodity.

There could have been no such primacy when obsidian first came into use, since there were no settlements at all on Melos at that time, as far as we know. The material must simply have been collected by outsiders who made trips to the island for that purpose.

It has recently been argued[38] with great ingenuity that this was the situation even in later times when there was an important centre of population at Phylakopi and settlement elsewhere on the island too. This view is based on the theory that an organised obsidian trade would have left more and different traces in the archaeological record than are in fact found. Among expected signs which are absent from the quarry sites are boundary walls, harbour installations, workshops and living quarters. Few tools have been found, such as would have been required for extraction and, although there is evidence of production activity, the different processes do not seem to have been specialised and there are only limited signs of standardised production methods such as might have been expected in an organised industry. Moreover, the quantity of waste material discovered on the sites is said not to support the idea of regular activity over a long period.

This analysis, though based on meticulous research, suffers from the fault of many archaeological 'models' in that it projects the expectations of a modern mind onto an ancient situation. In addition, it is entirely negative. In fact, the remains observed to date are far from incompatible with the controlled exploitation of the obsidian sources by local inhabitants. Apart from anything else, the obsidian trade was not necessarily centrally organised. It might well have consisted of a number of private operators, who worked without close co-operation, but together formed a kind of 'industry'. Quarrymen need not have lived at the site and could have taken their tools away – especially if they were useful for other tasks as well. The extracted material was certainly not all worked at the quarry site, witness the workshop debris from the site at Phylakopi. Much may have been carried away for this purpose; some may have been sold or traded on the spot. Raw material for export may have been more easily channelled through the most conveniently situated port at Phylakopi. If control of the sources were needed, we should first remember that visitors were only likely within the sailing season, and probably during the hours of daylight, when lookouts could have been posted with plenty of time to alert protection squads.

In time (by EC IIIB at the latest), when there was a large and presumably authoritative centre of population at Phylakopi, it seems inconceivable that the trade in obsidian, whether in the form of raw material or finished artefacts or both, was not exploited by the Melians (i.e. in effect by the main administrative centre at Phylakopi) for their own advantage. The very close links between the pottery of Mainland Greece in EC IIIB (contemporary with early Middle Helladic and Middle Minoan)[39] are probably due in large measure to a cultural fraternity which was fostered initially by the obsidian trade. The Mainland at that time was much more backward in metal technology and resources than Crete and its need for obsidian correspondingly greater.

A more complex question arises here, namely how far the 'obsidian connection' affected the Cycladic islands other than Melos. They were certainly themselves dependent on Melos for supplies and probably picked up other influences in the process. The only other excavated settlement of the EC IIIB period is Paroikia on Paros and it is very interesting that some of the vases from that site were apparently imported from Melos.[40]

Like so many things, this question will only be clarified as the years pass and more material is excavated, but meanwhile it seem probable that Melos played a leading role as a centre of communications within the island group and that transmission of ideas between the Mainland and the Cyclades and within the islands themselves was stimulated by the movement of obsidian. In these circumstances, it is not unlikely that the predominant role of Melos helped to stimulate the creative local ambience on that island, which the innovative nature of EC IIIB pottery seems to suggest.

(v) Marble figures[41]

Marble figures and marble vases are the most attractive of Cycladic products in the Early Bronze Age and the former, in particular, continue to be greatly admired as works of art. Their precise role in the context of Early Cycladic culture is somewhat elusive, though undoubtedly important.

The development of marble working in the Cyclades was certainly stimulated by the existence of marble sources[42] on many islands. Emery (Naxos) and obsidian (Melos) are also extremely useful manufacturing aids which are both found in the islands. In powdered form, emery could have been used as an abrasive for rubbing and drilling, and both it and obsidian for incising and cutting into the stone. The hardness of emery makes it very suitable for shaping-tools. Pumice was another available abrasive agent (Thera).

Cycladic marble is not of uniformly fine quality. The best is found on Paros and Naxos and it can be no accident that the majority of marble finds come from these islands, where most pieces are likely also to have been made. These objects are the earliest truly 'luxury' goods in the ancient Cyclades and, in spite of uncertainty about the organisation of

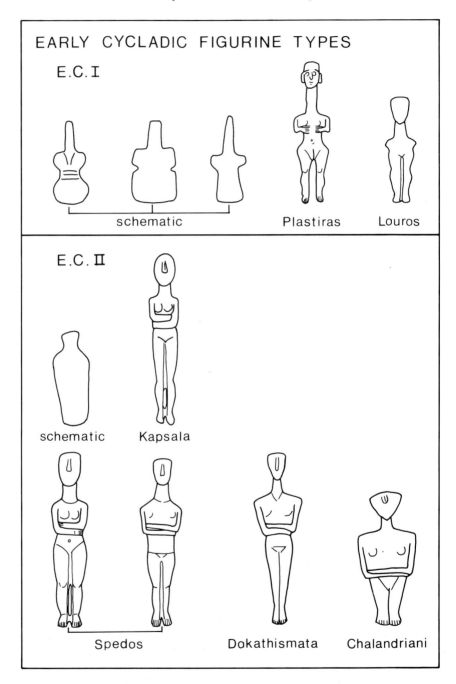

EARLY CYCLADIC FIGURINE TYPES

E.C. I

schematic Plastiras Louros

E.C. II

schematic Kapsala

Spedos Dokathismata Chalandriani

93. Marble figure types of EC I and II. (British Museum).

manufacture (see below), it seems a reasonable supposition that the exceptional prosperity of Naxos and Paros in the Early Cycladic period was based, in part at least, on their production.

Many Cycladic marble figurines and vases are known. Their appeal over the years has encouraged illicit excavation and export on a large scale, and numerous pieces (including a not inconsiderable number of fakes) are now in foreign museums and the hands of private collectors. In such cases, neither the provenance nor the nature of the associated finds are known – both vital elements for accurate interpretation. Accordingly, our understanding both of the chronology of types and of the ways in which these objects were used, is slight by comparison with the total number of finds, though just enough figurines have been found in systematic excavations to provide a key.

General types of figures (Fig. 93)

The broadest division of Early Cycladic figures is that between the 'schematic' and the 'naturalistic' types. A glance at some typical pieces (Figs. 94, 95) is enough to identify the distinction. The former represent the human body in an extremely stylised way, without detailed or realistic representation of the separate parts. The latter, of which the standing female with folded arms is the 'canonical' type, are recognisably human, if somewhat limited in iconographic range. Both are considered further below.

Chronology

This broad classification seems also to be of chronological significance in the Early Cycladic period. Marble objects are not found at all in the earliest stages of EC I,[43] but schematic figures appear in the second EC I group, while the first of the naturalistic (though of 'pre-canonical' type) together with marble vases, only in the third.

The schematic types thus begin earlier and they are always more common in EC I. The naturalistic pieces seem to start later, and certainly achieve the canonical form later, when they are the dominant type in EC II. Schematic versions nevertheless continue to be made.

There remain problems over the origins and early history of both types, which arise from the more general uncertainty about the transition from the Neolithic to Bronze Age in the Cyclades which was discussed in an earlier chapter.[44]

Schematic figures from Late Neolithic Saliagos are identical in form and suggest a very early origin, though they do not appear at the later Neolithic site of Kephala. A naturalistic type is also found at Saliagos, though not in a form which provides a convincing connection with Early Cycladic pieces. The most tantalising of earlier finds are terracotta heads from Kephala, which are close in style to those of the later naturalistic class of Early Cycladic figures. Since only heads of the terracotta figures survive, we cannot tell what the rest of the body was like. Nevertheless these finds from Kephala give a hint that naturalistic figures may have been made in the Cyclades continuously from the Neolithic period and that the present absence of finds from EC I contexts is due either to chance or to their early manufacture in a perishable material (see below).

The production of marble objects seems to have ceased or sharply declined with the disturbances of EC IIIA and not to have revived until the later Bronze Age, when a new type of schematic figure (Fig. 137) has been identified in the course of recent excavations on Kea.[45] There are no figures from known EC IIIA tombs, and marble vases never copy pottery forms of that period. The earlier figures however were certainly collected and kept by people in the islands in the intervening period, since a few are found in later contexts in the Ayia Irini settlement.

Schematic figures[46] *(Fig. 94)*

Several varieties have been distinguished but their basic characteristics are simply described. The head is only rarely indicated: most types have a narrow projecting prong which represents both head and neck together. The arms are normally shown by stumps, which either project from the torso or else are formed by the upper borders of a notch or inlet of varying width at the waist. The base is flat or rounded and no legs are indicated.

Marble beach pebbles are quite often found in graves and these may have been selected for use as figurines, without further treatment.

Naturalistic figures[47]

Two varieties of 'pre-canonical' naturalistic figures make their appearance in EC I. The so-called Louros type is still fairly schematic in character. The head is defined, but without features; the legs are shown, but the arms are merely stumps. The Plastiras form has arms which meet across the chest, and other facial and anatomical features are indicated.

The 'canonical' or standard folded-arm figure (Fig. 95) is a product of EC II, when it was quite widely exported in the Aegean area and inspired a locally-produced variant in Crete (the so-called Koumasa type).

The figures, which may be up to 1.50m in height, though the very largest are rare, are usually female and naked. The basic form is straightforward, the four varieties (five, including Koumasa) being distinguished by details of proportion, shape, decoration and anatomical detail. The figures stand, with arms folded, left over right, on the stomach. The heads are ovoid or sub-triangular and are tilted backwards. Only the nose is indicated sculpturally. Sexual char-acteristics are regularly shown and some figures are obviously pregnant. Most of them cannot stand because the soles of their feet are not flat.

All these features can be individually varied and the figures differ considerably in depth of profile.

Surviving detail is usually either in relief or incised but there is plenty

94. Marble schematic figurine from Paros. Height: 0.134m. (Ashmolean Museum).

95. Marble 'canonical' folded-arm figurine from Amorgos. Height: 0.19m. (Ashmolean Museum).

of evidence also for painted decoration – hair, necklaces etc. – which would have considerably modified their appearance.

Complex figures and groups

A substantial number of figures are associated with the canonical folded-arm type on general stylistic grounds, but include more complex and varied compositions. There are several musicians, standing or seated (Fig. 99), a cupbearer, one figure on the head of another, a group of three, two of whom are supporting the smaller third on their outstretched arms.

96. Marble 'hunter-warrior' figure.
Height: 0.25m. (Goulandris
Museum).

There are a number of examples of the hunter-warrior[48] (Fig. 96), whose
distinctive feature is a baldric slung over one shoulder. Some have belts,
penis sheaths and daggers in addition.

Methods of composition[49]

Careful study of the figures has yielded exciting information about the
sculptors and their methods.

As early as EC I, a system of proportions was employed, involving the

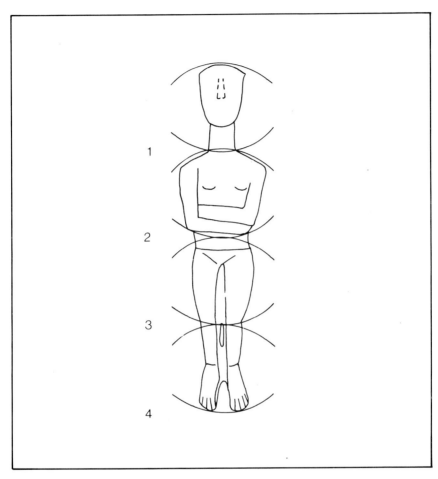

97. Folded-arm figure designed on four-part grid. Height: 0.256m. (After Getz-Preziosi 1977b, 74).

division of the figure into three parts. The dividing lines coincide with key points on the body of the figure – the base of the neck, the top of the pubic triangle. At a point near the waist the figure usually has an overall width of one sixth of its height.

In the canonical figures of EC II, a four-part scheme is adopted (Fig. 97), the dividing lines occurring at the base of the neck, at a mid-point in the abdomen, and at the knees. The maximum width is often one quarter of the total height. A simple form of compass was probably used to mark these divisions on the block of marble before carving began, since there are several examples of drawn arcs reflected in the figures themselves (Fig. 97) – in the curve of the shoulders or on the knee-caps, the latter being sometimes emphasised with incision. A ruler would also have been

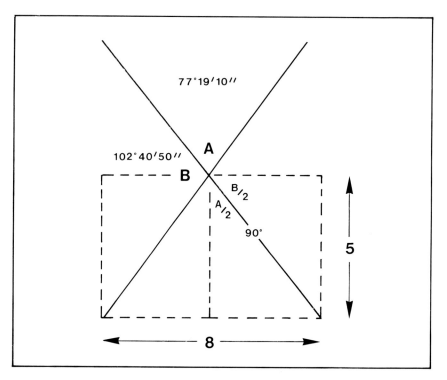

98. The derivation of harmonic angulation in the construction of Early Cycladic marble figures. (See also Fig. 100c). (After Getz-Preziosi 1977b, 78).

required to establish the length of the units and the total length and width of the basic block.

Further indications of systematic technique come from the measurement of key angles in the structures of the figures (Fig. 100c). These seem to show the use of what is called 'harmonic angulation', where all the major angles are those formed from a rectangle of proportions 5:8 (Fig. 98). For example, the angle at the junction of shoulder and armline in all figurine types is commonly angle B of the 5:8 rectangle. Angle B is the more popular for the pubic triangle in EC I.

All the measurable angles are usually either one of the major angles derived from the rectangle or else directly related to them.

As in the case of the pubic triangle cited above, certain values are consistently favoured for certain body angles at particular periods. Such practice would have required the use of an instrument for measuring angles.

Complex figures demanded a somewhat different approach because of their different postures and because the profile view was often as important as the frontal. Nevertheless they were similarly designed on a modified version of the four-part scheme described above. The basic four

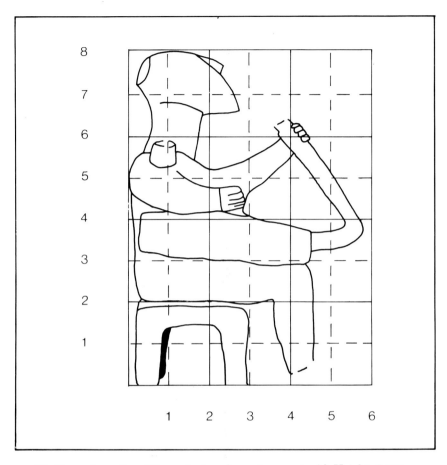

99. Harp player from Thera, designed on a four-part grid. Height: 0.165m.

units of height were further subdivided; the width allotted three basic units, similarly subdivided. Significant points in the composition are closely related to cardinal points on the grid.

The harpist figures (Fig. 99) essentially follow the four-part system except that the third dividing-line comes at the top of the seat, not at the knees as in a more normal type. As for the vertical divisions, the centre line is the key point of the composition since the front leg of the stool and the apex of the instrument are both located on it.

This approach to figure design is found consistently in the classic period of canonical figures, early and mature EC II. Varieties thought to be later (the Chalandriani and Dokathismata types) also show the application of proportional systems but these are sometimes unusual (e.g. with divisions into fifths or thirds) and they do not always follow the traditional interrelationships in detail.

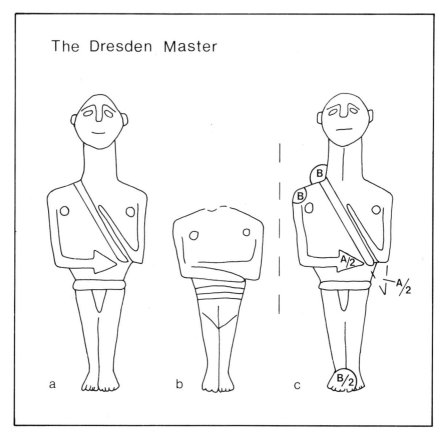

100. Early Cycladic marble figures by the 'Dresden Master'; (c) showing the application of harmonic angulation. Height: (a) 0.228m; (b) 0.161m; (c) = (a).

Individual artists[50]

Within the overall approach determined by the use of standard proportions and angles, there was plenty of room for variation – in the combination of those features, in the detailed shaping and modelling of the parts of the body, in the use and character of incised or painted detail.

On the basis of recurrent combinations of stylistic features, as well as such factors as size, figure-type, kind of marble used, it has proved possible to identify a number of individual artists, even in fragmentary works. We may briefly consider one of these, the so-called 'Dresden Master' (named after a figure now in Dresden), identified by Dr. Getz-Preziosi. The pieces attributed to him include a male and a (headless) female figure (Fig. 100). Although the figures are actually different sizes, key features in their composition (shoulder level, bottom of right arm, lower limit of pubic area) occur at the same points. The figures also make use of harmonic angles to produce closely similar overall forms. The heads have distinctive features – large size and extensive facial detail – which clearly distinguish them from the work of other sculptors. Other characteristic features are the small, widely-spaced breasts which are common to both male and female figures in this artist's repertoire.

The homes of individual sculptors like the Dresden Master are difficult to locate with certainty, when the provenance of so many pieces is uncertain, there was some export trade, and there is always the possibility that travelling craftsmen were involved.

The Dresden Master may have come from Amorgos, since two of his works are said to have been found there, and a third on nearby Keros. Three other pieces, perhaps from his hand, were recently discovered on Kea.

Craftsmen and manufacturing methods[51]

The process of manufacturing begins with the acquisition of suitable stone. In many cases beach pebbles were probably used but there may also have been some limited quarrying, particularly for material for the larger figures.

Working materials to which Early Cycladic sculptors would have had access include emery, obsidian and, later, bronze. Modern experiment has shown that blocks of emery, which is an exceptionally hard stone, are useful for detaching sizable fragments in the initial shaping. Obsidian is good for shaving and making incisions. Bronze tools may well have been advantageous, particularly in detailed work, but were by no means essential. Powdered emery or pumice were available as abrasives for smoothing the surface and polishing respectively.

Thus the sculptor would have begun by choosing a design and sketching it out on his block of stone. Then the main lines of the figure would have been formed by detaching pieces from the core. The surface was then shaved and worked with abrasives as required, and incised and painted detail added.

Experiment has shown that an inexperienced, though not incom-petent, worker can produce a schematic figure in about five hours, a simple naturalistic figure in about twenty hours and a canonical folded-arm figure in about sixty hours. These times could presumably have been reduced substantially by experienced craftsmen.

Sculptors, incidentally, apparently went in for repairs as well as original work, since a number of figures have holes bored either side of a break (Fig. 101) for the insertion of a binding agent.

While the experiments mentioned above suggest that it would have been technically possible for humble individuals to have made their own figures, this seems on balance unlikely, especially in the case of the canonical pieces. It is hard to know what value ancient islanders put on

101. Fragment of Early Cycladic
marble figure with borings for repair,
from Amorgos. (Ashmolean Museum).

their time. They were probably prone to illness, had short lives and
needed to work hard at the most basic and essential tasks. The
manufacture of a figure requiring many hours of work would most likely
have been entrusted to a specialist craftsman. That there were at least
some specialists is strongly suggested by the corpus of the Goulandris
Master, which now numbers about 120 pieces. Each island may have had
one or two sculptors, except in the case of the smaller communities which
could either have imported figures or have been visited occasionally by
travelling craftsmen who made them on the spot.

We have already referred to the fine marble and prosperity of Naxos
and Paros. There was perhaps a concentration of activity on those islands
but it was certainly not confined to them.

Uses of the figures[52]

The last and most tantalising aspect of the figures is the question of their
function. The vast majority come from graves, although they are by no
means rare at settlement sites. The settlement finds indicate that the
figures were used in the course of daily life and the fact that several show
evidence of breakage and subsequent repair supports this idea, always
assuming that the breakages did not occur during the manufacturing
process. The grave finds show that the figures could play some part in the

burial rite, but their absence from the majority of excavated graves suggests, at first sight, that it was not an essential part. It is, however, conceivable that it was in fact the custom for every burial to be accompanied by a figure but that the poorest people could only afford to have them made of perishable material (perhaps wood) which has not survived. If they were really only placed in a limited number of graves, they may have been a mark of wealth or of special status in the community. The chief difficulty in this view has been that one would expect terracotta to have been used since the material was so common. Until recently no Early Cycladic figures of this kind have been known, though some of the recent finds from Mikre Vigla seem to be of that date and the Kephala heads can legitimately be brought into the discussion. None the less there are still none from graves, unless fragments have previously been mistaken for sherds of coarse pottery which, at Mikre Vigla at least, is quite easy.

The variety of types is also interesting. Although the canonical folded-arm female type and the schematic figure, which were probably simpler representations of the same form, are in a considerable majority, there remain the significant body of males, as well as the complex figures and groups, which are different from the standard.

In attempting to interpret the figures – and many different suggestions have been put forward – we can make use of the evidence of the objects themselves and the contexts in which they have been found. We can also gain useful hints about their possible functions from observing the ways in which figures are or have been used in other better-known cultures.

The two most important aspects requiring explanation, both closely related, are the identity of the figures and the intention behind deposition in the grave. As for the latter, it may simply have been felt appropriate to bring personal possessions along with the dead person because of their intimate connection with him or her. If there was belief in an afterlife, the buried objects were probably intended to serve the dead there and the figures would take on the tasks of servants or, as has sometimes been suggested, concubines. If the grave goods were not directly for the service or use of the dead person they may have been intended as gifts to the deities who controlled the destinies of men. In this case they may have been representations of the deities or of servants or worshippers, the latter symbolising service or worship to the deity from the occupant of the grave.

Any explanation of the Cycladic figures needs to take particular account of their sophisticated character, the female nature of the dominant type and the mixed find-places (settlements as well as graves).

The widespread use of female figures with explicit sexual characteristics seems easily explained in the context of a relatively primitive agriculturally-oriented society, where the fertility of humans, animals and the land was of paramount importance and must have held a prominent place in religious thought and activity. The time and effort spent in collecting and working the material for these sophisticated figures suggests that they were of more than casual importance to their owners, and their appearance in graves suggests that they had some role in the transference of human beings from this world to the next.

If it is correct that these figures had a ritual purpose, the finds in settlements are probably from the remains of small shrines in individual houses – or possibly sometimes public centres of ritual. Some of them may have been cult figures; others servants or worshippers placed near the image of the deity or simply offerings in her own likeness. The non-standard figures, including the males, would fit in here, since they would be symbolically making offerings (the cupbearer), playing music (Fig. 99), hunting or going to war (Fig. 96) in honour or under the patronage of the deity.

The reason why some of the contents of these shrines were transferred to graves may have been that dedications made in them by individuals to mark their own respect for a deity were regarded as being specially connected with those individuals and were thus put in their graves at death.

There is a possible analogy in a similar practice in the Late Bronze Age in the Aegean, where small clay figures are found in graves and in settlements, as well as in public shrines. No public shrines are certainly known from the Early Cycladic period, though it has been quite plausibly suggested[53] that there was one on Keros, where an exceptionally large number of marble figures and vases have been found in a context for which there seems no other explanation.

Conclusion

Because of their good preservation, attractive character and intrinsic interest, it is easy to overemphasise the importance of marble figures in the context of Early Cycladic civilisation as a whole. Nevertheless they do give us important insights into several aspects of that civilisation – technical competence, craft specialisation, the export trade – but perhaps above all some feeling of the human concerns of the early islanders and the ways they expressed these in their relationship with the divine.

(vi) History and foreign relations[54]

The Early Bronze Age in the Cyclades lasted for about 1,200 years. The most important developments are simply stated – a considerable increase in population and the number of settlements; the appearance of an increasingly rich and characteristically Cycladic material culture; the opening up of regular contacts with peoples outside the islands and progress towards more sophisticated social organisation.

The archaeological finds are numerous and include some strikingly attractive and interesting objects, in particular the marble vases and figurines. On the basis of the full range of finds we can trace a broad historical story and form a reasonably detailed picture of certain aspects of contemporary life – burial customs, for example, or the exploitation and distribution of Melian obsidian. But it is as well to be clear that our understanding is dependent on and limited by what is available for scrutiny. What is missing, whether through archaeological neglect (the environmental and anthropological evidence from early excavations, often the coarser pottery) or because of its perishable character (wooden objects, foodstuffs) might radically alter our view of life in Early Cycladic times. The external relationships of the Cyclades which we can discern in the distribution of obsidian might prove to be quite different from those reflected in the import/export of food or woodwork, if such exchanges were known to have taken place. The balance of our overall view, which is necessarily somewhat crude, would thus have to be adjusted.

Twelve hundred years is a long time. That Early Cycladic history can be sketched in a few lines is another reminder, not only of the superficial character of our historical understanding, but also of the relatively slow cultural developments, at least by the standards of modern times.

As shown in Chapter 2, Early Cycladic culture can be divided into four stages (EC I, II, IIIA, IIIB), which provide a chronological basis for charting changes in material culture and for locating events. It is worth reviewing this sequence from a more broadly historical standpoint.

Late to Final Neolithic

In the later Neolithic (LN II/Final Neolithic), the islands, with the possible exception of Melos, seem to have been thinly settled. Kephala on Kea is the only excavated site, unless Saliagos is now to be down-dated. This was a small hamlet of perhaps 50 people on a barren headland by the sea. They lived in simple stone-built houses, cultivated crops, reared animals and collected shellfish. Their cist-tomb cemetery was nearby.

That they had some contacts with the outside world, the more distant ones probably indirect, is shown by similarities in pottery with other parts of the Aegean and by evidence for the export of Melian obsidian, which probably explains the greater intensity of settlement on that island.

Early Cycladic I

Not long after – or possibly even before – the abandonment of Kephala, there was a perceptible increase in the number of settlements in the Cyclades. In view of some similarities between the material culture of Kephala and that of EC I,[55] this seems likely to represent a growth in the indigenous population rather than the arrival of settlers from elsewhere.

The settlements at this time were no bigger than Kephala. We know little about them and most of our information about contemporary life comes from the cemeteries of cist graves. The limited size of these early cemeteries (15-20 graves) is probably another pointer to the restricted scale of the settlements to which they belonged.

It is certain that the efforts of the inhabitants were largely devoted to food production, though the gradually increasing sophistication of some of the artefacts, especially those in marble, show that the society whose structure, capabilities and preoccupations they represent was far from primitive.

The most important aspect of EC I is that it sees the development of all those aspects of material culture which we have come to regard as characteristically Cycladic. Cist tombs become widespread. Bronze comes into use, though in a very small way. Vase forms are introduced which provide the basis for subsequent developments. Marble vessels and figures begin to be found in the second and third phases of EC I and gradually increase in range and quantity.

The nature of contacts between the Cyclades and other areas in EC I is somewhat ambiguous. There are some very general similarities between EC I pottery and that of Mainland Greece and north-west Anatolia at the transition from Neolithic to Bronze Age. These can be seen in the heavy burnished fabric used, the rolled-rim bowl and the standard lug form. There are also some connections between Cycladic and Anatolian figurine types.

Graves at Ayia Fotia, near Siteia on the north coast of Crete, have Cycladic pottery but this is mostly EC II, and certainly no earlier than the end of EC I. The same is true of material from a small number of sites elsewhere in the Aegean, e.g. Palaia Kokkinia near Athens and Pyrgos in Crete.[56]

Iassos,[57] in Caria on the Aegean coast of Turkey, has produced finds which relate more closely to EC I. Some of the pottery and stone vase forms are like the Cycladic and some of the graves are Cycladic-type cists. It is possible that this material indicates the presence of a number of Cycladic settlers on a site which also had a local population. But the reasons for such a situation are not obvious, especially in view of the present lack of other evidence for direct contact between these two areas.

No imports from abroad have been found in the Cyclades in EC I contexts.

The limited evidence available suggests that foreign relations were not well established and had little influence on local culture. Some of the general similarities that exist may have been the result of independent invention rather than direct imitation – or of very indirect contacts. Such journeys as took place would have been encouraged by the need for distribution of Melian obsidian.

Early Cycladic II

EC II sees the expansion of Cycladic culture in almost every sphere. The number of sites continues to grow, most obviously on Naxos and

Amorgos. There is evidence of more substantial and sophisticated architecture – best represented for the moment at Ayia Irini,[58] where the houses of this period are neatly constructed and apparently laid out to a regular overall plan (Fig. 40). We may suspect also that settlements were larger, but it is not easy to prove this when so few have been excavated and none completely. Some of the cemeteries were certainly sizable; that at Chalandriani on Syros was huge, with over 600 graves of which the majority were EC II.

In other aspects of material culture, the range of finds and types is greatly expanded, though the basic forms in pottery and marble are derived from those of EC I. The two most obvious features of this expansion are the increased numbers of bronze objects and the development in marble of the canonical folded-arm figurine and other more complex figures or groups in a similar style. We should not forget either the small items of jewellery – beads, pendants and ornamental pins in various materials – which help to fill out our picture of a society where keeping alive was no longer the sole preoccupation.

The new capabilities in the field of metal-working are important for several reasons. Their very development involved a search for raw materials, requiring both exploitation of those that were available in the Cyclades and the acquisition by trade of those that were not. The products themselves improved the technological basis of virtually all the crafts, including those less immediately obvious such as ship-building, by making available more efficient tools. They may also have stimulated warfare – 'improved' can hardly be the right word – and certainly added a new dimension to ideas of wealth and 'luxury' in material possessions.

It would be foolish to see the search for metals as the only reason behind the increased foreign (and inter-Cycladic) contacts of EC II, but it must have been an important incentive. There are many other possible contributory factors whose weight we cannot assess – continued demand for Melian obsidian, the desire for fine Cycladic marble and possibly other objects, the migration of some Cycladic people to trading stations or to combat the effects of over-population in the islands.

Whatever the complex of reasons, the archaeological evidence clearly indicates a greater ease of movement in and out of the islands and the wider dissemination of both artefacts and ideas.

Links with other areas are usually observed in exported or imported objects, or else distinctive forms (of vases, weapons etc.) which, while probably manufactured in the places where they were found, nevertheless duplicate those of other regions in ways which suggest ideas, techniques or influences exchanged or held in common. These have been discussed in more detail in the relevant sections, but examples are the Cycladic marble figures from both Crete and the Mainland, as well as local copies of them in Crete; bronze weapon and tweezer types shared between the Cyclades and Crete or the Cyclades and north-west Anatolia; pottery forms common to both the Cyclades and Mainland Greece (the saucer and sauceboat). All these links connect the Cycladic period chronologically with EM II in Crete and EH II on the Greek Mainland.

A number of sites[59] however, all round the Aegean, show signs of more intensive relations with the Cyclades. Two of these are in Attica – Ayios Kosmas, on a promontory in the Saronic gulf not far to the east of Athens, and Tsepi near Marathon on the east coast of Attica. Ayios Kosmas was termed a Cycladic 'colony' by its excavator, chiefly because of discoveries in the cemetery of Cycladic-style cist graves. The finds from these graves included figurines, pottery and stone vases of Cycladic type, though possibly manufactured locally (some of the stone objects are of non-Cycladic material). Many features of the burial practices were as found in the Cyclades themselves. Cycladic material was however much less evident in the settlement. At Tsepi, no settlement has yet been discovered, but the numerous graves and the finds from them are both Cycladic in character and of EC II date.

In Crete, a cemetery at Ayia Fotia near Siteia also has strong Cycladic links. The graves are not built cists like those in Attica just described, but pits or partly rock-cut tombs which are not standard Cycladic types, although there are some Cycladic parallels. The finds however, mainly pottery, contain much that is very Cycladic in character and was probably imported. On the north coast of Crete, Ayia Fotia is well situated for communication with the Cyclades.

Archanes is in central Crete and lies some 15 km to the south of Knossos. The site of Fourni, north-west of the modern town, is an extensive burial ground ranging in date over much of the Bronze Age. There are no cist graves here but important Cycladic finds have come from EM III levels in a local built tomb and its associated structures. The finds included nearly 1000 blades of obsidian (55 from the tomb), 13 marble figurines and one of ivory, three stone vases, and other objects, as yet unpublished, which are said to be directly comparable with Cycladic.

The Archanes material is of great interest for a number of reasons. If there were islanders buried in the cemetery (and, in that case, they were certainly not in a majority) they may have been involved in the trade or working of obsidian. It would however seem very odd for this valuable commodity to be found in such quantity in a cemetery and this objection is not entirely met by the undoubted connection of craft activity and ritual[60] which can be observed at other Bronze Age sites in the Aegean, and indeed apparently in another instance (weaving in a mortuary context) at Archanes itself.

As regards a possible Cycladic presence in the cemetery, the other finds, especially the figurines, are of greater interest than the obsidian, since they would naturally form part of a truly Cycladic burial assemblage in the islands. This is not however quite conclusive since Cycladic objects, as we have seen, are quite regularly found abroad and were presumably prized as fine things. But the combination here of a number of different, Cycladic-style finds, together with the large quantity of obsidian, is persuasive.

There may be some significance in the date of the deposit, which must be late EC II, if not EC IIIA, since it is EM III in Cretan terms, although the EM III period cannot yet be very precisely correlated with the Cycladic sequence. If these finds are in fact EC IIIA from a Cycladic viewpoint, they might represent the arrival in Crete of a group of island refugees from the troubles of EC IIIA (see below).

This idea receives a little support from the character of the figurines from Archanes. While they include standard Cycladic types (brought with the incomers?), there are also two examples of the so-called Koumasa variant, which was manufactured only in Crete. This type has a later history than the purely Cycladic forms and is found in deposits as late as MM I, though also earlier. The Koumasa figures could then represent a Cycladic tradition, originally established in Crete by those who fled there in EC II/IIIA.

Within the Cyclades themselves there are no such obvious signs of the influence of external cultures, though Ayia Irini, no doubt because of its proximity to the Mainland, seems to have closer artefactual connections with that area than do the rest of the Cyclades.

Although Archanes provides more evidence to support speculation than the sites in Attica with Cycladic connections, the questions that all of them pose are the same.[61] Were islanders present and, if so, what were they doing there? In the case of Archanes a tentative solution has been suggested – that there was a group of refugees who managed to retain some of their native cultural traits and had brought with them, or managed to import, an island product.

In the case of the Attic sites, the dating does not seem to allow the suggestion that they were refugee settlements, except possibly Ayios Kosmas, where some of the local material is EH III.[62]

If refugee settlements are unlikely, we must consider other solutions. In a cultural sense, it seems highly likely that those buried in the tombs at Ayios Kosmas and Tsepi were islanders, for why should locals adopt Cycladic burial practices as well as using Cycladic objects as grave goods? But it does not seem possible to decide whether this was due to the expansion of the Cycladic cultural area by the movement of people from the islands, conceivably as a response to over-population, or to the establishment of permanent enclaves in an essentially alien cultural environment, perhaps for trading purposes. The fact that no non-Cycladic graves have yet been discovered at the site may make the latter suggestion rather unlikely.

Such is the picture of population growth, material prosperity and wide exchange of objects, materials and ideas which the archaeological finds of EC II date present. The following period could hardly provide a greater contrast.

Early Cycladic IIIA

The archaeological evidence for change at the end of EC II has already been summarised in Chapter 2 – the abrupt arrival of distinctive new pottery forms and fabric of Anatolian (and especially Cilician origin), new metal types, and perhaps the apsidal house form from the same source. The recent results[63] of analysis of the metal from which bronze objects in the EC IIIA fort at Kastri on Syros were made suggests that, in this case, even the raw material may have been imported, again from an Anatolian source. Old sites were abandoned (possibly Phylakopi and Paroikia; later Ayia Irini) or fortified (Mount Kynthos, Panormos) and at least one new one (Kastri) situated with regard exclusively for defence and equipped with a defence wall and towers.

Parallel with the appearance of these intrusive features, several traditional elements of Cycladic culture decline or disappear. Some cist tombs within older cemeteries have EC IIIA material but the numbers are few indeed in comparison with graves of the preceding period. There may well have been a decline in the population of the islands in EC IIIA, but it is also possible that much more casual and thus untraceable forms of burial were employed in these troubled times. No marble objects can be certainly dated to EC IIIA and it seems that this highly sophisticated traditional craft came to an end – a dramatic change indeed.

We have seen in the previous section how some islanders may have fled from the Cyclades to Crete, even possibly the Greek Mainland – a development which fits well with the abandonment of Ayia Irini during EC IIIA. Other main sites (Phylakopi, Paroikia) may have been temporarily deserted at this time, since there is very little EC IIIA material from either, in spite of the fact that it is quite widely distributed in the Cyclades. But it is also possible that the new features did not penetrate to all islands in equal measure.

The cause of the complete disruption of Cycladic culture which these changes represent can hardly be in doubt. It must be due to the movement of substantial numbers of intruders into the Cyclades from their Anatolian homelands, which we know themselves to have been afflicted by disturbances at the same time.

Although the historical emphasis now is rightly on change and disruption, it must not be forgotten that there are, from the start of the period, signs of continuity in island culture – in the fact that EC IIIA pottery makes its initial appearance (at Ayia Irini) together with material of late EC II, and in the direct reflection of one or two EC II forms in pottery as late as EC IIIB.[64]

Since the diagnostic pottery of EC IIIA is, in a sense, not Cycladic but Anatolian, when it is found elsewhere in Euboea and on the Greek Mainland its presence is more likely to be due to the further movement of Anatolian groups than to contacts with native islanders. In any event, we cannot distinguish between the two and there are in effect no Cycladic exports of this period. As for imports from neighbouring areas, there are none at all – a situation which is hardly surprising at a time when normal communications must have been virtually brought to a standstill.

It must here be mentioned that a different view of the history of this period, to which reference has already been made,[65] sees a great cultural 'gap' (the term is ambiguous) in the Cyclades between the end of EC II and EC IIIB. This theory depends partly on the argument that the EC IIIA-related finds on Mainland Greece are dateable to EH II (not EH III, as suggested here) and that, since the next Cycladic relationships which can be observed are with the early Middle Helladic period, there must be a lengthy period in the Cyclades of which we have no knowledge whatsoever, either because there was nothing to know, or because the characteristic material has not yet been recognised.

In fact, however, it can be satisfactorily maintained that EH III, not EH II is the correct Mainland context for the EC IIIA-related material. But, even if this were not so, the absence of import-export relationships is no kind of an argument for a gap in the local culture, especially where, as here, all the archaeological evidence shows that normal patterns of life and contacts were totally disrupted. Most significant of all however are the incontestable signs of continuity (from EC IIIA to B) in Cycladic pottery which show that, however deprived the Cyclades may have been in this period, neither the population nor their traditonal culture were entirely wiped out.

EC IIIA is thus a highly critical time, since it saw not only the fragmentation of the rich culture of EC II and a sharp reduction both in population and in the standard of living, but a virtually complete break in contact with the outside world.

Early Cycladic IIIB

This final stage of the Cycladic Early Bronze Age, contemporary, as we have already seen, with the first Middle Bronze Age phases on Crete and the Greek Mainland, has two particularly important features. One is the appearance of town centres; the other the mixture of change and innovation in the material culture.

The towns themselves are indications of more settled conditions since, in other circumstances, their construction and development would have been very hazardous. Although the evidence is somewhat fragmentary, since the remains of the two main sites of the period (Phylakopi and Paroikia) – to which should perhaps be added the refoundation of Ayia Irini at the start of Period IV – lie beneath substantial later strata, it seems that these EC IIIB settlements were larger and more substantial than the villages of earlier times. This was no coincidence as the tendency was now for the entire populations of all but the largest islands to be accommodated in single centres. This trend was apparently initiated by the need for protection in the unsettled conditions of EC IIIA but, by EC IIIB and Middle Cycladic times, the administrative advantages had probably become evident too.

There is no doubt that some aspects of the culture of Early Cycladic IIIB were derived from that of EC IIIA. This is at present chiefly evident in the pottery and has been discussed in (ii) above. As might be expected, the connections with earlier material are particularly strong in the pottery of the first stage of EC IIIB, showing that, whatever the disturbances, features of earlier Cycladic culture did in fact survive.

This is less evident in other areas, largely perhaps for lack of evidence, for little is available apart from the pottery. As for burial customs, there are no cists of this period, but the use of such tombs at Ayia Irini in the Middle Cycladic period, and elsewhere in the Cyclades later in the Bronze Age, proves continuity of the tradition. Two new forms of grave appear – the rock-cut chamber tomb and the urn. Urn burial has an earlier history in Anatolia which could stand behind its introduction in the Cyclades, especially if the contacts of EC IIIA continued to any degree: there are also urn burials at Late Neolithic Kephala. Chamber tombs might simply represent a local development in places where it was found that the rock was soft enough to excavate easily. Indeed, in this sense they could be connected with the cists, where some degree of excavation was always involved.

That the survival of cultural features could be patchy seems to be shown by differences between Ayia Irini and Phylakopi. At the former site, some EC IIIB features (incised pottery, the duck vase shape) survived into the Middle Cycladic period, whereas at the latter they virtually disappeared after early EC IIIB.[66]

As for foreign contacts, relations with Crete, which had been severed in EC IIIA, were still not reopened and, as a result, almost no MM IA pottery has been found in the Cyclades. But the relationship of MM IA to Mainland material (which does have Cycladic connections) shows that EC IIIB was at least partly contemporary with MM IA, and incised pottery of early EC IIIB type has been found in Crete.[67]

By far the closest connections of the EC IIIB pottery are those between the 'Geometric' or 'Rectilinear' class, which belongs to both phases of EC IIIB, and the early Middle Helladic matt-painted pottery of the Mainland, which is probably derived from it[68] (Fig. 102; cf. Fig. 66).

The strong relationship of the Cyclades with the Mainland, to the exclusion of Crete, may have had something to do with the fact that obsidian (see (iv) above) was still much in demand in Middle Helladic Greece, which was considerably more backward in all respects, including metal technology, than Middle Minoan Crete.

Contacts outside the Aegean are not strong but are suggested by two Cycladic vases supposed to have come from the Balearic islands.[69] There are also some limited similarities between EC IIIB Geometric and pottery from Tarsus in Cilicia.[70] The significance of this is still very obscure but could turn out to be important in view of the specifically Cilician connections of some of the new pottery of EC IIIA.

Summary

The Early Cycladic period thus follows a charmed course. Emerging from the Neolithic background, EC I sees the appearance of several

102. Barrel jar in the matt-painted
style (Middle Helladic), from Lerna.
(American School of Classical
Studies).

characteristic features of true Cycladic culture in a setting where outside
contacts were very limited. In EC II, we can trace the consolidation and
enrichment of that culture and an expansion of overseas contacts. The
picture undergoes a dramatic change in EC IIIA, when invaders crush
Cycladic individuality and introduce new cultural features and chaotic
conditions to the islands. EC IIIB sees the re-emergence of stronger
communities, now larger and town-based for safety, and the survival of
some traditional elements. This solid, if unspectacular, regrouping is the
basis for further developments in the Middle Bronze Age.

6

The Cyclades in the
Middle Bronze Age[1]

The picture of Middle Cycladic culture drawn in this chapter will inevitably seem more lopsided than that of the Early or Late stages. This is because, apart from the sites themselves, the range of material recovered for study is rather limited and interpretation is heavily dependent on the information that can be gleaned from pottery. A few years ago the bias would have been even more evident, but Caskey's excavations at Ayia Irini have provided much new material which is now in the process of publication. This is particularly valuable, not only for the additions to the general body of knowledge but also because comparison of finds from Ayia Irini, which is situated at the north-west limit of the Cycladic group, with those from islands further south (Melos, especially) can provide a real test of the unity of Cycladic culture at this period.

Background and stratigraphical basis

After the Anatolian incursions of EC IIIA when Cycladic life was seriously disrupted, EC IIIB saw the development of a more stable situation. Rather more sites are known and the two excavated settlements (Phylakopi and Paroikia) have substantial architecture apparently without fortifications. This probably indicates that some progress had already been made towards the Middle Cycladic climate where we find larger and better organised communities with a greater capacity to produce non-essential goods and to engage in trade and other foreign contacts. Evidence of the latter can be seen in the clear influence exerted by EC IIIB Geometric pottery on the formation of the matt-painted style of the early Middle Helladic period on the Greek Mainland.

The major settlements of Ayia Irini and Phylakopi provide the stratigraphic key to the Middle Cycladic period, as well as the bulk of the finds, though there are difficulties in relating the sequences at the two sites.

Phylakopi, Ayia Irini and the early Middle Cycladic period[2]

At the end of the second EC IIIB phase (City I-iii), Phylakopi was destroyed, probably by an earthquake, which seems to have razed the whole site. There may have followed a period when it was deserted, though, if so, it cannot have been for very long, since the pottery of early City II has some links (Fig. 58) with that of late EC IIIB. For instance, the barrel jar shape which is common in EC IIIB Geometric is also found in Middle Cycladic Dark Burnished pottery, and the beaked jug which occurs in Middle Cycladic Cycladic White fabric is clearly related to, though distinct from, the EC IIIB form.

The first excavators of Phylakopi thought that the degree of continuity from City I to City II (EC IIIB to Middle Cycladic) was very strong, and particularly evident in the continued use of Geometric pottery. Careful study of their report however shows that there were no clearly stratified levels which can be used to define their earliest subdivision of Phylakopi II (II-i). Recent investigations at the site, although admittedly restricted in extent, have not revealed any Geometric pottery in Middle Cycladic strata – a fact which suggests that there was a definite break between the final City I levels, where Geometric pottery is standard, and the earliest levels of City II, where it is entirely absent. Further study of the Phylakopi pottery has also shown that the so-called matt-painted class of Geometric pottery supposedly characteristic of this early Middle Cycladic phase (II-i) is very hard to isolate. It could in fact therefore simply be a minor pottery group contemporary with the standard Middle Cycladic classes, rather than an important class peculiar to the II-i phase.

This rather abstruse problem is unlikely to be resolved satisfactorily without a wider reinvestigation of the Middle Cycladic strata at Phylakopi, since it is possible that genuine II-i levels exist in parts of the site not so far excavated and/or that they originally existed in most areas of the settlement but were subsequently removed during levelling operations prior to rebuilding. It must also be said that recent finds from Thera (Ftellos)[3] include both EC IIIB and early Middle Cycladic elements and may thus represent just such an intermediate phase, though the stratigraphy of this site is not entirely clear.

At Ayia Irini, the EC IIIA phase (Period III), which is distantly related to though essentially earlier than City I-ii at Phylakopi, was followed by a period of desertion. The pottery relationships of Period IV are primarily with early Middle Cycladic Phylakopi (City II-ii), with the use of Middle Cycladic Dark Burnished and Cycladic White fabrics. The true 'Geometric' pottery of later Phylakopi I (EC IIIB) is not found at Ayia Irini, though there is a fabric known as Yellow-slipped ware which has Geometric patterns to some extent related to those on the Phylakopi material. This class of pottery is however more closely connected with the matt-painted pottery of the early Middle Helladic period on the Greek Mainland which was itself influenced by and later than the Phylakopi Geometric. Other pointers too indicate that the Keian class may be of later origin than the Phylakopi material. The Ayia Irini group does not appear to include one of the most characteristic shapes of the Phylakopi Geometric – the beaked jug – while it does have shapes (e.g. the barrel jar) which continued in use at Phylakopi in early Middle Cycladic times. Polychrome decoration is common at Ayia Irini, whereas it never occurs at Phylakopi in the EC IIIB stage.

So far, this discussion of the pottery has suggested that Ayia Irini Period IV is more or less contemporary with the earlier stage of Phylakopi II (=II-ii, not forgetting that we have discounted II-i as a meaningful subdivision) and is thus essentially Middle Cycladic, though it might overlap slightly with late Phylakopi I and start just before the end of EC IIIB.

This analysis is supported by the occurrence of imported Minoan pottery of MM IB-II date at the two sites. At Ayia Irini this occurs only in Period IV; at Phylakopi it is not found before the early Second City. There is none at all in late City I (EC IIIB).

An apparently serious difficulty however is caused by contexts of incised pottery at the two major sites. At Ayia Irini it occurs throughout Period IV (early Middle Cycladic), whereas at Phylakopi it is never found after I-ii (early EC IIIB). A similar contradiction is provided by the occurrence of the distinctive duck vase shape (Fig. 65). At Phylakopi this is rarely if ever found after I-ii (early EC IIIB), whereas at Ayia Irini it occurs in Period IV and is even made in the standard Middle Cycladic Dark Burnished fabric.

There seem to be two possible explanations of these inconsistencies. One is that the suggestion made above about the likely relationships of the phases under discussion is wrong and that Period IV at Ayia Irini in fact overlaps to a much greater degree with phases I-iii and I-ii at Phylakopi. The other is that these peculiarities reflect in a more complex way the fact that Cycladic culture, although broadly unified, was locally modified according to the differing character and differing histories of the individual islands. Thus the use of certain EC III features (incised pottery, the duck vase shape) continued at Ayia Irini, which was reoccupied at a time when they were still in use, whereas they disappeared at Phylakopi, perhaps because of the serious interruption of the life of the site at the end of EC IIIB in the destruction of the First City.

In fact, these are not strictly alternative explanations and there may be some truth in each, though any radical realignment of the relative chronology seems unlikely. For although it might resolve these relatively minor problems, it would automatically create new and more fundamental inconsistencies. Nevertheless the question, though complex, is worth attention for it illustrates the nature of the problem and the kinds of conclusions that archaeologists attempt to draw from pottery evidence.

The later Middle Cycladic period

The sequences at both major sites allow a stratigraphic distinction between early and late phases of the Middle Cycladic period. At Ayia Irini, this is Period V; at Phylakopi II-iii. The material distinction is of course provided mainly by the pottery. The earlier Middle Cycladic phase has local Dark Burnished pottery and the earliest type of Cycladic White (the so-called Curvilinear style), as well as imports of Classic Grey Minyan from the Mainland and MM IB-II pottery from Crete. Late Middle Cycladic, on the other hand, has much less Burnished ware, a later (Naturalistic style) variety of Cycladic White, MM III imports and locally-made vases much more heavily influenced by contemporary Cretan pottery. A rather dull-surfaced red-washed pottery seems to have largely replaced the Dark Burnished and was quite widespread, and there are the beginnings of the light-coloured but rather pinkish fabric ('Later Local') which became basic in LC I.

The end of the Middle Cycladic period is marked at Phylakopi by a widespread destruction of the Second City, probably by an earthquake. There is an interesting alternative suggestion – that the destruction was the result of a Minoan attack, presaging the Minoan domination of the site in LC I, and to be associated with the sharp fall in Cycladic, and especially Melian, imports to Knossos which occurred at the end of MM III or the very beginning of LC I. At Ayia Irini the change is less clearly defined, although there was a radical architectural realignment of the site at the beginning of the Late Cycladic period (Period VI).

Archaeological characteristics of the Middle Cycladic period

The settlements[4]

As mentioned in Chapter 4, a count of Middle Cycladic sites shows a substantial increase over the total for EC IIIB, indeed over all EC III (A and B) sites taken together. Even so there seems rarely to have been more than one major site per island – only when it was exceptionally large and fertile (Naxos: Fig. 51) or had special importance of another kind (the obsidian of Melos).

The distinctive features of sites of this period are their relatively large size, their carefully organised architecture and their defensive character, which sometimes included built fortifications. All this suggests strong and coherent local organisation.

Middle Cycladic Phylakopi (City II) was in the same promontory location as its predecessor but may now have been defended by a wall.[5] It is likely that City II was a good deal larger than City I and it certainly had a carefully gridded plan and well-built houses (Figs. 43, 44). It was the only site of any size on Melos at this time and virtually all the island's population must have become concentrated here. Consequently more transport was needed for working distant and now uninhabited agricultural land and the increased rearing of cattle (as traction animals) is reflected in the animal bone finds from the site.[6]

Ayia Irini was sizable and had fortifications from near the beginning of the Middle Cycladic period, but the architecture of the settlement is not very well known. Paroikia on Paros, on a hill by the bay, has produced a fair amount of Middle Cycladic material and the site presumably advanced in sophistication from its already developed EC IIIB state. Akrotiri on Thera was a substantial settlement already in Middle Cycladic times and more will be learnt about it in the future. Even now it is clear that parts of the settlement, which was rebuilt in 'Minoan' form early in LC I, go back to the Middle Cycladic period and the early LC I destruction deposits contain much pottery that would be equally at home in the late Middle Cycladic.

Other sites which have produced Middle Cycladic finds (e.g. Vryokastro on Tenos, Rizokastelia and Mikre Vigla on Naxos) are certainly in defensive positions. They may well have been important settlements, but we cannot tell much more about their character until excavations are carried out.

The local pottery[7]

Dark Burnished (Figs. 103-107)

Pottery with a thick lustrous coat, ranging in colour from black through shades of brown to red, is characteristic of the Middle Cycladic period, and particularly of its earlier stage. Although Ayia Irini and Phylakopi both produced this type of pottery and have many characteristics in common, it is quite easy to distinguish the fabrics of the two sites. That from Phylakopi is slipped as well as burnished and often has a very highly lustrous finish, while that from Ayia Irini is usually burnished only and less lustrous. Some of the vase shapes are distinctly Cycladic (the barrel/ovoid jar: Fig. 103; the 'Cycladic' bowl: Fig. 104) but the most interesting feature of developed Dark Burnished is its clear relationship to Classic Grey Minyan pottery of Mainland Greece (e.g. the kantharos and ring-stemmed goblet shapes which were frequently imported into the islands). Some of the Cycladic shapes are direct copies (Fig. 105, with plain stem) and the use of similar sharply angled forms is also characteristic.

Some of the pottery had painted decoration, usually in white but sometimes also in black paint (which did not show up so well against the usually dark surface). Some of the designs are simple and linear (bars on rim, festoons on body, spirals: Figs. 103, 104); some are more ambitious (occasional foliates). At Phylakopi, there is an interesting series of sherds

103. Dark (red) burnished ovoid jar with light painted decoration (Middle Cycladic) from Ayia Irini, Kea. (University of Cincinnati).

104. Cycladic bowl (Middle Cycladic). (British Museum).

from large vases with birds and other motifs (Fig. 106). A comparison of these with similar decoration found on other classes of pottery suggests that such elaborate decoration is probably quite late in the Middle Cycladic period. Fluted relief decoration is also found (Fig. 107).

The Ayia Irini stratigraphy has shown that Dark Burnished pottery is much more common and more sophisticated there in the earlier Middle Cycladic period. It seems likely that this is true of Phylakopi also, since the character of such pottery at that site is otherwise quite similar. A class of dull Red-washed ware probably replaced the fine Dark Burnished on Melos late in the Middle Cycladic period and similar Red-painted pottery is found in early LC I deposits at Akrotiri.

105. Red slipped and burnished stemmed bowl (Middle Cycladic) from Ayia Irini, Kea. (University of Cincinnati).

106. Dark (red) burnished sherds with white-painted motifs (Middle Cycladic) from Phylakopi, Melos (C. Renfrew).

Cycladic White (Figs. 108-111)

This is a most distinctive and often very attractive class of pottery. The fabric is variable in quality but, at its best, thin and with a fine non-gritty biscuit, a smooth, sometimes self-slipped surface and a consistent yellowish-white colour throughout. Designs are painted in matt black-brown paint. Sometimes burnished red elements are included in the designs (the so-called 'Black-and-Red' style: Fig. 108), which occurs from early Middle Cycladic but is much more common in the later

107. Fragment of dark (brown) burnished bowl with fluted decoration (Middle Cycladic) from Phylakopi, Melos. (C. Renfrew).

part of the period and in the early Late Cycladic. Some pieces are plain and undecorated. Coarser vases with thicker less consistent biscuit, greyish or yellowish in colour and with much cruder decoration, seem to belong to the later stages of the style, though it is difficult to demonstrate this stratigraphically. The class is at present best known from Phylakopi, though similar material is reasonably common throughout Periods IV and V at Ayia Irini. Most of the Kea material is thought to have been imported from Melos.

Some of the shapes are the same as in Dark Burnished (e.g. the Cycladic bowl) but Mainland Minyan vases were not copied; some (the hole-mouth or bridge-spouted jar) are clearly derived from Cretan forms; some are distinctly local, especially the beaked jug (Fig. 109) which, though distinct from the EC IIIB version, is obviously descended from it.

The designs can be divided into two groups. The first and essentially earlier consists of abstract curvilinear motifs (Fig. 110), frequently arranged in zones, and often ultimately derived from Cretan MM II prototypes. The second and later (Fig. 108) contains more naturalistic, especially floral, patterns and is related to MM III. Figured scenes are few but very striking (Fig. 111). A charming lion's head comes from recent excavations and shows a somewhat crude but fresh and lively approach, which is distinctly local.

108. 'Black-and-Red' style jug (Middle or Late Cycladic), from Phylakopi, Melos. (National Archaeological Museum, Athens. Photo: T.A.P.).

Later Local pottery (see Chapter 7)

One further group of pottery needs to be mentioned here. Its name is derived from the original Phylakopi report, where however it was applied to a rather more extensive body of material of LC I-II date. In the context of the Middle Cycladic period at Phylakopi, it refers to a relatively small class which has some clear connections with Cycladic White, with which

109. Cycladic White beaked jug
(Middle Cycladic) in the Curvilinear
style, from Phylakopi, Melos.
(Ashmolean Museum).

it shares a few shapes (e.g. the hole-mouthed jar) and decorative motifs.
The fabric is fairly fine, usually buff in colour and decorated with matt
paint. Spiral decoration is very common. Later Local pottery anticipates
in all respects the major local decorated pottery class of LC I which is
closely related to that of Cretan LM IA, and the range of shapes includes
the semi-globular cup, so common in LC I. Tortoiseshell ripple
decoration is common. Although the term 'Later Local' has been applied
only to the Phylakopi pottery, material with similar characteristics is
known from late Middle Cycladic Ayia Irini, where Minoan and
Minoan-influenced material is predominant by the end of Period IV.

A wide range of coarse shapes is known and there are other decorated
classes. Among these is the Yellow-slipped (Ayia Irini) mentioned above.

Ceramically, then, the Middle Cycladic period can be viewed as
follows. The early stage sees the rapid development of Dark Burnished
ware which has distinct local characteristics at the two major sites. This
pottery is considerably less evident in later Middle Cycladic times.
Cycladic White also occurs throughout the period but there are earlier
and later features and the absence of Minyan-related elements may be
significant. The Curvilinear style of decoration precedes the Naturalistic

110. Cycladic White bowl (Middle Cycladic) in the Curvilinear style, from Phylakopi, Melos. (National Archaeological Museum, Athens. Photo: T.A.P.).

and the finer ware seems generally to be earlier. Use of the 'Black-and-Red' decorative system occurs from an early stage but is much more common later, and in early Late Cycladic times. At the end of the Middle Cycladic period we find the introduction of a new class (called 'Later Local' at Phylakopi) whose closest connections are with the LM IA-derived pottery of the early Late Cycladic period.

Middle Cycladic burials and religion[8]

In EC I-II all known Cycladic graves were either simple burials or stone-built cists. A few EC IIIA cist burials are known and the rock-cut chamber, which is definitely attested on Melos (at Aspro Chorio and probably Phylakopi) in EC IIIB, may have originated in this period, if the EC IIIA-type pottery in chamber tombs at Manika in Euboea is a reliable guide. Jar burials within the settlements are known from EC IIIB Phylakopi (Fig. 57), Paroikia and perhaps also Akrotiri. A double cist with EC IIIB pottery is known from Amorgos.

To date, Middle Cycladic burials, early and late, are known chiefly from Ayia Irini, though important discoveries of early Middle Cycladic cists on Thera have recently been reported and there is material from Aila, Naxos (see below).

The Ayia Irini finds show that the use of the traditional cist tomb (Fig. 112), as well as the more recently introduced practice of jar burial (Fig. 112) continued in Middle Cycladic times, and cist tombs of late Middle

111. Fragments of Cycladic White panelled cups (Middle Cycladic), from Phylakopi, Melos. (C. Renfrew).

112. Middle Cycladic cist and jar burials from Ayia Irini, Kea. (University of Cincinnati).

Cycladic or early Late Cycladic date have been found too at Aila on Naxos. Platforms are also associated with some of the graves, as in the Early Cycladic period (Fig. 56). Burial is usually single and contracted. The jar burials (as the other graves) are almost all extramural, in contrast to EC IIIB Phylakopi and Paroikia, where they are intramural.

As the Middle Cycladic period progresses, the tombs become more elaborate and various, though all are probably, in one way or another, developments of the cist – large shafts with built stone linings and cover slabs, or more complex built tombs (see Chapter 7). These tombs, especially the later ones, contained a good deal of jewellery and metal objects, which hint at a material improvement in Middle Cycladic prosperity which has not previously been evident.

One tomb (Nô. 1) which, with its platform, was found in a room of the town, may have been the focus of some ritual ceremonies. Apart from this the only evidence for religious activity in the Middle Cycladic period is the knowledge that the Temple at Ayia Irini goes back to that phase. Although the Middle Cycladic finds from the building give no direct proof of ritual use, there are hearths which could have been associated with sacrifice, and it would be surprising if the function of the building was not the same then as in the later period.

Pottery, history and external relations[9] in the Middle Cycladic period

The reader will now be painfully aware of the dependence on pottery which was mentioned at the beginning of this chapter. Most of the discussion so far has been devoted to that and the sequences at the two major sites. Let us now consider some other aspects of the Middle Cycladic pottery and see what it may be able to tell us, first about the chronology of the Cyclades relative to other areas of the Aegean in the Middle Cycladic period; secondly about the nature of island life.

Finds of Cycladic pottery on Crete and the Greek Mainland give a satisfactorily consistent picture of the relative chronology. Early EC IIIB incised material occurs in late EH III or earlier Middle Helladic contexts on the Mainland and in MM IA in Crete. EC IIIB Geometric ware is closely related to earlier Middle Helladic matt-painted pottery on the Mainland in forms and decorative motifs. The Cycladic material seems somewhat earlier and probably acted as a formative influence on the Mainland style. Some Cycladic Dark Burnished pottery was exported to Mainland Greece (in particular to Athens and Lerna).

In the Cyclades, there is a striking lack of imported material in EC IIIB. But Middle Minoan (mostly, if not all, MM IB-II) pottery is found in early Middle Cycladic contexts, as are imports of Classic Grey Minyan and, to a much lesser extent, Mainland matt-painted.

Cycladic White pottery of the earlier (Curvilinear) variety has been found in an MM IB context at Knossos in Crete and the later (Naturalistic) type in late Middle Helladic at Lerna in the Argolid. Late Middle Cycladic pottery in the form of panelled cups and Cycladic White sherds with Black-and-Red style decoration are found in late Middle Helladic or early Late Helladic contexts on the Mainland and in MM IIIB-LM IA on Crete. A substantial number of Cycladic container vessels have recently been identified from MM III Knossos.

Thus early EC IIIB covers the end of EH III and the beginning of MH I. It is also, for the most part, parallel with MM IA (there is very little MM IA imported pottery in Phylakopi II-ii or Ayia Irini IV – indeed virtually none at all from either site – and the explanation must be that none was imported, although the period certainly ran parallel to the phase(s) in the Cyclades (EC IIIB and probably part of IIIA) before those when pottery of the subsequent Cretan styles is found).

Late EC IIIB coincides with the earlier part of the Middle Helladic period and later MM IA; early Middle Cycladic with MM IB-II (and possibly the end of MM IA) and with mature Middle Helladic. Late Middle Cycladic is related to MM III, late Middle Helladic and perhaps the beginning of LM IA.

The pottery finds indicate that Cycladic relationships were strongest with the Mainland in EC IIIB/early Middle Cycladic times, when Cycladic Geometric pottery influenced the formation of the Mainland matt-painted style and Dark Burnished was closely related to Mainland Grey Minyan. Cretan connections were not prominent yet, though there are signs of them already in certain pottery shapes and in the origins of some of the designs on Cycladic White pottery.

In late Middle Cycladic the Mainland contacts continued – there are Cycladic finds from that area and Mainland elements are prominent in late Middle Cycladic Akrotiri – but were really eclipsed by those with Crete. There is a much stronger incidence of Cretan imports in the islands and of Cretan influences on Cycladic shapes and decoration. It seems clear that the Cyclades were being increasingly drawn into the orbit of Crete.

It is never easy to determine just exactly what such pottery relationships represent in real human terms. But since they are virtually the only evidence we have, some attempt must be made to interpret them in this way.

It is usually thought – and reasonably so – that the essential impetus for the expansion of Cycladic external relationships in the EC II period lay in the importance of island obsidian as a commodity much in demand in other areas of the Aegean. This is probably true, in spite of the fact that the obsidian sources were controlled by only one of the Cycladic islands, namely Melos.

With the development of the Cretan palaces in the Middle Bronze Age, Crete became better able to organise the acquisition of raw materials for bronze production and the processes of production themselves. This may have led to a decline in the demand for obsidian by Crete, but at a time when Minoan political expansion was not fully under way. In the Middle Bronze Age, Mainland culture was much less sophisticated. Society was still essentially village-based, as it had been in the Early Bronze Age, and there were no coherent central organisational units, like the Cretan palaces, to encourage greater specialisation and the rapid development of skills and more efficient use of resources. In these circumstances, it is likely that the Mainland demand for obsidian would have remained high and contacts with the Cyclades, especially Melos, frequent. This may well be why what seems an essentially Melian ceramic style (EC IIIB Geometric) was able to play such an important role in the development of Mainland Matt-painted. It is also true that, probably before the end of the early Middle Cycladic period, the Cretan palaces had suffered a series of disastrous destructions which must have greatly reduced their external activities. During the later Middle Cycladic period, however, the Cretan palaces were rebuilt in their final and most sophisticated form and overseas contacts were greatly expanded. It is at this time that Cretan connections tangibly replace those with the Mainland. It was also at this time that Mainland contacts with Crete developed, Mainland culture, including the bronze industry, grew more sophisticated, and the need for obsidian probably declined.[10] A curious feature of the MM III Cycladic imports to Knossos, mentioned above, is that they cease at the end of MM III or the very beginning of LM IA, just at the time when Cretan influence in the islands was increasing rapidly. If the Cretans took over administative, and perhaps military, control of the Cyclades at this time, they may have interrupted local production of the commodities which they had previously imported, or else have started to organise the importation to Crete themselves and in their own vessels (of both kinds!).

Within the Cyclades, we have seen that, although the overall classes of Middle Cycladic pottery can be distinguished throughout the islands (and this is true not only of Ayia Irini, Phylakopi and Paroikia, but also of surface finds from unexcavated sites), there are nevertheless some distinguishable local characteristics and it is likely that these will become continuously more prominent as our knowledge of Middle Cycladic material culture grows.

The study of the physical and stylistic characteristics of local island ceramics is at an early stage, but it is possible to discern some exchange of material between the islands.[11] Melian sherds are found on Naxos (Mikre Vigla, Rizokastelia) and a good deal of the pottery from Ayia Irini is thought to have come from Melos. Dark Burnished and Cycladic White from Crete and the Mainland is also thought to be Melian. Melian, Naxian and Theran vases have been tentatively identified among the container vessels from MM III Knossos. It is hard to tell whether this apparently pre-eminent situation of Melos in the pottery export market is real or whether it is simply due to our failure yet to appreciate the extent of the existence of similar locally-produced material at other sites. If it is real, it would certainly suit the proposal made above of the important role of the obsidian trade of Melos and the island itself in the Middle Bronze Age. The island would have had a rate of development and a degree of prosperity much in advance of other islands, which would have been to some degree dependent on it.

One sign that the islands were developing a rather more sophisticated culture in the Middle Cycladic period is the increasing interest in naturalistic and figured designs for pottery decoration. It is not possible at present to analyse this in any detail but the contrast with the unrelieved geometry of the EC IIIB period is quite striking and suggests a much more conscious concern with physical surroundings and the natural world – perhaps something that grew with the increasing leisure brought about by greater prosperity.

Another element in the advancement of the Cyclades in Middle Cycladic times (as in other periods) may have been the seamanship of their inhabitants. Seamanship is vital to islanders in a way that it is not to Mainlanders or to the people of Crete (almost a continent in itself) and their skills may have resulted in them being employed as carriers by their less experienced neighbours.

Summary

Enough has already been said about the complexities of the Early to Middle Cycladic pottery sequence. It seems that what we call the Middle Cycladic period did not begin until the Middle Helladic and Middle Minoan periods were each beyond their initial phase. Then we may divide it into two stages; the first corresponding to a mature phase of the Protopalatial period in Crete (MM IB-II) and mature Middle Helladic (Classic Minyan) on the Mainland, the second to Middle Minoan and MH III.

Middle Cycladic culture displays elements both of continuity and of the disruption which one would surely expect following the serious incursions and consequent instability of the EC III period, itself still inadequately known. General continuity may be seen in the cist graves and certain pottery types obviously related to those of EC IIIB.

Disruption and change is suggested by the new settlement pattern and the changed character of the settlements themselves – larger, more centralised, more defence-conscious – as well as by the development of new and distinctive classes of pottery, namely Dark Burnished and Cycladic White. The technical sophistication sometimes evident in the pottery may be derived from more efficient and centralised production. There is also a greater sophistication of decoration and a new interest in figures and motifs from the natural world, as if the islanders were moving away from an existence where they were totally pre-occupied with subsistence and self-protection.

The new strength of these local centres led to the development of local traits which we can at present only discern in the pottery but which no doubt extended to other areas of material culture as well. The apparently greater extent of Melian external contacts may reflect the greater authority of that island deriving from its control of the obsidian sources.

It has also been suggested that these obsidian sources provided, or rather continued to provide, the basis for whatever influence the Cyclades possessed in the Aegean world of the second millennium BC and further that, since the Mainland was at the time in a considerably less advanced state of material culture than was Crete and had a much less well-developed bronze-working technology, a continued requirement for obsidian encouraged a close relationship with the Cyclades in general and Melos in particular. In this context we may interpret the close ceramic connection that can be observed between the islands and the Mainland in EC IIIB to early Middle Cycladic.

In the later Middle Cycladic period, relations with Crete, again mainly discerned in the pottery (though possibly also in the more sophisticated architecture of some of the island settlements, which some have thought influenced by the fine masonry of the Cretan palaces) became much closer. The revived Cretan palatial system of the Neopalatial period resulted in increased influence over the islands, at the same time as expanded contacts with the Mainland. By the end of the Middle Cycladic period, the islands seem to be declining into a position where local initiative was secondary to the influence of Crete.

7

The Cretan Connection

The Cyclades at the beginning of the Late Bronze Age[1] (LC I-II)

In terms of calendar years, this phase may be dated to c. 1550 – c. 1400 BC. It is represented by the LC I and II phases in the relative archaeological sequence in the islands and is marked most clearly by two features. The first is a series of architectural changes at the three major sites (Akrotiri on Thera, Ayia Irini on Kea and Phylakopi on Melos; the second the appearance in quantity of Cretan objects and other cultural features and local copies of them, with a consequent decline in local invention and originality.

Both these statements require amplification, for inevitably neither is as definitive as it seems. The Second (Middle Cycladic) City at Phylakopi was completely destroyed (it is usually thought by an earthquake, but human (Cretan) agency is also a possibility: see Chapter 6). The succeeding Third City (Fig. 45) was a rebuilding of this and is dated by finds of LM IA and related pottery, which is found in only very small quantities at the end of the Second City. A defence wall was added about now, presumably at the time of the rebuilding.

At Ayia Irini there was certainly considerable architectural change between the Middle and Late Bronze Age (Periods V-VI) and there was serious destruction during, though not at the end of, Period V. Some of the Late Cycladic buildings were aligned quite differently from their predecessors (Fig. 113), and the full town plan that has been recovered in the excavations is essentially a creation of the early Late Cycladic period (Fig. 46). The fortifications were also reorganised/repaired at this time.

At Akrotiri, the town as revealed in recent excavations (Fig. 144) acquired its most characteristic features in a rebuilding following earthquake destruction early in the Late Bronze Age, perhaps at about the same time as Phylakopi was being rebuilt. Although this reconstruction involved a good deal of alteration, including the destruction of some older buildings, the general layout of the town appears to have been settled much earlier, in Middle Cycladic times.

No doubt we shall, in due course, learn more about the extent, nature and exact dating of the changes at these three sites, but meanwhile it is

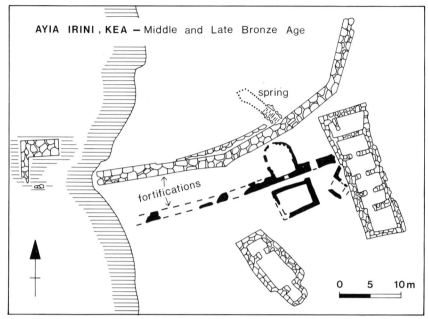

113. Middle Cycladic (black) in relation to Late Cycladic (outline) structures at Ayia Irini, Kea. (After Caskey 1971a, 370).

quite striking that, in each case, a serious destruction of the settlement in late Middle Cycladic or very early Late Cycladic times was followed by planned rebuilding on a large scale. At Ayia Irini and Phylakopi this was accompanied by the construction or reconstruction of fortifications.

Earthquakes are normally accepted as the causes of these destructions, not least because it is difficult to conceive of a human agency powerful enough to inflict such general devastation. But it is exceptionally difficult to identify the causes of a destruction by archaeological methods and we should not exclude the alternative – especially since the rebuilt towns are associated with a marked change in material culture – the replacement of local features with Cretan. The fortifications also suggest that the contemporary Aegean climate was not entirely peaceful.

The new Cretan features may vary to some extent from island to island. The most evident is the pottery: there are many imports from Crete and local production is heavily influenced by Cretan shapes and designs. The long held view of a total domination of Cycladic by Cretan taste has been questioned by the excavators of Ayia Irini and also needs to be modified in view of the considerable number of Mainland imports now identified, both there and elsewhere, in the early Late Cycladic period. It is also noteworthy that the pottery from Akrotiri has many purely Cycladic features. It is not always easy to distinguish Cretan from Mainland pottery, but work at Ayia Irini has shown that Mainland imports are about as common numerically as those from Crete in LC I

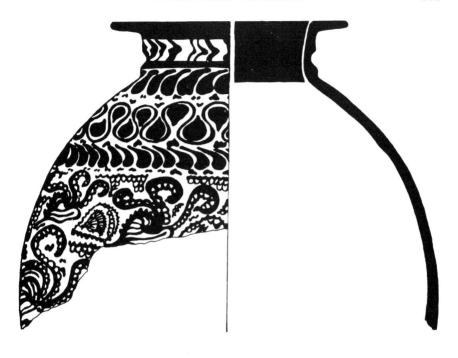

114. Imported Cretan alabastron in the Marine style (LM IB) from Phylakopi, Melos. (After Renfrew 1978b, 408).

and may even exceed them in LC II. While such imports are probably also more prominent on other islands than was previously recognised, it is fair to observe that Kea had always had particularly close links with the Mainland because of its geographical proximity, and these may well have continued in the early Late Bronze Age.

In terms of architecture, as we shall see, the designs of the buildings at Akrotiri, as well as the details of their masonry and construction, are much more strongly Cretan in character than those of the other two sites, betraying once again that particularly intimate relationship of this site with Crete which is shown also by the evidence of the other finds.

There are other Cretan features too (see further below) – some imports and local imitations of Cretan stone vases, a cache of bronze vessels on Thera which closely resemble contemporary examples from Crete and, perhaps more striking, the widespread introduction of figured fresco decoration on the island in a technique and in styles that must have been initially inspired by Crete and which reflect many aspects of Cretan life, though, once again, local and/or Mainland elements are more evident than first thought.

The fact that frescoes are very much more common at Akrotiri than elsewhere may be due, to a considerable extent, to the miraculous preservation of that site under volcanic debris. But it is probably also another sign of the close links between Thera and Crete.

So much for LC I and some general aspects of the material culture. Before going on to look at some of these in more detail, we need to consider the next phase – LC II. Akrotiri was abandoned at the end of LC I, as a result of the activity of the island's volcano, but both Ayia Irini and Phylakopi continued occupied and each site has distinct deposits of the period. The most chronologically diagnostic feature of these deposits is that they contain imported LM IB pottery from Crete (Fig. 114: as opposed to the LM IA of LC I) and local imitations of that style. At Ayia Irini, where the range of material culture is better known than at Phylakopi, LC II seems to have been at least as rich as LC I, and the same may well have been true of the Melian site. Many of the Kea frescoes belong to that period and there is thought to have been a resurgence of local pottery styles. It is interesting that Mainland influences may have been even stronger than Minoan.

The end of LC II is of particular significance. At Ayia Irini the site was razed, probably by an earthquake, and at Phylakopi we know of some destruction levels with burning and of the fact that the town as a whole was rebuilt in the following period – though the precise extent of the LC II destruction has never been quite clear.

As well as these two stratigraphical breaks, the character of the material culture of the following phase (early LC III) is once again crucial to our understanding of events. This character is strongly Mycenaean, with no Minoan admixture (see Chapter 9) and at Phylakopi included the building of a Mycenaean palace. One if not both of these islands must have been forcibly taken over by conquerors from the Mainland.

Evidence so far has been drawn from only three islands, and the lack of finds from elsewhere in the Cyclades is quite striking. There are however signs that this is at least partly due to chance since Naxos, the richest of the Cyclades, which must certainly have been important at this as at other times in antiquity, has recently begun to produce early Late Cycladic finds (e.g. Grotta, Mikre Vigla).

Other islands are however largely barren of such material – a fact which makes the abundance of LC I sites on Thera quite extraordinary, especially so in view of the extreme difficulty of site location on an island whose Bronze Age ground surface is largely covered by immensely thick deposits of volcanic debris. This is an important confirmation of the unique status of the island, which we have already been led to suspect on the basis of other finds. There are, in fact, at least nine sites (Fig. 115) in addition to Akrotiri, though some of these are indicated only by chance finds. Excavated evidence from three suggests that the island was quite widely populated by rural farmsteads which were presumably administratively dependent on the metropolis at Akrotiri. We do not have the field evidence to show whether this was true of the other islands at the time; if so, it may have been due to the more settled conditions imposed by the rule of Crete. It may be, however, that Thera was unique

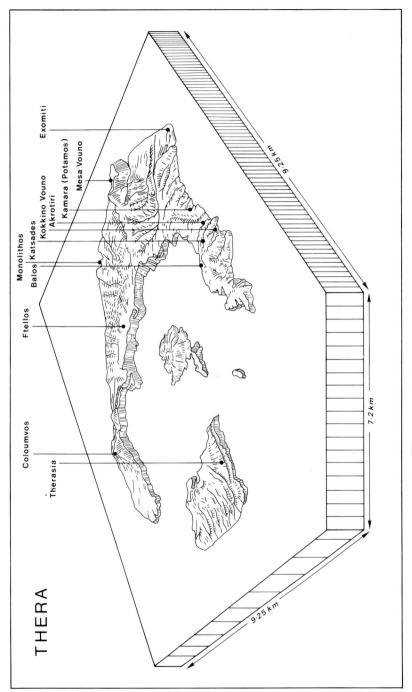

115. Thera, showing locations of Bronze Age sites.

in this respect, since one might have expected at least some evidence from elsewhere to have come to light, had it existed. Recent survey work on Melos suggests that there was very little settlement there at this period outside the main centre, and analysis of animal bones from Phylakopi, which shows that traction animals were important, points to the conclusion that the inhabitants at this time were still living in the town and travelling to work their fields – a situation which suggests a different climate to that prevailing on Thera and could again lend credence to the idea of special Minoan preference for the latter island.

We may now move on to consider the particular character of the various aspects of Cycladic material culture in the early Late Bronze Age.

Site plans and architecture[2]

The description in Chapter 4 of Bronze Age architecture in the Cyclades covered many of the important remains of this period, since it encompasses the best preserved buildings and town plans from the whole of the Bronze Age in the islands. Here we are more concerned with the general nature of the developments of LC I-II and the question of whether they represent simply a continuation of local island traditions of town planning, house design and architectural technique, or whether there is reason to suspect substantial influence from outside.

The significant breaks in the histories of all three major sites at or near the end of the Middle Bronze Age, and the subsequent widespread rebuilding, have made it rather difficult to make clear comparisons between Middle and Late Cycladic architecture. At Phylakopi, where comparison is perhaps easiest, a system of block construction, already developed in the Middle Cycladic period (Fig. 43) was retained in the early Late Cycladic (Fig. 116), the later walls in many cases following the lines of the earlier, which were used as footings. No constructive comparison can really be made between this plan and those found in other areas of the Aegean. Cycladic sites are not so different from the best known of the Cretan towns (Gournia, Palaikastro) but there is no reason why the most distinctive overall feature, viz. block construction, should not have developed independently, since it is much more economical of both space and materials than a more scattered collection of independent buildings without party walls. A large building (Fig. 117) in the administrative centre of the site was constructed at this time (see below, pp. 193-4).

There are, however, one or two important and distinctive developments in the Late Cycladic period, which are found earlier in Crete and therefore probably derived from that source (for illustrations, see Chapter 8). Mainland architecture of this period is very badly known but seems to have been much less sophisticated, although itself gradually coming under Cretan influence. These developments[3] are the use of

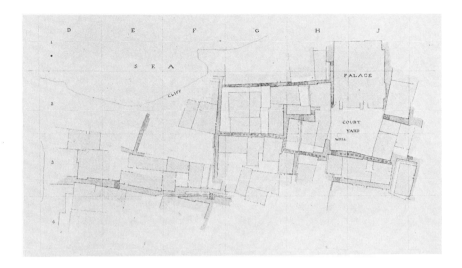

116. Phylakopi, Melos. Block plan of City III (Late Cycladic). (Atkinson *et al.* 1904, 51).

figured fresco scenes to decorate the interior walls; the use of ashlar (squared-stone) masonry; the appearance of peculiarly Cretan room units (the lustral basin; the pillar room) and some distinctive individual architectural elements (the pier-and-door partition). These might also lead us to suspect that other features (e.g. lavatory installations) might be derived from the same source, but there is no good reason why they, and other more minor constructional features (e.g. the use of dowels to join wooden insert-frames to ashlar blocks), should not have been of purely local origin.

The most interesting fact about the definitively Cretan elements is that they are far more evident at Akrotiri on Thera than at any other Cycladic site, and Akrotiri is also the only site where independent buildings (the West House, the various Xestai), in many ways comparable to the Cretan 'villas', are found within the settlement in combination with block construction.

Other sites had fresco decoration – probably a good deal more of it than their inferior state of preservation might suggest – but only limited use of ashlar, and that fairly crude and always in combination with smaller stones – no lustral basins, almost no pier-and-door partitions, and no independent buildings (apart from the Kea Temple and, possibly, the Phylakopi mansion).

The slighter effect of Cretan architectural taste and practices on Phylakopi and Ayia Irini may be due, in some measure, to their greater geographical remoteness and the peculiar characteristics of the stone used for building (easily split schist slabs at Ayia Irini; beach boulders sometimes at Phylakopi; both to be compared with the easily cut

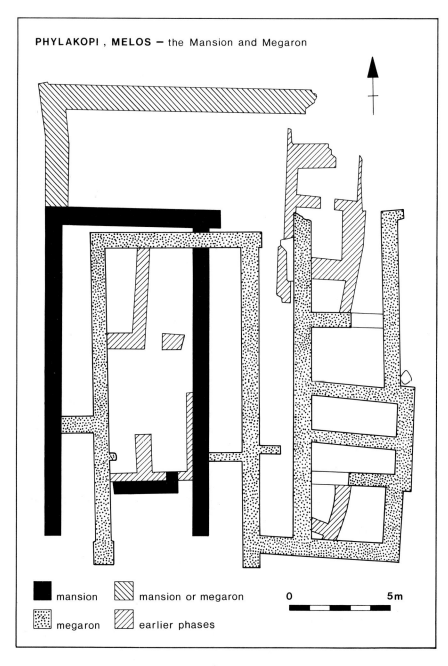

117. Phylakopi, Melos. Administrative centre – walls of the 'Mansion' (LC I) and the 'Megaron' (LC III). (After Renfrew 1978b, 409).

118. *above* Red-and-Black style bridge-spouted jar (LC I or II) from Phylakopi, Melos. (Dawkins and Droop 1911, pl. III).

119. *right* Monochrome rhyton (LC I or II) from Phylakopi, Melos. (Dawkins and Droop 1911, pl. II).

volcanic rock on Thera), but the other features of plan and construction mentioned above would not have been subject to those factors and indicate that both they and the very widespread use of extremely fine ashlar construction are due to some very special connection of Akrotiri with Crete.

Fortifications (not so far found at Akrotiri) are an aspect of Cycladic architecture hardly attested in Crete,[4] and the character of contemporary Mainland fortifications, although they presumably existed at sites such as Mycenae in LH I, are unknown. The constructional style of the LC I wall at Phylakopi is not distinctive. On Kea quite good ashlar masonry in large blocks was used and there were projecting towers.

Local pottery[5]

The pottery in use in the Cyclades at the beginning of the Late Cycladic period was not radically different from that of the late Middle Cycladic. Indeed many of the shapes (the beaked jug, the hole-mouthed jar) and decorative motifs (black with red circle elements, foliate bands, floral sprays, for example) represent continuity of local practice, whether truly local or already Cretan-inspired, in the later stage of the Middle Cycladic

120. *above* Jug with light-on-dark decoration (LC I) from Akrotiri, Thera. (École Française d'Athènes).

121. *right* Beaked jug or nippled ewer (LC I) from Akrotiri, Thera (C. Doumas).

122. Kymbe (LC I) from Akrotiri, Thera. (C. Doumas).

period. The shapes fulfil, perhaps more satisfactorily because the range is larger, the same basic functions of ceramics; the decoration reflects more effectively the interests of the islanders in their natural environment: flowers, grasses and crops; birds; fishes and sea creatures, as well as a few more fantastical figures (griffins) and the usual range of abstract motifs.

At Phylakopi, the main class of pottery is called Later Local. The fabric was derived from Cycladic White; indeed, as we have already seen, it had been introduced before the end of the Middle Cycladic period. The parallel class at Ayia Irini is Cycladic Painted, which varies in fabric from coarse to fine and, because of the character of the local clay, is often covered with a thick creamy slip. Pottery of both these classes may

123. *left* Imported Cretan rhyton (LM I) from Akrotiri, Thera. (C. Doumas).

124. *above* Jug (LC I) from Akrotiri, Thera. (C. Doumas).

be decorated either in a red-and-black (Fig. 118 – more common on Melos) or a single-colour scheme (confusingly called 'monochrome' in early reports: Fig. 119). The Thera material seems roughly comparable, though there the use of a light-on-dark decorative system (Fig. 120), of a kind that was standard on Crete in the Middle Minoan period, is also prominent, though not dominant.

Almost the only colours used are red and black, with occasional details in white sometimes on Theran pottery (Fig. 122). The true Black-and-Red style (burnished red, matt black) survives; otherwise vases decorated in one colour are usually in matt paint, the remainder in matt and/or lustrous, the tendency to use lustrous paint becoming stronger with the passage of time.

There is no doubt that the vast majority of the vases used in the islands at this time were locally produced – virtually all the undecorated pottery and perhaps over 90 per cent of the decorated too. But careful analysis of the shapes and decorative motifs and systems show that, by and large, these were borrowed from elsewhere – chiefly from Crete.[6]

125. Imported Mainland panelled cups (LH I) from Akrotiri, Thera. (After Marinatos 1968-76, V, pl. 62a,b).

One or two of the vase shapes – the beaked jug (Fig. 121) is the most obvious example, another being a modest spouted bowl – had been local inventions, and a few others (the kymbe: Fig. 122) were created or popularised in the islands (in the case of the kymbe, on Akrotiri) at this time. But the great majority of shapes in use (Vapheio cup, bridge-spouted jug, stirrup jar) were Cretan in origin. So were the motifs used to decorate them (large linked spirals, tortoiseshell ripple, leaf-patterns), though here too we can find a few examples of local choice (continued use of the Black-and-Red style, popularity of dolphins, certain matt-painted motifs). Two different decorative systems have been distinguished among the material from Akrotiri: one employing an essentially zonal arrangement of chiefly geometric motifs, which is derived from Crete (Fig. 123 (import); cf. Fig. 118); the other treating the whole surface as a single field and using pictorial (mainly plant and animal) motifs, which follows a local Cycladic tradition (Fig. 124). This Cycladic style seems much more prominent on Thera than on the other islands – and least evident on Kea. We have already noted at Akrotiri the use of a light-on-dark decorative system. The excavations at Ayia Irini have shown[7] that, in LC II, there was a significant revival of local initiatives in the field of decorated pottery.

There is one problem here, closely related to the question of imported pottery in the Cyclades, which we must go on to consider. Can we really be sure that Crete was the source of these undoubted external influences? In LH/LM I-II there are very many similarities between Cretan and Mainland pottery and even experts find it difficult to tell the two apart. Connections between Crete and the Mainland were very close; many features of Mainland culture were being developed under influence from Crete and it has been suggested that some Cretan potters were actually working on the Mainland. Accordingly, where features which appear in the Cyclades are seen both in Mainland and in Cretan pottery, the source might be either.

We can look to the imported vases[8] themselves to throw some light on this question. Until recently, it has been assumed that virtually all the influence reflected in early Late Cycladic pottery was Cretan. Now the picture is rather different. Although no thorough study has yet been published, it is clear that there is much Late Helladic pottery among the published and unpublished sherds from Phylakopi. The excavators of Ayia Irini inform us that, in LC I, Mainland imports approximately equal Minoan, and may surpass them in LC II: there is also a class of pottery (both local and imported pieces) which reflects styles found in the LH I-II Shaft Graves at Mycenae and Lerna (Fig. 125). At Akrotiri, a limited statistical analysis suggests that Mainland imports accounted for about 2.5 per cent of the total number of vases and that Minoan were two and a half times as many again. This – and the other strong evidence of Minoan influences on Cycladic material culture – suggests that, in doubtful cases, external influences are much more likely to be from Crete than the Mainland, though this was no doubt modified by the geographical proximity of any given island to one or the other (Kea to the Mainland, Melos to Crete). As far as pottery goes, therefore, the old view of formative Minoan influence seems to hold good, but must now make allowance for the substantial Cycladic connections with Mainland Greece which imports (and Cycladic vases found on the Mainland) affirm.

A few imports from further afield[9] (Cypriot sherds on Thera and Melos; a plain Syrian amphora and Syro-Palestinian stone and other vessels from Akrotiri) are evidence of more wide-ranging contacts (possibly via Crete), though hardly of serious cultural influence.

Obviously Cycladic objects abroad at this time are very few indeed – a few vases and sherds among material, much of which could be late Middle Cycladic, from Attica, the Argolid and Crete.[10] The most striking are the Theran bird jugs from Grave Circle B at Mycenae.

There is some evidence for interchange of pottery between individual islands.[11] Melian material is known from Kea (a good deal, including the Black-and-Red griffin jug, but mainly Cycladic White), as well as Naxos (sherds, so far) and Thera (though most of this may be later Middle Cycladic). There is an obviously Theran sherd from Phylakopi and probably a few from Naxos. Exports of Keian vases are not yet identified, though there may be some from Melos. Melian material seems easily the most prominent, though the role of Melos as main production centre of

Cycladic White pottery remains to be demonstrated conclusively, and I suspect that the fabric was locally manufactured to a considerable extent.

Frescoes[12]

Ever since the late nineteenth-century excavators of Phylakopi discovered part of a frieze of flying fish in a marine setting, and fragments of other scenes, it has been known that Cycladic buildings were sometimes decorated with painted murals at the beginning of the Late Bronze Age. These paintings were inevitably compared to and their inspiration sought in the figured scenes which decorated the Cretan palaces and villas from the time of the second palaces (MM IIIA, though non-figured decoration goes back much earlier). The Cretan material itself, although much greater in quantity, is nevertheless very fragmentary and much reconstructed.

Now, as well as extensive, if fragmentary, scenes from Ayia Irini and some new pieces from Phylakopi, we have a wealth of well-preserved (and painstakingly reassembled) pictures from Akrotiri.

Akrotiri was no doubt exceptional in the extent of its painted decoration, as in other aspects of material culture, but the far from insignificant remains from Ayia Irini and Phylakopi show that such decoration was by no means uncommon in the Cyclades at this time.

Most of the painted scenes came from upper floors, where the most important rooms were located. Some of them were miniature friezes c. 0.20-0.40m high, on occasion set at eye level, below the lintel height of any doorways, and thus interrupted by them or by windows. Whole walls were also painted and occasionally there were individual scenes in panels (e.g. the fishermen). There are ornamental borders, dado courses, and examples of window recesses and door lintels being enlivened with decoration on painted plaster.

The scenes were painted[13] in a limited range of colours provided by earth and mineral pigments (white, red, yellow, blue and black is the range from Kea). The colours were normally applied in true fresco, some in tempera after the plaster had dried. A thick coarse coat formed the basis and was then topped with a layer or layers of often very pure lime plaster to provide the surface for decoration.

The subjects are quite various and the categories into which they can be divided (inevitably these sometimes overlap) indicate this: narrative, human, the natural world (animals, flowers, landscape); marine; inanimate objects; subsidiary ornament.

Narrative scenes

These are best represented by the miniature fresco[14] (part of which is sometimes referred to as the ship fresco) from Room 5 on the upper floor

126. Fresco of Nautical Festival (LC I) from the West House, Akrotiri, Thera. (National Archaeological Museum, Athens. Photo: T.A.P.).

of the West House (see Chapter 8) at Akrotiri, although fragments of figures from Ayia Irini and Phylakopi show that such were found on those islands as well.

In the West House, the pictures are from the north, east and south walls, and the west wall may have been decorated too. On the north wall is a hill-top scene. The two figures on the summit have long coats as opposed to those who are still climbing and wear kilts, and it has been suggested that these differences in dress show that the figures are representative of two different groups, possibly Mycenaeans and Minoans, who are known to have favoured these respective types of dress. It could however be some kind of ceremony in which the celebrants and participants are distinguished by dress or in which people of different social classes are involved.

A second scene, which may have joined the one just described, is in a seaside location. Inland, there is a fenced enclosure with two trees inside, probably an animal fold, and rows of animals with herdsmen. Buildings in the vicinity include one which may be a well or spring chamber, since there are women with jars on their heads. On the shore is a line of eight warriors, armed with scabbards, long spears, large dappled oxhide shields and boars' tusk helmets. All these items of equipment are usually associated with Mycenaeans.

In the sea is a scene of disaster – a shipwreck or the aftermath of a battle. There are ships with their gear in disorder, fallen figures and weapons. This scene has some resemblance *inter alia* to that on a silver vase found in Grave Circle A at Mycenae (sea battle before a walled city) and may represent a traditional art theme rather than a specific incident.

On the east wall is a different scene – a subtropical landscape with a river, various vegetation, rocks, birds, a panther and a griffin.

On the south wall is the Ship Fresco (Fig. 126) which shows a fleet sailing in ceremonial array from one town to another. The first town, surrounded by a river on the further bank of which are some country dwellings, consists of a cluster of flat-roofed buildings. People stand on the roofs and in the doorways, watching the ships. The town is on a promontory with reddish rocks, perhaps reflecting the volcanic geology of Thera.

Eleven ships are shown. Seven are large and, of these, six have limited adornment in the form of painted motifs or shaped and painted prows, and one has very elaborately ornamented rigging. Only one of them has its sail hoisted. One other smaller boat seems to be at the tail of the procession, off the port of departure, while one more is being paddled and two are anchored off the town of destination. The larger boats have ornamented stern cabins for the captain and awnings under which warriors sit, their helmets hung up and shields stacked behind (dappled oxhide). The steersmen wear kilts, the warriors longer garments.

This second town is also on a promontory. The rocks of the tip are multicoloured (as also in the volcanic Cyclades, e.g. on Melos) and there seems to be a watchtower on one peak. This has been compared, quite convincingly, by Doumas[15] to the ridge of Mavro Rachidhi, near Akrotiri, where he would locate the ancient harbour of Thera. Twenty-five figures or so line the shore, unarmed and wearing kilts. The town is roughly similar to the first but rather more elaborate. Again figures can be seen in windows and on roofs, looking towards the approaching fleet. Both the architecture and the figures are more obviously Minoan than in the departure town.

The subject of the piece is not essentially a military one but some kind of formal ceremonial.[16] This is shown by the fact that the one boat (in particular) is so highly ornamented; the military occupants are not in a state of readiness; no enemy is visible; the boats are being paddled in a most awkward and inefficient way by rowers leaning out over the sides. There are parallels for such ceremonial paddling in antiquity and also for what seems a most appropriate occasion, namely the Annual Resumption of Navigation – after the long lay-off in the close season. The setting may be Thera itself (both towns) or possibly Akrotiri and a town in Crete – though this seems much less likely, since ships could not be paddled very far in this fashion – if indeed a precise setting is intended at all. An interpretation which suggested Libyan personnel and a Libyan locale is now largely discredited.

A great deal of interest has centred on the apparent juxtaposition of both Minoan and Mycenaean elements in these frescoes,[17] the latter being very surprising in view of the fact that Mycenaean pictorial art was in its infancy at this time. There are no substantial fresco remains from the Mainland for another hundred years at least, though a few earlier fragmentary pieces suggest that we may still have a good deal to learn about its earlier stages. The elements referred to are both iconographic and stylistic. Some details of dress and weaponry are apparently Mycenaean. The depiction of warriors and the very warlike nature of the 'shipwreck' scene are much more akin to the taste demonstrated in later Mycenaean frescoes and other media than in Minoan art. It has also been suggested that the paratactic (linear) composition of the group figure scenes (especially the warriors on the shore line in the shipwreck scene) are characteristically Mycenaean in their awkward formality.

There are of course plenty of Minoan things too. Many of the figures wear the Minoan kilt, some of the women the characteristic open bodice. Some of the architecture is shown with beam ends and horns of consecration on the roofs.

If these deductions about personal origin are correct, we have the odd situation of kilt-wearing Minoans (usually thought of as the superior race at this time) crewing ships carrying Mycenaean warriors. The frescoes seem to confirm what other archaeological evidence (e.g. the pottery already discussed) increasingly emphasises, namely that the Mycenaean presence in the Aegean islands c. 1500 BC was much more significant than previously thought.

A final item of interest in the ship fresco concerns the stern cabin (*ikrion*, see below) on the flagship, the most highly decorated vessel. This

127. Fresco of Boxing Children (LC I) from Block B, Akrotiri, Thera. (National Archaeological Museum, Athens. Photo: T.A.P.).

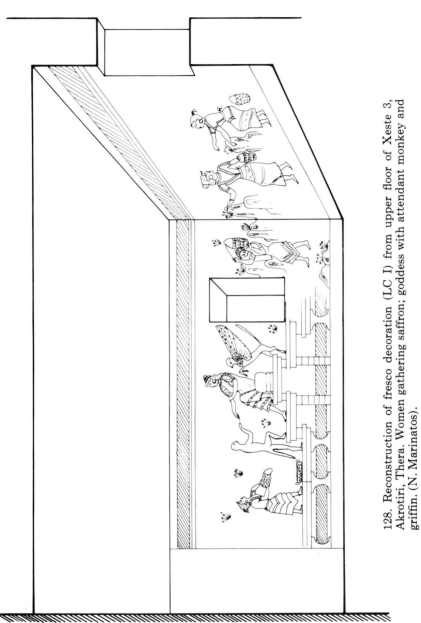

128. Reconstruction of fresco decoration (LC I) from upper floor of Xeste 3, Akrotiri, Thera. Women gathering saffron; goddess with attendant monkey and griffin. (N. Marinatos).

specific *ikrion* (recognisable because of the so-called 'waz-lily' motif attached to it) reappears as the major motif (Fig. 132: repeated eight times at large scale) of the decoration of Rooms 4-4a, on the same floor of the same West House where the frescoes just described were found. It seems likely therefore that the owner of the house was the same man who occupied the stern cabin on the flagship – the admiral of the fleet.[18]

Another miniature series, extensive but much less well preserved, has been found on Kea. It shows buildings, animals, and human figures occupied in various ways. The conjectural restoration allows for scenes of hunting, the preparation of meat, the making of offerings and general celebrations – presumably episodes in a festival.

Human figures (larger scale)

Two fishermen, naked and carrying their catch, come from the north-east and south-west corners of the same room as the miniature fresco. They seem ordinary enough, apart from their blue heads with sparse locks – a feature found elsewhere in the Theran scenes – and are probably purely decorative. They resemble a scene on a painted pottery stand from Phylakopi (Fig. 13) which was probably based on a fresco prototype (it has a border pattern – an uncommon feature for a vase scene).

From the upper storey of B 1 there are two children, apparently boxing (Fig. 127). Their heads are treated in a somewhat similar way to those of the fishermen, but their hair is more copious. They may be just playing or engaged in some ritual of deeper significance.

A 'priestess' figure was found in Room 4 of the West House although her precise original location is not clear. She is clearly performing a ceremonial act. She wears a long saffron-coloured robe with blue-and-white patterned upper sleeves. Her head is treated in the manner described previously. She has a large earring and carries an offering in a dish, or perhaps incense in a brazier.

Other scenes with figures are more elaborate. Different but related compositions come from the walls of a lustral basin in Xeste 3 and from the room on the floor above it. On the upper floor is a scene of a rocky landscape planted with crocuses. Finely dressed and bejewelled young women are seen picking the crocuses, putting them in baskets and taking them to a wooden structure. There are delicate touches like the necklace swinging from a stooping girl and a dropped basket.

An older woman with very elaborate dress and jewellery (with representations of ducks, birds and trees) also forms part of this scene (Fig. 128). She is seated on the stepped wooden structure, flanked by a monkey and a griffin. She thus seems to be the so-called Mistress of Animals, a goddess well-known from Crete who always appears flanked by wild creatures. The girls are picking saffron (used in ancient times both as a colouring agent and for medicinal purposes) and offering it to the goddess as part of some rite, perhaps fertility, if the pairs of animals usually seen with the 'mistress' have connotations of mating and

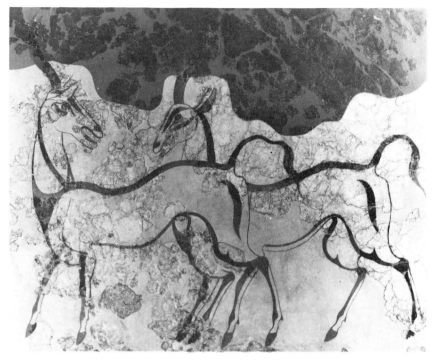

129. Fresco of antelopes (LC I) from Block B, Akrotiri, Thera. (National Archaeological Museum, Athens. Photo: T.A.P.).

procreation. On the walls of the lustral basin are other crocus-gatherers, including a girl seated on a rock removing a thorn from her foot and an altar with horns of consecration.

Another scene (from the Room of the Ladies in a building in the southwest of Block A), again evidently ritual in character, shows women in procession, one stooping forward and offering objects to another (a priestess or deity). Behind the priestess are three tall formal plants (papyrus). The upper part of the scene is filled with four-pointed stars linked by red-dotted lines, the whole being divided from the main scene below by a triple wavy line of dark and light blue, running at an uneven height. A new processional scene (nature unspecified) is reported from Xeste 4.

The natural world

One unusual (at least to our eyes) fresco has a close parallel from the House of the Frescoes at Knossos in Crete. It is from an upper storey of B 6 and shows monkeys climbing and collecting food in a rocky landscape.

Monkeys appear in other frescoes from the site. In Xeste 3, Room 2, probably upper floor, they are performing human activities. One has a

130. Fresco of vase of flowers (LC I)
from a window sill in the West House,
Akrotiri, Thera. (National
Archaeological Museum, Athens.
Photo: T.A.P.).

harp, another a sword and scabbard. The scene also contains complex
landscape elements.

The tropical landscape which formed a section of the miniature fresco
has already been mentioned. From B 1 (on walls adjacent to that on
which the boxing children were depicted) came scenes showing two
antelopes (Fig. 129). The creatures are drawn economically, in free
outline with very sparing details, and are attractive in their direct
simplicity.

Vases of flowers are found decorating the window recesses in Room 4 of
the West House (Fig. 130) and a number of other fragments of as yet
incompletely restored scenes from Thera show natural or animal
elements. However, one of the most attractive and decorative nature

131. Flying Fish fresco (LC I) from Phylakopi, Melos. (Atkinson *et al.* 1904, pl. III).

scenes from Akrotiri comes from three walls of a small room in D 2. A rocky landscape is shown in rather garish colours. Clumps of lilies grow out of the rocks. Swallows fly above and among the plants, sometimes cavorting in pairs. The flowers are easily paralleled in Crete (and on a light-on-dark frieze from Phylakopi) but the birds are a distinctive local type, also seen on Theran vases.

A scene with blue birds (at least 22) is also known from Kea, though there they are larger, and the main elements in a frieze.

Marine life is not yet attested as a major fresco theme on Thera. At Phylakopi (G 3, 6 and 7) the miniature frieze of flying fish (Fig. 131) has rockwork above and below and sponges and sea eggs in the field; and the Fisherman Vase (Fig. 13) was almost certainly based on a wall-painting. From Kea a panel or frieze from Area J showed dolphins.

Inanimate objects/abstract motifs/relief frescoes

Purely inanimate scenes are represented by the *ikrion* scheme (Fig. 132), already discussed in connection with the miniature fresco of the West House.

Abstract decorative motifs seem to be found only very occasionally, on small pieces of plaster which were applied to door lintels or furniture.

Dado panels, with a veined effect intended to represent marble and sometimes interspersed with plain painted panels, are quite common. Most scenes have borders of some kind – simple straight lines (single or

132. Fresco of *ikria* (stern cabins) (LC I) from the West House, Akrotiri, Thera.
(National Archaeological Museum, Athens. Photo: T.A.P.).

multiple), wavy lines, spiral between lines (monkey fresco), ivy leaf (boxers and antelopes).

Cretan and Mainland links[19]

A number of iconographic and stylistic features which appear to link these frescoes with either Crete or Mainland Greece have already been mentioned. Since the chronological priority of the Cretan frescoes to both Cycladic and Mainland examples is clearly established and since there are strong Cretan elements of technique, style and subject in the Cycladic work, it is hard to doubt that they were inspired by Cretan models, though the circumstances in which this might have occurred are interesting to consider further below.

The Mainland links however seem undeniable and they extend to a series of minor details of representation, as a leading authority on Aegean frescoes (M. Cameron) has shown. The strangest features of these apparent connections are that Mainland frescoes are barely known before c. 1400 BC, though painting in Crete in the period c. 1450-1400 BC (after the Mycenaeans had taken over the islands) seems to show evidence of Mycenaean taste, including, for the first time in Crete, some of the 'Mycenaean' features of the Theran frescoes which are discussed here. The same scholar has suggested a most interesting explanation – namely that these features are in essence Cycladic and were developed in the islands in the period we are now considering. On this argument, the subsequent emergence of Mainland fresco work was directly influenced by Cycladic painters who transferred not only the essential Cretan style, but their own modifications of it as well.

It is also feasible, I suppose, that the 'Mainland' features were borrowed from Mainland Greece in a period (LH I) when, although we have virtually no material evidence of Mainland palaces or fresco painting, it is not impossible that they existed.

Religious elements in the frescoes[20]

Some, even a good deal, of the subject matter of the frescoes seems to have ritual connotations. We should beware however of automatically assigning such a significance to every single scene.

Certain features can be shown (horns of consecration; 'goddess' flanked by animals) or reasonably supposed (blue, shaved heads) to have such associations and it is probably relevant that frescoes are often found in areas which appear, on the basis of other kinds of evidence (e.g. special vessels) to have been the locations of ritual activities (see below, pp. 185-9).

Much of the argument over this topic is somewhat subjective, and it is complicated by the fact that distinction between the sacred and the secular is by no means as easy in a prehistoric context as it is in modern society. Religious practices were very closely interwoven with the activities of daily life. Thus religious themes might well have been chosen for essentially decorative purposes, and the latent religious connotations of essentially decorative scenes would have been brought out by their location in 'shrines'.

Of all the scenes that have survived, that of the saffron-gathering in Xeste 3 is perhaps the clearest example of a ritual representation: saffron is being picked and then offered to a figure whose attendants (a monkey and a griffin) surely mark her out as divine. The presence of a monkey in this context makes us wonder about the other scenes (several) in which monkeys are involved.

In the West House, we have noted the festival interpretation of the ship procession from the miniature fresco (a festival too perhaps on Kea), but the relationship of the other two scenes is not clear. Is the 'sea-battle' a real event? Does the intervening tropical landscape provide some rather obscure thematic unity (in terms of aggression or aquatic scenery, or both)? Elsewhere in the house the gesture of the 'priestess' surely shows that she has been correctly identified, but her association with the *ikria* is mysterious. The suggestion has been made that it reflects a ritual relating to the fleet, carried out either at the harbour or in the West House (home or headquarters of the admiral).

The boxing children are thought to have been involved in an initiation ceremony ('boxing' scenes are found on ritual vases in Crete). The Spring fresco may represent fertility or vegetation rites, though it is undoubtedly a beautiful decorative scene, to our eyes.

One fresco which must be purely decorative is the groups of rosettes with relief-line border, from Xeste 3.

Other finds and aspects of life in the early Late Cycladic period

The finds from Akrotiri provide the clearest picture of the character of daily life in the Bronze Age in the Aegean, and that site and subject will be discussed in the following chapter.

At this point, however, we need to survey the remaining archaeological evidence from the Late Cycladic period, before considering what conclusions about historical developments and Aegean interrelationships may be drawn from it.

Burials[21]

Not many burials of the early Late Cycladic period are known. An earlier cemetery of cist tombs at Aila on Naxos continued in use in LC I. On Melos, some of the rock-cut chamber-tombs may belong to this period but none are firmly dated.

At Ayia Irini, where there is rather more to go on, the finds suggest features of both continuity and change. The use of simple cists seems to die out and there are no more platforms; but a few jar burials are still

133. Grave 29 (probably Late Cycladic) at Ayia Irini, Kea. (University of Cincinnati).

found (now inside the settlement). There are however some quite complex stone built tombs which may have been richly furnished, though all had been robbed of most of their contents before excavation. These are apparently the end result of the gradual elaboration of the cist, a trend whose beginnings can be seen in some of the Middle Cycladic tombs. Grave 28 is a shaft grave, partially lined with neatly cut courses of stone and topped with large cover slabs. This tomb was later (perhaps in LC II) covered by a tumulus which was itself given a border of upright slabs. Grave 29 (Fig. 133) consists of a double compartment, one of which is an entrance shaft, the other the burial chamber. It has a paved floor and is also covered with slabs.

Religion[22]

Evidence for religious life in this period has accumulated in recent years, with discoveries at Ayia Irini and Akrotiri. The only public (presumably) shrine so far discovered (though there was another at Phylakopi in LC III) is the Temple at Ayia Irini (Figs. 134, 135). The building – long, narrow and subdivided into a number of rooms – is an independent structure, situated just inside the main gate of the town (Fig. 46). Some of the rooms have stone-built platforms along the walls. Widespread evidence of burning suggests sacrificial hearths, and the discovery of large numbers of drinking cups and container vessels indicates that libations were also a standard part of the ritual.

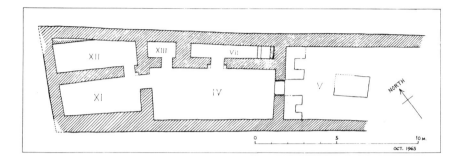

134. Plan of the Temple at Ayia Irini, Kea. (University of Cincinnati).

135. The Temple of Ayia Irini from the east. (University of Cincinnati).

The Temple was built in the Middle Bronze Age, though it was subsequently extended in LC I-II, to which period the most interesting finds also belong. These are fragments of at least 55 terracotta figures (Fig. 136), from 0.60m high to life-size, built up in coarse local clay on wooden armatures and then fired, often imperfectly, by some means not yet understood. They are distinctly Minoan in style – female figures with long flaring skirts and breasts left exposed by the familiar Minoan open bodice. Some were dancing. The surviving remains look rather crude but at least some of the figures were originally coated with a surface layer of more refined clay and then painted. Fragments of one show that the flesh

136. Terracotta statue from the
Temple at Ayia Irini, Kea.
(University of Cincinnati).

was coloured white, the bodice with yellow ochre and there was a red
necklace. Some, if not all, the figures seem likely to have stood on the stone
platforms in the Temple. Careful study has suggested that new figures
were continually added to the group and worn pieces were repaired. Thus
none of the pieces are to be considered replacements and we must think
of a steadily growing company. Signs of repair and repainting suggest
that the figures were used in some way, even if just moved about.

All the figures are more or less similar in character. No one stands out
as more important than the rest and thus likely to be the cult statue, if
indeed there was such a thing. The discovery of a number of terracotta
feet in another building nearby has occasioned the suggestion that the
cult statue was in fact kept there, rather than in the 'Temple' itself. It
may have been made of a variety of materials, mostly perishable
(perhaps mainly wood, which is the material of which the most ancient
cult statues of later Greece were made), but including terracotta feet.

There are several features of the Temple and its contents which show that the impetus for their adoption came from Crete – the style and dress of the terracotta figures, as well as the terracotta feet and stone libation tables, both of which are found in ritual contexts in Crete. Unless however we are to believe in a complete Minoan takeover of the Cyclades, these Cretan features were presumably grafted on to a local religious tradition, which no doubt anyway had some basic elements in common (the worship of a mother goddess, for example). Shrines with platforms on which ritual objects (including figurines) were placed are known from Minoan (and Mycenaean) sites. It is unusual however to find so substantial a building exclusively devoted to ritual, and the size and number of the terracotta figures is quite unparalleled.

Also in the Temple were a limited number of objects (including an attractive terracotta dolphin) which were probably offerings to the deity. There were also signs of 'industrial' activity, consisting of colouring matter, presumably for the statues to be painted or repainted in situ, and objects associated with metal-working.

The latter are particularly interesting since finds from Crete (in particular the palaces) and now from Akrotiri[23] strongly indicate a very close connection between ritual and economic/industrial activity, which is sometimes taken to mean that economic life was essentially controlled by a priesthood.

This mixture of the sacred and the secular – not least the fact that ritual meals involving the use of everyday kitchen equipment appear to have been common – has made the recognition of 'shrines' very difficult and is again a salutary reminder that we should not impose our own preconceptions in attempting to interpret the practices of a prehistoric society.

Of the items of equipment which have been identified in Crete as having specifically ritual functions (vases, horns of consecration, stone offering vessels etc.) a high proportion have been found in various contexts at Akrotiri (see Chapter 8), and a number, including the terracotta feet, which have not yet turned up at Akrotiri, on Kea.

Several centres of religious/economic activity have been identified at Akrotiri on the basis of caches of ritual objects (as defined above), fresco scenes with apparently religious connotations (see above) and certain architectural features of proven ritual significance (e.g. the Minoan 'lustral basin'; see Chapter 4). In all cases ritual is associated with activities like the making and/or distribution of bread, as well as eating and drinking.

On similar grounds, a shrine has been identified in House A at Ayia Irini, where objects connected with weaving and metallurgy were found together with domestic pottery and ritual items.

At Phylakopi, pillar rooms like those used in Cretan ritual are known but no shrines like the above are yet identifiable. Nevertheless it may be that records of the early excavations should be reassessed in the light of our new knowledge of this subject. Apart from the linkage between ritual and domestic contexts, we have evidence of shrines within houses (or

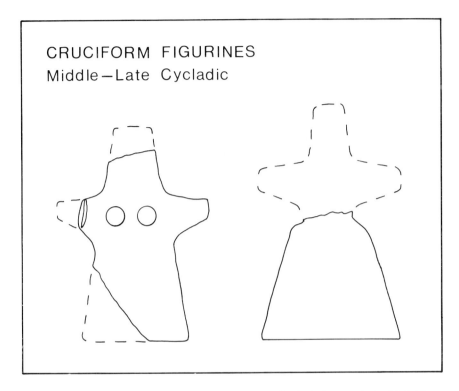

CRUCIFORM FIGURINES
Middle—Late Cycladic

137. Marble cruciform figurines (Middle to Late Cycladic) from Ayia Irini, Kea. (After Caskey 1971b, 120).

blocks) at all three main sites, as well as of the public Temple at Ayia Irini.

Another site, Mikre Vigla on Naxos, appears to have had a small shrine on the summit of the hill which the site occupies. Small coarse clay figures of various types were offered here. They are not well dated but some should belong to the early Late Bronze Age and recall dedications in Minoan peak sanctuaries.

These finds present something of a puzzle. As in so much else, the ritual life of Akrotiri seems highly Minoan in character. Ayia Irini gives a hint of this too, but has unique features – the Temple itself, the statues, perhaps also the use of a distinctive type of cruciform marble figurine (Fig. 137)[24] (the sole descendant of the Early Cycladic tradition) of which examples were found in the House A 'shrine' mentioned above. The situation at Phylakopi is unclear; the finds from Vigla unique in the Cyclades. Thus the extent to which Cycladic ritual was Minoanised in LC I-II is debatable. The Minoan elements may in some cases have been entirely superficial and the situation probably differed from island to island.

138. Imported Cretan 'blossom' bowl in steatite from Akrotiri, Thera. (C. Doumas).

139. Waste cores drilled out in the manufacture of stone vases, from Ayia Irini, Kea. (University of Cincinnati).

Non-ceramic objects[25]

In general, there are perhaps two really striking features about the minor material culture of LC I-II. The first is its range and quantity, especially as compared with the Middle Cycladic period: the second, the extent of

Cretan imports and Cretan influence that are apparent – and this in spite of the Mainland connections discussed in respect of the pottery and frescoes.

Stone vases[26]

Fine stone vases are known from all three major sites. Some are of characteristically Cretan types (Fig. 138) and were made on Crete and exported (possibly sometimes made in the Cyclades by Minoan or Minoan-trained craftsmen from material imported from Crete). But there were local industries too, on occasion copying the fine Cretan types but in local stone, sometimes providing coarse vases (mortars, for instance) for local domestic use. On Kea, numbers of waste cores (Fig. 139) have been found in local stone. These had been drilled out in the process of hollowing the interiors of the vases. Some vases came from even further afield – the Syro-Palestinian area – perhaps via Crete.

Metals, including weights

There seems to have been some resurgence in the availability of bronze in the Late Cycladic period and there are a number of finds from excavated sites throughout the islands. Moulds, crucibles and slag, although not all well-dated, are enough to attest local production at the major sites, though the most sophisticated pieces were probably imported from Crete. Most of the raw material is shown by analysis[27] to have come from the Lavrion area (South Attica) – a marked change from the use of local sources (perhaps now worked out) which were exploited in the Early Cycladic period (see Chapter 5). An ingot found on Kea could have come from Cyprus, again perhaps via Crete, and seems to indicate the use of imported material too.

In the context of the bronze types known from Crete and the Mainland, the Cycladic finds bring no surprises. There are few weapons, though perhaps there would be more if more graves were known. The tool types are predictable – knives, chisels, hooks, pins, needles. Sickles (Fig. 140) in bronze replace the earlier type with obsidian blades. One or two bronze statuettes have been found, which reflect Minoan religious iconography. A spectacular series of bronze vessels (Fig. 141) has been found on Thera. The types were already known either from Crete or the Shaft Graves at Mycenae (where the parallels are assumed to be Cretan imports). Crete certainly led the Aegean in bronze production in this, the time of the second palaces, and it is not surprising that the finest Cycladic finds probably came from that source.

Precious metals are virtually unknown at present in LC I-II but one other metal, lead (raw material again mainly from the Lavrion), was in quite common use – for rivets to repair broken objects; for door swivels or hinges; occasionally for other objects, but mostly for weights (Fig. 142). A large number of such weights, mostly flat discs, have come from Akrotiri,

140. Bronze sickles, knives and other tools from Akrotiri, Thera. (C. Doumas).

Ayia Irini and Phylakopi – the first two sites having the most. The weights mostly represent a Cretan metrological system[28] whose standard base unit was just over 60 grams. This is a further piece of evidence for the adoption of Cretan practices in LC I-II, but also for widespread trading within the Aegean, in a presumably peaceful political situation. The need to operate other metrological systems is indicated by a minority of weights which do not conform to the Minoan. These could either belong to other local standards – for more specialised commodities and thus less frequently used – or to truly foreign systems.

Other objects and materials

Among other material objects, those of wood are best discussed in the context of the site at Akrotiri, where they were recovered in remarkable circumstances. Because there are no direct parallels from other sites, they are hard to assess in comparative terms.

Considerable quantities of minor items in stone or terracotta (hammers, mills, loomweights etc.) have occasional Minoan parallels but are objects developed for their suitability for common tasks and thus often of similar character at different periods and at sites in areas far removed from each other. Obsidian was still employed,[29] though perhaps less so with the greater availability of metal tools.

Bone and ivory were used for handles, buttons, plaques, and occasionally furniture inlays. Comparisons are not very instructive but it may be noteworthy that ivory-working had reached a sophisticated level in late palatial Crete and that its first occurrence in the Cyclades comes at the time of maximum Minoan influence.

A few Minoan sealstones have been found, though rarely in comparison with their ubiquity on Crete. Some faience rhyton attachments probably came from Crete, where the material is much better attested.

141. Bronze jug (Cretan) from Akrotiri, Thera. (After Marinatos 1968-76, IV, pl. 95).

Scripts[30]

In view of the numerous Cretan links so far mentioned in this section, it comes as no surprise that such evidence as there is for writing in the Cyclades at this time is in the Minoan Linear A script which was in use in contemporary Crete. There are fragments of inscribed clay tablets from Ayia Irini and Phylakopi (Fig. 143) and vases from Akrotiri and Ayia Irini with Linear A signs. Some vases have other marks, less standardised, presumably indicating manufacturer, ownership, destination, quantity or contents.

Study of material from Crete has shown that the tablets were mainly, if not exclusively, used for keeping records of produce – agricultural or manufactured – as part of a storage and redistribution system. No archive has yet been discovered in the Cyclades to indicate its use on the islands on such a large scale. But such may yet be found and it is particularly interesting that the fragments recently found at Phylakopi came from the area of a large and probably administrative building (since it was on the site later occupied by the Mycenaean palace) which

142. Lead weights on the Minoan standard from Akrotiri, Thera. (C. Doumas).

belongs to early LC I. In any case it is clear that the islanders were familiar with Cretan script, unless of course Cretans were always on hand to translate or were in charge of the operations in relation to which it was used.

The influence of Crete

The discoveries surveyed in the earlier parts of this chapter show that there were significant changes in the Cyclades in the hundred and fifty years or so of the early Late Bronze Age. The islands became more prosperous in a purely material sense; settlement may have become more

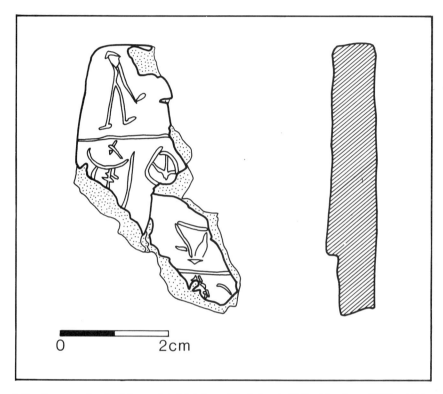

143. Fragments of a Linear A tablet from Phylakopi. (After Renfrew 1978b, 419).

scattered (if the Thera pattern is at all representative of other islands); but most striking of all is the strong Minoan influence visible in most areas of material culture. Our view of the strength of this influence must however be somewhat modified by recently acquired evidence of large quantities of Mainland imports and other Mainland links (e.g. in the frescoes) at the same time, and the likelihood that the islands were not all affected to the same degree.

Contacts with Crete were by no means a new development of LC I-II, since Minoan imports occur regularly throughout the Middle Cycladic period and they and their influence on local ceramic production had already become more evident in late Middle Cycladic. Nevertheless the quantities of pottery imported and the range of imports and copies of other objects are immensely more prominent at the beginning of the Late Bronze Age, especially since they are accompanied by evidence of the use of Cretan administrative systems (Linear A script, Minoan metrology) and by the adoption of some aspects of Cretan religious practice (see above), as well as some distinctively Cretan architectural forms, especially on Thera (see Chapter 8).

This archaeological evidence has often been interpreted in the light of the persistent and frequent references in later Greek authors to an ancient tradition recording a thalassocracy (sea empire) of King Minos of Crete and presumably the establishment of Cretan colonies in the Aegean.[31]

While the archaeological discoveries seem in general to fit the picture presented in the sources, some crucial questions arise. Exactly what was the thalassocracy? In other words, how is the archaeological evidence to be interpreted in human terms? What do we mean by a 'colony' and can the Cycladic settlements of this period be so described? Why were the Cretans so involved in the Cyclades? Was there any real difference in character between the various island settlements?

That Cretans and Cycladic islanders were closely involved with each other is evident – but why? There is certainly no single explanation but there are a number of likely contributory factors – trade in commodities desired by either party; imperial expansion on the part of palatial Crete; colonial settlement to relieve unacceptable population pressures in Crete; control of the Cyclades to protect sea routes against pirates or hostile powers.

Trade[32]

It is not easy to see what the Cyclades themselves might have produced which was not readily available in Crete – except services (slaves? seamen?). Obsidian was still in quite wide use in the Late Bronze Age and could have been a factor. But the marble for which the Cyclades had been famed in the Early Cycladic period was no longer seriously exploited even by the islanders – and the islands with the richest marble resources (Naxos and Paros) are those which have to date shown least signs of Minoan contacts. In spite of the apparent improbability that the Cycladic islands would have yielded substantial agricultural surpluses for export, there is evidence from recent analysis of animal remains from Phylakopi to suggest that sheep-rearing on Melos was developed significantly in the Middle and earlier Late Bronze Age, and one might guess that the intention behind this was to produce an attractive commodity for export.[33] We may also recall the Cycladic container vessels found in MM III Knossos, which show that there were some such export products in an earlier period.

However, with specific reference to Crete, it is hard to see sheep as a major Cycladic export, since it has been shown that large numbers of sheep in Crete contributed to a highly organised wool-production industry there, although that was apparently later than the expansion of the Melian industry.

Other suggestions for Cycladic exports[34] have included saffron (shown being picked on the Thera frescoes) and perfumes (possibly processed in the 'fire-boxes' from Kea), as well as andesite, a volcanic stone used for industrial purposes (millstones), of which pieces have been found in the Argolid.

This is not an impressive list. But an explanation connected with trade becomes much more probable if the Cyclades are seen not as one half of a bipartite relationship with Crete so much as a series of calling places between Crete and Mainland Greece. If this is right, Cycladic commodities for export may have existed but would have been much less important, the materials being carried originating largely either from Crete or from the newly emerging Mainland of the Shaft Grave period whose Cretan links are clear. The main island contribution to this system might have been in ships and seamen – a situation which would have allowed many islanders to see and absorb Cretan ways and styles.

It has been sensibly pointed out that the three islands with which we are now familiar as the most prosperous in LC I-II are convenient stopping points (approximately one day's sailing apart) on a route between central Crete and the Saronic gulf (Aegina, Athens) – or the Argolid (Fig. 2), if the stop at Kea was omitted. We need not however postulate a highly organised timetable of four-day sailings from Knossos to Athens (or three to the Argolid). Vessels might well have diverged from the direct route to carry products between islands, or never even intended to complete the whole run. The stepping-stone route would have been a nautical convenience – but a distributive one as well, since not all the cargo would be going direct from Crete to the Mainland or vice versa. Some items would be dropped off in the islands, others picked up and others again, as already indicated, simply taken from one island to another. Leisurely voyages of this kind are still undertaken in the islands. In the summer of 1981, I saw the same kaiki from Kalymnos selling melons and other simple produce in the harbours of both Amorgos and Ano Kouphonissi, and no doubt it made many other calls as well.

The numerous finds of lead weights (on the Minoan standard) from the Cyclades, Kea and Thera especially, is good evidence of intensive local trade. As we have seen, the bronze, lead (and silver) in use in the Late Bronze Age Aegean seem mostly to have come from Lavrion in Attica and this would certainly have been taken to Kea and then southwards via the route described. In this way, many of the Cretan objects known from the Mainland and the Cyclades at this time would have reached their destinations. This would be true also of the less tangible ones (people, fabric, oil, agricultural produce) of which evidence cannot be recovered archaeologically.

In the ways suggested above, a considerable variety of products could have been traded through and with the Cyclades, many of them Minoan, at a time when Mainland material culture was much less sophisticated than and indeed basing itself upon that of the Cretan palaces. Might this trade network, if such it was, have involved some kind of 'colonial' settlement of the islands, or is there some other reason why the Cyclades might have been 'colonized', if indeed they were?

Colonies?[35]

Strictly speaking, the term colony indicates a new settlement, founded by a mother-city on foreign soil. This definition clearly does not fit any of the Cycladic sites which all had long histories of their own, not radically influenced from outside. It is conceivable, however, that at the beginning of the Late Bronze Age, the local inhabitants were completely displaced by Minoans (this could explain the destructions which are followed by the appearance of Minoan pottery in quantity), or that the Minoans took control of them and left a select body of administrators (plus garrisons?) in charge, or that Minoans were present in other capacities, as traders or as emigrants who had come peacefully as a result of contacts originally established for the purposes of trade. All these situations could be regarded as aspects of colonialism, though there is also the entirely non-colonial explanation – that the islanders were so overawed by the superior civilisation of Crete that they copied almost all its material aspects, and others (religion, administration) as well.

It is not realistic to attempt a choice between these possibilities. The original suggestions of Cretan colonialism were based, from an archaeological point of view, on the intensity of Cretan imports and influences in the early Late Bronze Age and these could form part of any of the 'colonial' options outlined above. They do not however seem to exclude the completely non-colonial explanation. Nevertheless the penetration of Cycladic life by Minoan techniques (fresco-painting, weaving, stone vase-making), practices (religion, administration) and domestic objects (conical cups, loomweights), which are not in themselves overtly desirable objects – in addition to the plethora of imports and imitations – suggest a more radical involvement with Crete than could be created by regular calls of trading vessels (only for six months of the year anyway, we should remember).[36]

If we accept the possibility of some form of colonisation, there are other plausible causes for it than solely the organisation of trade. Simple territorial expansion of an important power could well be one,[37] though we might perhaps wonder in this case why it did not happen earlier. Protection of trade routes could be another. Both Ayia Irini and Phylakopi had defences in LC I-II, suggesting that protection was required on occasion, and the Aegean has often, through the ages, been infested by pirates.[38] The islanders on their own might have been unable to combat such threats and perhaps invited aid. Finally, the resources of Crete itself may have become stretched with a growing population, to the extent that settlers were encouraged or driven to seek new homes outside the island. A recent review[39] of evidence for Cretan population levels and pressure on resources at the time supports this view. Total expulsion of the local population seems out of the question, because distinct local elements remain in the pottery, which is our best guide, and these even increase on Kea in LC II. Besides, we have also seen proposed important

Cycladic initiatives in the style of fresco painting, elements of religious practice which were not strictly Minoan and a local origin for some other minor objects.[40]

Another question that must be posed is whether the nature of the Minoan presence was the same on all the islands. They certainly do not seem to have been present in force everywhere. As well as the smaller islands, Paros seems a striking exception; Naxos too since, in spite of recent discoveries, the island still has not produced the amount of Minoan material that such an attractive centre would seem to warrant. There are also indications (which have been discussed above but need now to be drawn together) that the intensity of Minoan influence was not the same everywhere. This is a difficult question to assess at present but will become easier as the various categories of artefacts are subjected to further study and more sites are excavated. Nevertheless three factors seem positively to point to such a differentiation.[41] These are (1) The considerably greater amounts of Mainland pottery at Ayia Irini than elsewhere; (2) The much more thoroughly Minoanised civilisation at Akrotiri, particularly evident in the architecture (and note the apparently greater degree of Minoanisation in the ritual objects at Akrotiri as opposed to Ayia Irini); (3) The lack of consistency in the intensity of individual island contacts with Crete, as shown by the pottery.

All these propositions are unfortunately disputable: (1) There may prove to be very much more Mainland pottery on Thera and Melos than previously thought; (2) The existence of Minoan elements, indisputable at Akrotiri, is more contentious at other sites because locally available stone was responsible for some of the non-Minoan architectural characteristics; (3) There is always a degree of chance in the relative amounts of finds made on any island.

This evidence suggests to me that there were significant differences in the Minoan relationships with the various islands and, further, that Akrotiri was the major Minoan centre in the Cyclades. There were almost certainly inter-island rivalries and perhaps it is to these that the inconsistencies in the inter-island connections and the walls at Phylakopi and Ayia Irini point. A subtle policy of giving rein to these rivalries, so long as they did not affect Minoan interests, and at the same time of having a single key base in the islands on Thera, would have been effective and economical for Crete. In this scenario, the Mainlanders play a passive role, involved in trade and acquiring artefacts and expertise from the Minoans, though as yet without the power, organisation, or perhaps even inclination to challenge Minoan authority. Perhaps the Mycenaean warriors on the Thera ships, if such they are, were mercenaries.

Much of this interpretation of early Late Cycladic developments is speculative and could well be altered by future discoveries. But the main facts are clear – substantial developments in material prosperity and strong Minoan influence on many aspects of life, apparently deriving from the place of the Cyclades in a trading network involving also Crete and Mainland Greece, a process which may or may not have involved Minoan settlers in the Cyclades.

This period of stability came to a sudden end at all three major sites. In late LC II there was a destruction by fire (Mycenaean attack?) of at least part of the settlement at Phylakopi and Ayia Irini was devastated by an earthquake. Earlier however, at the end of LC I, the Akrotiri settlement, indeed the whole island of Thera, had been overwhelmed by the volcanic cataclysm whose effects, together with the details of life in the town of Akrotiri, will be considered in Chapter 8.

8
Akrotiri

More than any other discoveries in the history of Aegean archaeology, the excavations at Akrotiri[1] on Thera have illuminated the practical realities of life in a Bronze Age town. As we have seen, Akrotiri was probably in some ways exceptional. But there are enough similarities between this site and the contemporary townships on Kea and Melos to show that, while Akrotiri may have been more sophisticated and had a closer relationship with Crete, for most of the inhabitants the way of life was essentially the same.

Around 1500 BC, the settlement at Akrotiri was first rocked by earthquakes, then inundated with pumice and submerged under a layer of ash up to 60m thick. This cataclysmic eruption was followed by the explosion and collapse of the volcano at Thera's core. The details, chronology and wider effects of this series of volcanic events will be considered later, but first we shall look more carefully at the settlement itself and what was found in it. Architectural characteristics have already been described in Chapter 4.

The existence of important remains on Thera (and the islet of Therasia in the bay, which was part of the main island before the volcanic eruption) was known in the nineteenth century, when the commercial exploitation of ash and pumice brought deeply buried remains to light.

In 1967 the late Professor Spyridon Marinatos of Athens University, who had long wanted to investigate the possibility of a link between the destruction of many sites in Crete in the fifteenth century BC and the Thera volcano, began work near Akrotiri in an area where erosion of the thick ash layer gave the best opportunity of locating ancient remains beneath the surface.

Marinatos' choice of location was inspired, and his workmen quickly hit on ancient buildings. But the same factor that allowed access to the antiquities here (the eroded ash layer) has also meant that we are left without any idea of the extent of the ancient settlement and in what part of it (centre? periphery?) the excavated remains lie. The ash covering to either side of the ravine which is the site of the excavations is very much thicker, and work is impossible there without enormous expense.

The settlement (Fig. 144) does not appear to have been built to any

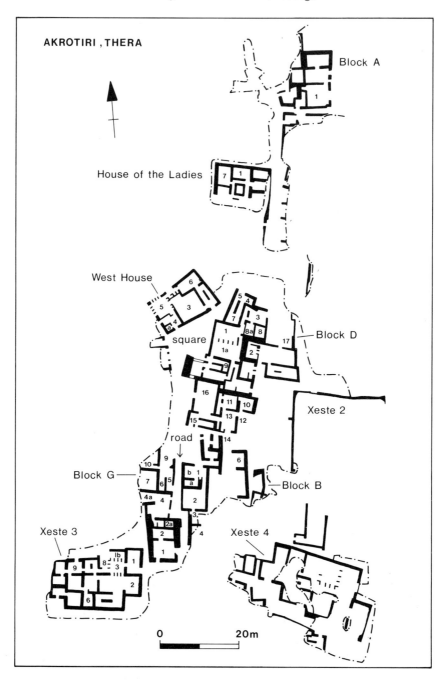

144. Akrotiri, Thera. Plan of the site in LC I. (After Marthari 1984, 120).

careful plan. The streets and alleys have no regular relationship to each other, and Block D, for example, has five separate periods of construction.

The buildings are either rather irregular blocks (like D) or else substantial independent houses (e.g. the West House).

Walls are often of miscellaneous small stones with a coating of clay (with straw tempering). Larger, shaped (ashlar) blocks are also used, especially as quoins. But properly cut regular ashlar masonry is also used for whole facades, occasionally entire buildings (Fig. 16). The division between floors is sometimes marked on the exterior by a projecting cornice of ashlar blocks. Buildings may be as high as three storeys, and sometimes have cellars.

Although upper-storey plans often reflect those of the ground floors, this is not inevitably the case, and light-framed walls of stakes and clay or fired/unfired bricks are found in some upper rooms. The general excavation plan therefore most closely reflects the ground-floor layout.

The following description begins from the present entrance to the site at the the south, but does not thereafter attempt to follow the spectator route round the excavation.

Architectural history

The Late Cycladic town is essentially a construction of the very early Late Bronze Age, following a devastating earthquake which seriously damaged the buildings then standing, which were presumably of Middle Cycladic origin.

After the earthquake some buildings were completely demolished (remains found under Mill House square), but many were rebuilt on the same general lines as previously, though with some alterations and often new entrances.

The new entrances were required because the debris from the earthquake was spread out over the streets and open areas of the town, thus raising the external ground level above that of the original thresholds (Fig. 145). This also had the effect of turning previous ground-floor rooms into half-basements. In one case (Delta 15) the entrance was adjusted to provide entry on to the landing of a staircase whose foot had originally been at the earlier street level.

Most of the settlement was either reconstructed or built for the first time (perhaps some of the more sophisticated ashlar buildings) in early LC I. There are some signs of building activity over a period of time in Block D, where different elements seem to belong to different periods.

A major earthquake, which preceded the final sequence of volcanic events, was largely responsible for the demise of the settlement, although there was some reoccupation by 'squatters', who adapted the buildings to their use. The site was finally overwhelmed (and preserved for the future) by the tephra (ash) ejected by the volcano.

145. Akrotiri, Thera. Platform of rubble from early LC I earthquake (associated with doorway at new level). (M. Marthari).

Xeste 3

This building (the first to the left on entering the site) was constructed entirely of carefully cut ashlar masonry, all brought from the same quarry so as to give a uniform finish. It had at least two and possibly three storeys. Against the south wall of the main building, poorer construction seems to be the work of squatters who came back to the settlement in between the first earthquake and the final destruction. Many simple tools were found within.

The entrance is at the south-east corner where, set back from the east facade, there is a doorway with a window to the side. Inside is a small anteroom, with paved floor and stone benches (Fig. 39) to either side. A staircase, with seven steps up to a landing and a return flight, leads up from the anteroom to the first floor. The walls of the stairway were decorated with a landscape scene. There was a second staircase in the north part of the building (Room 8). The most important room on the ground floor is Room 3, in the north part of which is a lustral basin. The room is a 'polythyron' (literally, 'of many doors') because the inner arms of its L-shape open on to a light well via a series of doors set between jambs. Individual doors could be opened to varying degrees, thus permitting fine adjustment of the amounts of air and light admitted.

The ground and first floors of the building had fine frescoes on the walls

146. Akrotiri, Thera. Lustral basin in Xeste 3.

including the splendid scene of girls gathering crocuses, as well as the 'mistress of animals' with monkey and griffin discussed in Chapter 7.

Access to the basin (Fig. 146), which was paved with schist slabs, was by a flight of five steps returning round a balustrade of finely cut stones. Such structures are known from Crete, where they are thought to have had some ritual function, but this is the first one to be found in the Cyclades.

A few finds have been reported, especially from Room 6 on the ground floor, where a collection of pottery included domestic storage jars. Room 9 contained a fresco with relief decoration.

Doors and windows are of standard types, often with stone lintels, jambs and sills/thresholds: these however usually had wooden fittings, either square or semicircular in section. The pumice fill of a window on the north side of Room 9 contained impressions of wooden cross-pieces which presumably formed part of a grating. Also from the window opening (possibly its original decoration) came fragments of a relief fresco with rosettes and a border.

To the north of the main entrance, Rooms 1 and 2 (also with fresco fragments in their upper levels) project to form the main east facade of the building. Room 2 has a large pillar set between the end walls of the room – the rest of the east side being quite open. On the top of the central pillar and on the sides of it and the end walls, a series of slots were cut, suggesting that the space was filled with some kind of lattice – either to shut this further entrance (if such it was) or partially to close the enormous windows.

The fine and consistent quality of the external masonry, as well as the frescoes inside and the lustral basin and the possibility of relatively free access from the east, all suggest that this building had, or could on occasion have had, some special ceremonial function, which the decoration of the lustral basin might indicate was to do with fertility rites. It is risky, however, to suppose that the whole building was devoted to such a function, or even that the the structure had a primarily ritual use all the time. There was a much greater intermingling of the sacred and the secular in ancient Akrotiri than we are in the habit of expecting today.

Block G (Gamma)

Outside the entrance to Xeste 3 is an open area. To the north, and divided from its north-east corner by a narrow passage, are the buildings comprising Block G. Many details of the excavation have not yet been reported, but the buildings (up to three storeys high) seem mainly of rubble masonry with the characteristic wooden inserts (see Chapter 4). They are fairly unsophisticated in character, though some fresco fragments were found. There was evidence of 'squatter' activity here, including blocked doors and makeshift walls which apparently belonged to a period of re-use between the first earthquakes and the final catastrophe. Some of this work could however be rather inferior building of the original period.

The rooms to the south of the complex (G 1-3) have very thick walls. An entrance to the south has a crudely built circular step and there may have been one also to the south-east. These rooms appear to represent a complete unit – with a staircase in the north-west corner to the upper floor and access from the staircase chamber also to the group of rooms to the north (G 4-10). Finds from the ground floor were mostly tools (anvils, pounders etc.) and G 1 might have been a squatters' workshop.

The rooms immediately to the north of those just described may also have formed a separate unit in the squatter period, since the north doors (out of G 4 and G 4a) were blocked and access apparently provided either from the staircase to the south or through the windows on to the street.

The most northerly section was entered by a door from the street which runs along the east face of the building. G 5 and 6 may have been a corridor, with fresco decoration, and a stair well. G 9 had food remains and a mortar and was perhaps a kitchen. G 10 contained clay pipes, probably belonging to a lavatory on the upper floor.

The open space opposite the entrance to Xeste 3 and to the south of complex G and the narrow alley that runs out of it to the northwest between the two buildings has already been described.

Telchines Road; Block B (Beta)

The most important road so far discovered in the settlement (dubbed 'Telchines Road') runs out of the 'square' up the east side of G, with Block B to the east forming a jog where rooms B 1-2 project forward beyond the south line of the building (B 3 and 4). The road is paved and a drain runs beneath it. North of B 1 the road runs into another small 'square'.

The precise interrelationship of the rooms B 1-8 is not entirely clear but they may form a unit with their own staircase (east of B 1); the staircase to the north (D 15) belonging to the adjacent unit.

B 1-2 were important both for their character and the finds in them. The upper storey was paved with fine thin flagstones. B 2 had a column in the centre (the column of wood, the base stone; the latter only surviving). The objects found round about it suggest that the column was the focus of some kind of ritual. There were many vases, both large and small, some of them very fine, including a nippled ewer, a strainer, a kymbe and also a number of stone vessels, among them a kernos.

At the north-east corner of the room a door gave access to B 1, which was subdivided by one substantial and other more flimsy walls. In the wall to the right of the doorway are two openings (doors or windows). In the north wall of B 1 is a large window looking out onto the courtyard. A small room (behind the projecting wall to the left) was divided by low partitions of unfired bricks, in which were kept vessels of ritual function (including more nippled ewers, and tables of offerings). In the north half, the function of the small room B 1b is not clear; the main area (B 1) was extensively decorated with frescoes. A single antelope at either side faces inwards to the window onto the square, a pair of antelopes are on the adjacent walls (Fig. 129) to the east and west, and the boxing children (Fig. 127) are located in the small space on the south wall, between the entrances to B 1b and B 1a.

Against the east outer wall of B 2 were remains, perhaps of a lavatory, on the upper floor.

The construction of the flagged floor/ceiling of B 2 (lower) is of interest. The roof beams of the lower floor were overlaid with closely set slabs and these again with branches and stones, clay and earth (in the manner of modern country roofs): the slab floor of the upper storey was laid on top of these.

The ground-floor rooms are equally interesting, though quite different in character. The plan did not correspond to that of the upper floor, since an additional later wall created a narrow passage in the centre. This was part of the early LC I rearrangement, when B 1 and 2 became half-basements, with the raising of the street level outside, and the building was otherwise altered to provide the large room on the upper floor. The column in the upper-floor room seems to have been set directly over a similar column in the room below.

The numerous vases discovered in this room were limited in type and mostly domestic tripod cooking pots, blackened by fire, and simple cups. It was identified as a 'plain kitchen storeroom'.

To the north of the dividing passage was a different kind of storeroom. Large clay storage jars were set in stone benches to either side of a narrow passage (Fig. 38). The mouths of the jars are more or less flush with the surfaces of the stone benches. On these benches rested plain rhyta for dipping into the jars and dispensing the stored grain, oil etc. in exact measures. Stone pestles for pounding grain were also there.

From Room B 6 in the east of the complex came the Blue Monkeys fresco and other landscape scenes, as yet incompletely published.

Another road or alley appears to have run from the square at the south up the east side of units B and D.

Xeste 4; Xeste 2

Before considering Block D, immediately to the north, we may briefly notice two other buildings, so far hardly investigated.

Well to the southeast is another fine structure called Xeste 4. This, like Xeste 3, is entirely constructed of ashlar masonry, all quarried from the same source. The division between the ground and first floors was marked by a projecting cornice. The upper-floor rooms included a polythyron like that already described in Xeste 3 and the building seems to have had important frescoes – fragments show greaves and feet of figures, presumably military and possibly lifesize. The building may be of early LC I origin.

Traces of other important buildings have also been found to the south and north, including another at least partly ashlar construction called Xeste 2 (to the east of areas B and D).

Block D (Delta)

The most complex unit so far revealed, perhaps partly because it is one of the most fully excavated, is Block D. It was apparently built in five different stages.

Where the Telchines Road broadens out into a square (Fig. 147) at the north end of Block B, the southernmost part of D includes D 15, whose adjacent door and window face south. This small room is a millhouse, one of several on the site, where grain was apparently ground, and possibly distributed to people who could wait in the square.

A slab-stone bench stood opposite the door (Fig. 148) and a millstone, on which the grinding would have been done, lay fallen on the floor. Beside the stone bench, on another bench built of stones and clay, stood

147. Akrotiri, Thera. The north-east corner of Triangle Square. (C. Doumas).

a large container vase with smaller bowls inside it, possibly for measuring. A flight of steps led upwards from just inside the millhouse door to the first floor.

The rooms to the east of the millhouse (D 10-13) are smaller and may form part of a unit with its main entrance to the street on the east. Room 14 had a quantity of animal bone, suggesting cooking, and 13 a niche full of loomweights.

North of the millhouse is D 16 – another place where the original ground floor became a semi-basement, while at the same time the entrance (D 15) was adjusted to open onto the original landing of a staircase. On the ground floor there was a large window in the wall onto the street. In the centre of the room was a column, the stone base preserved. The room was full of pottery – some large jars which had

148. Akrotiri, Thera. The millhouse in Block D. (C. Doumas).

apparently contained organic substances, others fine luxury vessels. Further finds included a few bronze implements and vases, some stone vessels and triton shells and ostrich eggs, the latter with ritual connotations. The beam slots of the upper floor of this building were found in the course of the excavation but there seem to have been no deposits definitely assignable to the upper storey.

Again a monumental porch, new in LC I, projects into the street, with doors to south and north (larger). From the porch further doors lead to passages and stairs or narrow storerooms inside the building.

The interrelationships of the east rooms are far from clear (D 9 etc.). Very large quantities of pottery were found in 9 and 9.1, but the most interesting room in the area is D 2 – an upper-floor room, whose means of access is uncertain. It was originally fronted by a polythyron system which was later converted into a wall with a door and window facing east. The jamb separating the two was plastered and painted red. The north, south and west sides of the room were lavishly decorated with the Spring fresco. Traces of shelving, high on the walls, have been recovered, and built-in to the south of the window there was a cupboard. The north wall of the room was flimsy, of wood and plaster, though decorated, and formed a closet between it and the main north wall (the north, south and west walls were of very solid construction). Access to the closet was by a narrow tunnel at the north-east corner of the room. In the room were very large numbers of vases, large and small, including some of ritual character, as well as other finds. Many of these were at a high level in the fill, having fallen from shelves. On the floor were large vases, some with traces of organic remains, also a bed – of which the outline was recovered by pouring plaster of paris into the cavities in the pumice. Under the bed more vases were stacked.

The tunnel into the small room was packed with vases and the room itself contained pottery and loomweights.

The remainder of the complex is best considered together. The main means of access were via the porch already mentioned, via D 16, and by another doorway in the monumental north-facing facade at the other end of the complex. This third entrance gave access to a narrow paved vestibule (D 4-5) from which a staircase ascended to a landing adjacent to D 1, a corridor beside it leading to the ground floor interior. The staircase is still visible, its stone treads cracked by earthquake. The bottom of the staircase was closed by a two-leaved door which pivoted on a lead hinge. The door leaves wore grooves in the lowest tread.

On the upper floor, D 7 had a hearth and, by the outer wall, the pipes of a lavatory system. The landing also gave access to another stairway further east which descended to a narrow landing (with an ascending flight opposite also). From this point a third flight descended east to D 3 which had a cellar beneath, probably approached by a ladder. The floor of D 3 was paved and had a rock-cut niche in one corner. Many vases came from the niche and the floor. In the cellar, under the floor slabs of D 3, was also a fine hoard of bronze vessels. D 8 and 8a are upper-storey rooms which produced various finds, and D 17 a storeroom with vases and other implements. The north-east area has not yet been fully explored.

The central part of the building (D 1-1a) has two ground-floor windows and a larger one at first-floor level in the west facade. The upper floor is a polythyron. This contained some large finely decorated storage vessels, some of them placed in the divisions of the polythyron, presumably for protection from earthquake damage. A bundle of loomweights came from a window sill.

The polythyron of the upper floor stands over a partition wall at ground-floor level. The south room contained two built ashlar pillars. Underneath the window onto the street was a hearth of stones and clay with a pitcher set beside it – perhaps with water for dousing/controlling the fire. To the north is a door into the unexcavated part of the ground floor and, to the south, two doors leading to passages/staircases. The room contained many vases, both local and imported.

Other important finds from D 1 included an impression of a wooden table with relief decoration (Fig. 149), a basket (Fig. 11), also recovered by plaster impression, and a partly carved antler.

Triangle Square and the West House

To the west of D 1 is a triangular square which consists of irregular

149. Plaster cast of wooden table from
Akrotiri, Thera. (C. Doumas).

paving stones laid on an artificial levelling fill. Opposite the porch to unit
D is part of the facade of a building not yet excavated and to the north of
that, forming the main north-west side of the triangle, is the important
and imposing building known as the West House.

Foundation trenches for its walls were cut into bedrock, about 1.5m
below the surface of the square. The trenches were considerably wider
than the actual walls and were packed with smaller stones.

The building is an independent freestanding structure, not built of
ashlar masonry, though there are some ashlar quoins. The main entrance
is at the east end, where a door with a window beside it leads to a
vestibule and stairway to the upper floor. From Room 6 at the top of the
stairway there is access to the large central room (3), with an enormous
window looking out onto the square, and to Room 5 at the north-west
corner. The window, timber-framed with stone surrounds, was
apparently divided into two by a large bipartite stone jamb.

Room 5 had a series of four small windows in each of the north and
west walls: these were closed by wooden shutters of which casts were
recovered from the pumice. Vases had been put on the sills of all the
windows. The room had a floor of schist slabs and a painted dado of
panels of imitation marbling alternating with narrower yellow painted
panels, the latter coinciding with the jambs of the multiple windows on
the north and west walls. There were cupboards and shelves in the east
and south walls. Painted fishermen came from the north-east and
south-west corners of the room and the miniature fresco frieze from the
north, south, east, and perhaps also the west wall of this room. Traces
were recovered of the stakes used in the make-up of the floors.

A door led into Room 4 which was divided into two by a flimsy brick
partition. Room 4a was a bathroom/lavatory with a lavatory installation
(Fig. 150) fixed in the south-west corner. Stone blocks had a gap between

150. West House, Akrotiri, Thera. Lavatory installation on upper floor. (C. Doumas).

them which may have been covered by a wooden seat. A drain pipe led to a pit in the street below which had a large slab cover and into which other drains converged.

A window in Room 4 (perhaps the bedroom) had the sill painted with vases of flowers (Fig. 130), and Rooms 4/4a and the partition which divided them were decorated with the *ikrion* motif (Fig. 132). The figure of a priestess may have adorned the doorway between Rooms 4 and 5.

Room 3 was large but it is not clear exactly what was found there, though it seems to have contained pithoi and other vases.

The ground floor had three windows in addition to that by the door. These three were all at street level, because of the LC I rearrangment. The effects of this are very evident here, since the original floor of Room 4 is 1.80m below the new street level, and the levels on the ground floor varied a great deal.

The ground-floor rooms contained, as usual, many vases and pithoi. Room 4/4a may have been the location of metal-working (cupellation of silver) as lead was found adhering to some vases.

House of the Ladies

To the north of the area just described (D North and the West House), and separated from it by an unexcavated part, through which runs the continuation of Telchines Road, is a building dubbed the 'House of the Ladies'. A section of the road uncovered here had two phases – one when the road consisted of rectangular slabs and with which a drain was associated, and a later in which the surface was formed of irregular stones. There was an open area to the west of the building.

The south and east sides have been badly affected by the torrent which has run through the site, and it is not clear exactly where the entrance was located, but a return staircase leads up to the first floor in the middle of the south side of the building.

The centre is occupied by a doorless square unit which may have been a light well. A passage surrounds this, giving access to the remaining rooms. Room 1 in the centre of the north side had the Ladies fresco which was probably of ritual character (west wall: four groups of three lilies; south: two flower groups, a gap, a woman walking left; north: two more females, one stooping, a seated figure). The room was divided into two units. One contained a large number of conical cups, as well as triton shells and ivory fragments. In the other (west) room were four brick-built compartments containing mainly pottery, including jugs and a rhyton. These compartments were covered by schist slabs. Three small rooms occupied the east side of the house and two larger the west. One of these, Room 7, had many finds, which had mostly fallen into the room below with the collapse of the middle of the floor. The finds included rhytons and breasted ewers, as well as kymbai and triton shells, some placed in a slab-built container in the east corner.

The ground-floor Room 7 was paved with schist slabs. Many vases had been stacked along the walls – some inside each other.

Block A (Alpha)

The last group of buildings – in the northernmost part of the area so far excavated – is centred round a storeroom complex. The outline of this block is clear, except at the north-west corner, where the rooms recede under a thick layer of volcanic debris. To the south and west the building is separated from other unexcavated structures by a narrow passage (south) and a roughly paved road (west). Finds are mainly from ground floors, though there were upper storeys, at least on the west, and some of the material in the fill is fallen from them.

151. Akrotiri, Thera. Room with storage jars in Block A. (C. Doumas).

The three rooms on the east are quite spacious, though decreasing in size to the north. A 1 had a large window in the east wall (the jambs are of small stones and clay packed between wooden uprights) and might have been a shop (Doumas). There was a built hearth against the west wall with a sunken stone vessel beside it. Various vases were found, among them large storage jars (Fig. 151) with organic remains, as well as smaller utensils, including the ubiquitous mortars and grinders. Many loomweights were discovered, mostly above floor level, suggesting that they had originally been associated with looms above.

The second room contained a similar array of storage vessels, pestles and mortars, other utensils, lamps etc., as well as some ritual vases (including a lion's head rhyton) in the fill of the room and evidently fallen from above. Some of the vases, especially the larger, stood within separate clay partitions. In one of these was a terracotta chest and, in another, a slab with weights on it, perhaps showing the position of a pair of scales.

The west rooms are smaller and less regular. One has access only from the south corridor and has reasonably been described as a porter's lodge. The first room (at the south-west corner of the complex) contained a milling installation for the grinding of grain. Access was via an anteroom with a bench and paved floor, to the north. The anteroom had a door, the millhouse itself a window. The floor of the millhouse was paved. A rectangular millstone was set in a structure of smaller stones and clay and portable mills were found on it and on the floor. Beside was a slab to receive milled grain. The room also contained (in the south-west corner) a decorated terracotta tub on a paved area, probably for storage, though usually referred to as a bathtub.

There were two further rooms to the north, of which the central one seems to have had a religious function on its upper storey, since a table of offerings and a nippled ewer were found to the east, fallen in the fill.

Life in Bronze Age Akrotiri

The repercussions of discoveries at Akrotiri will take a long time to absorb, but already they have thrown new light on some aspects of life in the prehistoric Aegean and provoked speculation about others. It seems fair to say that, whereas the miraculous state of preservation of the site has lent a degree of detail previously unavailable to our understanding of daily life, the apparently unique character of much of the material (and especially the architecture) uncovered arouses the suspicion, discussed elsewhere, that Akrotiri was not a typical LC I town – that its special relationship with palatial Crete gave it a peculiar authority and character. We shall combine consideration of these two aspects in the following brief discussion.

Architecture

We have already noted the distinction between independent buildings and blocks in which a number of partially separate units are combined. Within the blocks it is impossible to be sure of the 'house' divisions, even if these existed in the sense in which we understand them, but all types of accommodation seem to share the same division of functions between the ground and upper storeys. The ground floors contain storerooms (for produce and pottery), granaries, workshops, hearths, perhaps also shops and distribution centres; whereas the upper rooms are devoted to living accommodation (beds and bathrooms), leisure rooms (frescoes, paved floors) and ritual activities. If we had better preserved third-storey remains, it might be possible to make further distinctions. The proposal that weaving normally took place on the first floor suggests again that they were the site of quieter, cleaner activities.

The finds of furniture (Fig. 149), if limited, are very illuminating – beds, a stool and table, wooden shelving. It would be interesting to know how widespread was the ownership of such items, for there seems little sign of the stone-built benches that served for beds and furniture in other island settlements in the Bronze Age and often do still today.

Interpretation of the architecture in social terms is full of problems. There is no way of deciding how many people lived in the buildings so far excavated and the relationship of the inhabitants of the different buildings to each other is highly problematic. At the most basic level, it is likely that the independent villas and ashlar structures are either public buildings or the residences of important officials. The lustral basin in Xeste 4 and the *ikria* frescoes in the West House lend some support to this suggestion.

Religion and social organisation

The frequency of ritual objects should really occasion no great surprise; nor should it make us feel that the inhabitants of Akrotiri were religious maniacs in the way that the Minoans are sometimes made to seem. The ubiquity of ritual paraphernalia does not necessarily mean that the people permanently set aside large areas of all their buildings for virtually continuous ritual observances: rather that such observances played a relatively large role in their lives and no activity was performed without invoking them. In the same way we find today a flame burning before the ikon in the house, an ikon of the Panayia on the motorist's dashboard, blue beads on the donkey's brow.

It is a mistake to say that the millhouse was for production of grain for ritual purposes because ritual objects were found in the same building. The grain was for human consumption (though perhaps a tithe for the deity too) but it would be grown, reaped and milled under the protection of the divine.

An interesting recent analysis of the organisation of the Akrotiri settlement (by N. Marinatos) sees it as based on groups of inhabitants attached to shrines – the ultimate government thus being in the hands of the priests who controlled them.

The identification of the shrines is based on the assumption (quite well supported) that figured frescoes always have a religious significance and are usually found together with other evidence of ritual activity.

Although this theory is not perhaps as fanciful as it sounds, so baldly stated, it goes far beyond what can justifiably be said on the basis of the archaeological evidence and, at present, I must prefer a more modest explanation of the relationship between ritual activity and daily life of the kind offered above.

Daily life

Various daily activities find expression in the objects discovered. There are numerous vessels for the preparation and storage of food, and mills for grinding grain. Loomweights attest weaving, weights the existence of active trading, whether within the settlement or outside – probably both. A part finished vessel points to stone vase manufacture within the settlement, though there is little evidence for metal-working or other tool manufacture, at least in the parts of the site so far investigated.

A number of agricultural and fishing implements (sickles, fishhooks: Fig. 140), as well as animal bones, have been found at Akrotiri, and these raise the question of the occupations of the inhabitants of the town, and of its broader relationship to the other sites on the island.

It must remain highly improbable that, in spite of its relative sophistication, Akrotiri was fundamentally different from any other community in the prehistoric Aegean, which depended primarily on agriculture. Surely most of the town's inhabitants were occupied in this sphere of activity. It is thus likely that the implements found on the site represent the tools of trade of individuals who lived in the settlement and walked to the fields to cultivate crops or look after their animals. Although bone remains have been found on the site, there is no positive evidence that animals were kept there, whereas they have been commonly kept within villages and houses in rural Greece in recent times.

The smaller settlements at Balos, Ftellos and Therasia (see Chapter 4) seem like country farms – with architecture and finds less sophisticated than at Akrotiri. They have accommodation for animals and/or other signs of farming activities. It would be interesting to know what their relationship to the metropolis was. They must have been in close touch with the Akrotiri settlement and probably took in their surplus produce to be marketed there, even if production was not strictly controlled from the main centre, on the lines of the relationship between the Cretan palaces and their dependencies.

The Thera volcano and its effects[2]

The circumstances in which Akrotiri has been preserved for posterity themselves make evident the catastrophic nature of the eruption of the Thera volcano. It is time now to consider the details of this and the effects of the event and its aftermath on Aegean civilisation as a whole.

For thousands of years before the Bronze Age eruption, the volcano (or rather the series of volcanoes) of which Thera was formed had been quiescent, and there was no reason for the builders or occupants of Akrotiri to suspect that they were in danger – at least hardly more so than other inhabitants of the Aegean who are periodically subject to the ravages of earthquakes.

The first stage of the major Bronze Age activity (Fig. 152) was a very serious earthquake – presumably the one that drove most of the inhabitants away, killed the man in the farmstead on Therasia and was followed by the return of squatters to Akrotiri.

This was succeeded, after an interval of something between a few months and two years, by the eruption and collapse of the volcano.

Recent researches suggest that this final stage took place in three phases:

(1) The ejection of pumice into the air – which lasted only a few hours and resulted in falls of 0.5-5m thickness on the island. The cloud would

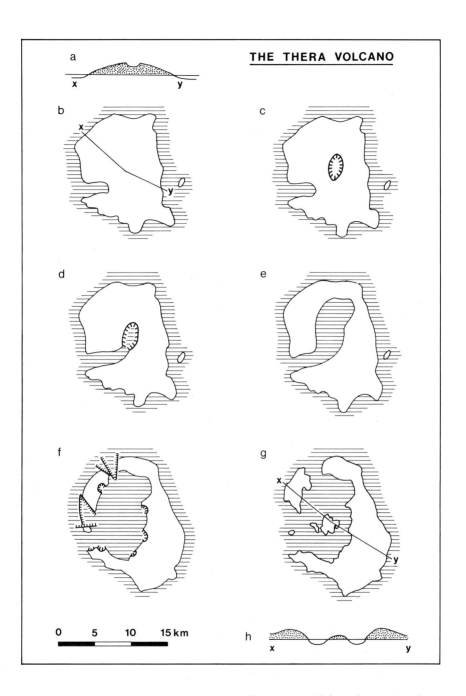

0   5   10   15 km

152. Phases of the volcanic catastrophe on Thera *c*. 1500 BC: (a-b) the island before 1500 BC; (c) opening of vent (pumice emission); (d) seawater inflow (base surge deposits); (e-f) collapse of caldera etc.; (g-h) present state. (After Pichler and Friedrich 1980, 17).

have been several kilometres high and much material carried in a south-easterly direction by the wind. This would have fallen in the sea or on other islands.

(2) Much more intense activity, caused by the intrusion of seawater into the chamber of the volcano. Ash rather than pumice was ejected, together with lumps of rock (old lava) from the walls of the chamber and vent, and the eruption took the form of a low-level spreading surge. Most of the material which did not land on the island would have fallen into the sea, as the ash was damp and heavy and was not projected high enough into the air for distant dispersal. The rock fragments in some cases acted like 'bombs', destroying buildings. This phase lasted a few days to a few weeks.

(3) In a development of the second phase, a chaotic mixture of ash, pumice and stone blocks poured out of the chamber, which was itself beginning to collapse. The material was ejected laterally rather than vertically up into the air.

This was the last main event, though the collapse of the crater continued in stages thereafter.

The most significant points of dispute in the investigation of this sequence have been the length of time that was involved (estimates have varied from a few days to several years); the nature of the dispersal of ash (over how wide an area, and to what depth); and the severity of tidal waves associated with the collapse of the crater (one enormous tidal wave or several smaller ones). These factors are of course directly related to the precise mechanics of the eruption.

The history of the Thera volcano is of enormous scientific interest *per se*, but it becomes of archaeological importance not only because it has preserved for us the Akrotiri settlement, but also because of its possible relationship to other events identified as approximately contemporary in the Aegean archaeological record.

It has long been known that very many sites all over Crete (including the major palaces) suffered damage, often by fire, during LM I. Most of these destructions happened in the later part of that period (i.e. LM IB), but some – perhaps significantly more than has often been thought – were earlier (LM IA). Some of these sites, especially in eastern Crete, were not then reoccupied until much later. It is also the case that, after LM IB (i.e. in LM II), there is good evidence that Mainland Mycenaeans were in control of Crete. These two facts have tempted scholars to connect the Cretan destructions with one or both of the above events (the Thera eruption and the Mycenaean takeover). In the case of the former link, it has been suggested that earthquakes associated with the volcanic activity of the Thera volcano rocked Cretan sites, setting some of them on fire; that the ash fall on eastern Crete affected that part of the island so seriously that its agricultural base was ruined and the area was totally abandoned for a time; and that an enormous tidal wave caused by a single gigantic final collapse of the Thera caldera ruined coastal sites in

Crete and the islands, as well as others not too far inland to be reached by its force.

Documented effects of the eruption of Krakatoa in the late nineteenth century have been adduced in support of these arguments. At Krakatoa, ash rose over 30 miles into the air and fell up to 3,300 miles away; associated tidal waves swept away whole villages; the sound of the final explosion was heard over 3,000 miles away. Nevertheless, the effects were considerably localised by geographical factors and cannot be used directly to interpret the likely situation in the Aegean.

According to this view, the subsequent Mycenaean takeover of Crete (and the Cyclades) was due primarily to the physical and psychological destruction of Crete by the effects of the Thera volcano, of which the Mainlanders took advantage at a time when they were, in any case, reaching an expansionist phase in their development.

The alternative interpretation of the evidence suggests that the physical side-effects of the Thera volcano on Crete were not great (although the psychological were probably extreme – an aspect of the situation largely neglected by most commentators) and that most of the LM IB destructions were considerably later than the volcanic catastrophe. Thus they are the work of Mycenaean invaders who attacked the island at that time.

There are a number of points where interpretation of the evidence may be disputed. One of the most important problems is a chronological one. The established pottery sequence for Late Bronze Age Crete divides the LM I period into two phases – A and B. Characteristic of the former is decoration in which plants and flowers are prominent, of the latter (Fig. 114) marine motifs (though these are not the only motifs used in each respective period). In the debris of the Thera destruction, only LM IA pottery has been found, whereas that from the Cretan destructions is in most cases LM IB. This evidence, if taken at its face value, would mean that the Thera eruption and the main (LM IB) series of Cretan destructions took place at different times and cannot possibly be connected. In the light of recent research it seems probable that this statement is correct and there was no connection. There are however various ways of explaining away this discrepancy. If there was a gap of several years between the original earthquake and virtual abandonment of Thera and the final catastrophe, which might have affected Crete, the LM IB style could have developed on Crete but would not have been found on Thera because there was no one there to import it – or the few inhabitants who were left were not in touch with the outside world.

The other argument sometimes advanced is that LM IB pottery was most characteristic of the Cretan palace centres (particularly Knossos) and might not have reached the Thera until later. This seems most improbable, since there are considerable quantities of LM IB pottery from other Cycladic islands in contexts which clearly follow those containing the LM IA material so characteristic of finds on Thera.

What then of the side-effects of the Thera volcano? Could they have been so relatively insignificant as compared to Krakatoa when the potential for damage was apparently so much greater? It does now seem that this was the case, though the not insubstantial evidence for damage at various sites in LM IA may well be the true archaeological reflection of these effects.

First, remains of the ash-fall on Crete have proved impossible to detect, except in microscopic quantities. Ash in the area of Crete was first identified from cores drilled in the sea bed where it was as thick as several centimetres in places. The distribution of cores containing tephra showed that the wind was blowing in a south-easterly direction at the time of the eruption and made more probable the theory linking heavy ashfall on eastern Crete with the desertion of sites there. But, in order to reach eastern Crete and to be distributed widely and thickly over it, the ash would have had to have been wind-borne, and recent research (above) has shown that only a relatively small part was ejected vertically and distributed in this way. The ash in the sea cores is however consistent with the more likely form of tephra ejection (lateral surge) which would have resulted in vast quantities floating on the sea (to the southeast, on account of the prevailing wind and currents) until it sank to the sea bed.

It also now seems likely that the collapse of the Thera caldera took place in gradual stages over a long period of time – perhaps causing minor tidal waves in the process – and that there was not a single catastrophic explosion and crater-collapse which would have generated a wave sufficient to devastate villages and towns on Crete.

Secondly, the archaeological evidence from Crete also seems to favour the 'Mycenaean' explanation of the LM IB destructions. There are increasing signs of at least some continuity of life in eastern Crete between LM IB and LM III (i.e. in LM II) and devastation and depopulation could equally well have been caused by marauding armies as by volcano-wrecked agriculture.

The nature of the LM IB destructions does not really favour earthquakes (too widespread) or tidal waves (some sites very remote from the sea; many destructions involving burning). It should also be remembered that exact contemporaneity of all these disasters, though not impossible, cannot in fact be proved archaeologically.

The chronological obstacle to assigning the causes of the Cretan LM IB destructions to the Thera volcano outlined above is quite decisive. It now looks certain that Mycenaean invaders (signs of whose presence we can see clearly in LM II Knossos) were directly responsible for many of these destructions and that the only ones which might be connected with the Thera volcano are those which can be dated to LM IA.

What of the other Cycladic islands? Phylakopi and Ayia Irini are of course the most likely to provide evidence. Neither suffered any major destruction in LM IA, though Ayia Irini was devastated by an earthquake in LM IB when some buildings at Phylakopi were also destroyed by fire, perhaps attributable to Mycenaean attack, since a

Mycenaean palace ('megaron') was built at the site not long after. Traces of ash have been found in a a probably LM IA level at Phylakopi but this need mean no more than the similar wind-borne traces in Crete which were discussed above – and, in any case, the ash seems to have been directed to the south east, and thus away from the islands, both by wind and by current. There is no evidence of destruction by tidal wave.

There is no doubt that the Thera catastrophe, as well as having wiped out life on the island for nearly 300 years, must have caused an enormous shock to the inhabitants of the south Aegean – a shock which we may imagine to have been related in contemporary thought with divine wrath.

The worst effects would have been felt in the south-east Aegean where the sun-obscuring ash cloud accumulated in the earliest stages of the eruption and to which subsequent flows of pumice and lava were directed.

Pieces of pumice set in cups in a shrine at Nirou Chani on the north coast of Crete are probably one tiny reminder of the divine terror inspired by these horrendous natural events.

It was not however these events that formed the course that life in the Aegean was to take for the next 400 years, but the newly-emergent Mycenaean power from the Mainland, already growing in strength and ambition, which moved into the vacuum caused by the decline of Minoan Crete.

9

The Mycenaeans and the Cyclades[1]

Early Late Cycladic III

The end of LC II, marked by the earthquake at Ayia Irini and a partial destruction at Phylakopi (III-ii), is a key point of change in the life of the Cyclades. Up to this time, the dominant external cultural influence had been Minoan; afterwards it was Mycenaean.

The devastation of Ayia Irini (end of Period VII) left for posterity the debris of a town filled with the material evidence of Cretan taste. Now parts of the town were repaired and rebuilt – indeed it may have become again, even if briefly, a reasonably prosperous and flourishing centre[2] – but the archaeological connections are entirely Mycenaean.

At Phylakopi the change is even more striking. A part of the town was destroyed by fire when LM IB pottery was in use – that is at approximately the same time as Ayia Irini. Some time later – early in the fourteenth century BC[3] – the area of the site where the LC I mansion had stood was entirely rebuilt to form a distinctive megaron complex, and this period (= LH IIIA:1) is marked, here and elsewhere in the islands, by the appearance of substantial quantities of Mainland pottery.[4]

Even the most superficial comparison between the plan of the Phylakopi complex (Fig. 154) and the main units of the Mycenaean palaces at, for example, Pylos (Fig. 155), Mycenae or Tiryns, can hardly fail to demonstrate the essential fact that there was now a Mycenaean palace on Melos. This is a clear indication that Mainlanders were resident on the island, since purely external political control would presumably have left the local population to run their affairs in their own ways (and from their own administrative buildings), so long as they did not obstruct the policies of their overlords.

There are other features too which emphasise the newly Mycenaean character of Phylakopi. The pottery is one. Virtually all the decorated vases now in use appear to have been imported from Mainland Greece and Minoan influence has been entirely supplanted.

A second building was erected soon after the megaron. This was a shrine complex (Figs. 156, 157), which will be discussed in more detail below. Here it is the fact of its existence and the overall Mycenaean character of the finds which concern us. These are best exemplified by the large wheel-made female terracotta statuette (0.45m high) which has been dubbed 'The Lady of Phylakopi' (Fig. 161). She is dated to the later fourteenth century BC (LH IIIA:2), is decorated with motifs found also on Mycenaean pottery of that period and resembles pieces found at Mycenae. It has been suggested that Mycenaean religious practices now replaced Minoan. If this was so, there must have been a very influential Mycenaean presence.

Nor are Kea and Melos the only islands which have produced evidence of Mycenaean activity in the Cyclades at this period. On Delos there is a large complex of buildings which has been called a 'palace', though it certainly does not include a classic megaron. On Naxos, the extensive coastal settlement at Grotta (modern Naxos) was flourishing now, although it may have been founded earlier.

Elsewhere in the Cyclades, finds of early LC III are mostly from surface exploration and thus not so informative as those from systematic excavations. Nevertheless, some eleven sites[5] have produced material which may be reasonably taken to show that they were first used during early LC III. Dating has to be in Mainland terms because there is no independent Cycladic sequence at this time. Only one of the eleven sites is definitely datable as early as LH IIIA:1 (early fourteenth century BC); the other ten having material of LH IIIA:2-B (c. 1350-1200). These represent over 20 per cent of known Late Cycladic sites and do not include either the major settlements where occupation continues from an earlier period or other sites where the nature of postulated Late Bronze Age occupation is very ill-defined. An interesting development is the first settlement on Thera (at Monolithos) since the LC I catastrophe. In spite of the inevitable qualifications, this evidence suggests that there was quite considerable expansion of settlement in the Cyclades soon after the Mycenaeans had taken control, and covering the periods LH IIIA:1-IIIB:1 (c. 1400-c. 1250 BC).

Some connection between these developments, the volcanic events on Thera described in Chapter 8, and the Mycenaean takeover of Crete seems obvious. The two Cycladic destructions, though only one of them (that at Phylakopi) can certainly be ascribed to physical attack, belong to the same span of time (LM IB)[6] as those in Crete. The same effects follow in both areas – pronounced Mycenaeanisation of material culture. This must represent the translation of the Mycenaean foothold in the Cyclades, which we have already seen represented by substantial imports of pottery in LC I-II, into a military and political takeover.

Evidence from other parts of the Aegean world (the Dodecanese, Asia Minor) fits in with this account – Mycenaeans replacing Minoans. Material from eastern Mediterranean and Egyptian sites shows that the Mycenaeans were becoming active in those areas from the earlier fourteenth century.[7]

The Cyclades now became a prosperous Mycenaean province, located on Mycenaean contact routes with Crete, Anatolia and ultimately Egypt and the eastern Mediterranean – a situation which lasted until the middle of the thirteenth century BC.

Middle Late Cycladic III: signs of trouble in the Aegean

After LH IIIB:1 (c. 1250 BC) there are a number of archaeological indicators that the stability of Aegean life was upset. To start with, a drastic reduction in the amount of pottery imported from the Mainland[8] suggests that communications had become more difficult; and the same conclusion is implied in a general way for the whole of the Mycenaean area, since the pottery is now less standardised and regional variations more apparent.

The character of some Cycladic sites[9] at this period is also significant. At Phylakopi, major fortifications were built (see below), the water-source at Ayia Irini was incorporated into the defensive system to ensure protected access, and Ayios Andreas (Siphnos) and Koukounaries (Paros) were also fortified. The two latter sites differ from Phylakopi in that they were probably settled now for the first time and were located in notably defensive positions – Ayios Andreas on a high inland acropolis, quite remote from the sea; Koukounaries hidden on a concealed cliff-top plateau above the bay of Naoussa (Fig. 153) and approachable only by a steep and easily defensible ascent. Another site that seems to come into this category but is less well known is Ayios Spyridon on Melos, and a further possible candidate is To Froudhi tou Kalamitsou on Siphnos.

That such defences were required, even if sometimes to no avail, is shown by the abandonment of Ayios Andreas soon after 1200 BC and, some years later, the destruction of the Koukounaries settlement in a massive conflagration, in which both men and animals, herded within for protection, perished. This can have been due to nothing other than hostile attack. The recent excavations at Koukounaries have provided a fascinating picture of life (by no means unprosperous) in a fortified Cycladic settlement of this period – and of its grim downfall.

In the last few years it has become clear that developments in the Cyclades are closely linked with, and in some ways parallel, the situation on Mainland Greece.[10] At Mycenae, some buildings outside the citadel were burnt down, possibly in an enemy attack, about 1250 BC, and the next fifty years saw a rash of fortification building at most of the major palace sites – building which frequently included defended spring chambers to ensure access to supplies of water. Ultimately these provisions failed to prevent destruction of all the palaces by about 1200 BC.

Late Late Cycladic III: renewed prosperity

The linkage between Mainland and Cycladic developments continues

153. Koukounaries, Paros, from the east.

into the twelfth century BC. Although the Mainland palaces, as such, had apparently all been destroyed and there was some dispersal of population to areas (including southern Anatolia and Cyprus, though mostly within the Aegean) remote from the former centres of authority, Mycenaean culture in this period (LH IIIC) was far from dead. There are many rich finds, especially from cemeteries, and evidence of widespread external contacts, both within the Aegean and beyond.

Within this period too there was a serious destruction of the shrine at Phylakopi, though it is not possible to tell whether it was due to earthquake or some kind of hostile action. The megaron might have been affected as well, but there is no archaeological indication of the date of its demise.

As we have seen, destruction or abandonment overtook certain Cycladic sites in the late thirteenth and earlier twelfth centuries, but there was some recovery. Koukounaries was reoccupied in a small way and there was limited rebuilding. There is still material from the Phylakopi shrine, which was reused in a contracted form, and two cemeteries on Naxos (Aplomata and Kamini) have produced rich finds.

It is very likely that the partial dispersal of Mainland population after 1200 BC brought new settlers to the Cyclades. Since sites were already strongly Mycenaean in character, such an influx is hard to demonstrate, but the impressive finds from the Naxos tombs[11] (large numbers of decorated vases, gold dress ornaments and cut-outs, distinctive swords) suggest the arrival of a new prosperous group. Who should these be but refugees from the Mainland, who may well have continued to operate the foreign trading contacts that had originally been built up in their former homes? The vases from these tombs have been carefully analysed[12] and shown to include stylistic elements from East Attica, Crete, the Dodecanese and Cyprus, as well as a few imports.

This period of revival may have lasted until the early eleventh century, when Phylakopi was probably abandoned; and Koukounaries as well.

Final Late Cycladic III: the end of Bronze Age civilisation in the Cyclades

Although it is possible to suggest that one or two Cycladic sites continued to be occupied by a few inhabitants (see below, Postscript) through the following two or three centuries until the next great resurgence of civilisation in the Aegean, it seems a more accurate interpretation of the archaeological evidence to say that life came to a temporary halt in the Cyclades in the first half of the eleventh century BC.

The process of transition from late to final LC III cannot yet be properly documented and the historical picture is obscure. Parallels with the Mainland LH IIIC pottery sequence[13] suggest that occupation on Kea continued rather later than elsewhere, perhaps until around the middle of the eleventh century. The pottery from the site is plain and restricted both in range of shape and decoration, and it comes mainly from the Temple, which was by now reduced to a single room built over a corner of the earlier edifice.

Although the relative chronology of events at the different sites is obscure, the overall picture is coherent, if depressing – declining prosperity, reduced resources, decrease or departure of population. On present evidence, it looks as if some sites were abandoned early and quite suddenly (Phylakopi?), while others suffered a slow and debilitating decline (Ayia Irini).

Life in the Cyclades under the Mycenaeans

The basic character of island life under the Mycenaeans was not radically different from the preceding period. The architecture of the islands, conditioned largely, as it was, by local traditions and resources, was not distinctly altered and, while features of Mycenaean rather than Minoan style, taste and technique, appear in most of the artefacts (e.g. pottery, figurines, dress ornaments) the significance of these can best be absorbed in a discussion of some aspects of Cycladic life and culture in LC III.

Material culture

Relatively little LC III pottery has yet been studied in detail[14] and generalisations are somewhat suspect. Nevertheless it seems that early

LC III sees a thoroughgoing transformation of Cycladic material culture which makes it indistinguishable from Mycenaean. The excavators of Ayia Irini have remarked[15] that 'Mycenaean cultural domination is complete. One looks in vain for signs of Cycladic artistic independence and creativity; they are dead.'

Still, for the moment, we should be cautious about assuming that things were the same in every island (or that local features will not be recognised without further study).

In middle and late LC III the situation is rather different and analysis of pottery from Koukounaries and Naxos[16] has shown up features local to these islands, though many too are shared across an Aegean community which stretched from eastern Attica to Rhodes and the Dodecanese. Perhaps the most striking ceramic feature of LC III (late) is the appearance of an elaborate pictorial style (Fig. 159 no. 6). The final stage of LC III is characterised by a drastically restricted range of shapes and decorative motifs. 'White ware' is the most prominent fabric on Kea, but we are not yet in a position properly to define the diagnostic pottery of this phase.

Other classes of object (from the Phylakopi shrine, Koukounaries, the Naxos tombs) also have a strongly Mycenaean character. Most of the terracotta figurines, for instance, found quite widely in the Cyclades, are of types familiar from Mainland Greece, though there is one small group of male figures which are paralleled only in very late contexts in Crete. The significance of this connection is at present obscure but it is just as possible, I suppose, that they are Cycladic objects as Cretan and they may help us to learn something about peculiarly Cycladic elements among the majority that seem of Mycenaean origin.

Architecture and fortifications[17]

With the exception of the Phylakopi megaron and some aspects of the Koukounaries fortifications, no Mycenaean features are immediately apparent in the architecture of LC III, the Cycladic villages continuing essentially in the form they had acquired in earlier times – blocks of small house units divided by streets or alleys, the overall configuration largely dependent on the local terrain.

The Grotta settlement on Naxos, where the first major building period seems to be LH IIIA, although the overall plan is unknown, appears to conform to this character. Recent aerial photographs show a substantial wall on the seaward side of the settlement. There is a good deal of evidence (largely unpublished) of occupation in late LC III and contemporary with the Aplomata and Kamini tombs which must have belonged to the settlement.

At Phylakopi it is not entirely clear how much of the town was rebuilt at the time of the construction of the palace, shrine and adjacent buildings but, with the exception of those buildings, the overall character of the site does not seem to have changed a great deal.

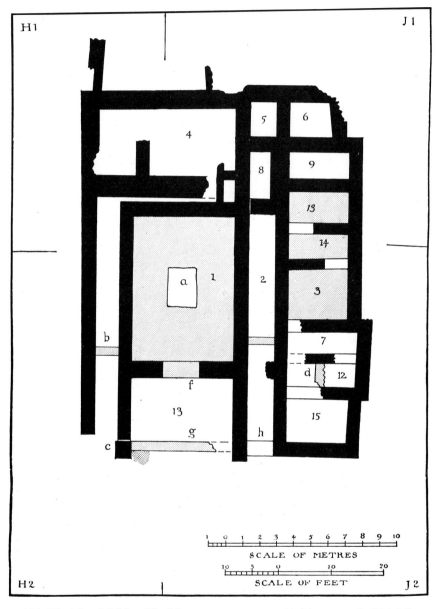

154. Phylakopi, Melos. The Mycenaean megaron. (Atkinson *et al.* 1904, 56).

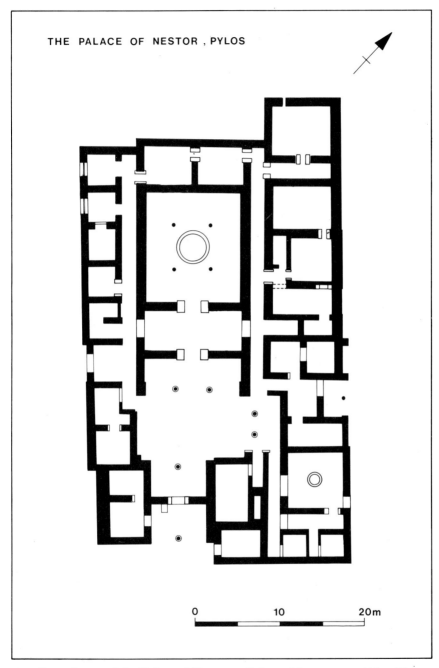

THE PALACE OF NESTOR , PYLOS

0   10   20m

155. Central part of the Palace of Nestor at Pylos, with megaron. (After Blegen and Rawson 1967, endpiece).

The megaron itself (Fig. 154), as has already been indicated, closely resembles similar structures on the Greek Mainland. The central unit consists of an inner hall (7.40 x 6m) approached by a doorway from a portico (6 x 4.60m). There is a large subdivided room behind the main unit and passages to either side. A number of small rooms open off the east passages. The outer entrance (to the portico) has a massive threshold block. The inner room had a thin concrete floor with a rectangular area in the centre of a different material (hardened clay). There was some evidence of painted plaster in the east rooms.

The details of furnishings and functions of the megaron unit are lost to us. Mainland examples (e.g. Pylos: Fig. 155) had fine frescoes on the walls, painted floors, a central hearth often between four columns, a throne and ritual apparatus. The surrounding rooms were for storage or domestic use. No administrative archive (like the Linear B material from Pylos) has yet been discovered, but it is still possible that such may be found.

The shrine was constructed at roughly the same time as the megaron, at the edge of the town (Figs. 156, 157). In its final form it consisted of a large room (6.60 x 6m: the West shrine), with a smaller service chamber to the west again. Another room (the East shrine) was attached to the north-east corner. Communication between the West and East shrines was not direct but via an outside court in which stood a prominent stone or 'baetyl' (0.47m high). The court had a stone bench.

The West shrine was built first (early LC III) and the East added later, though within the same broad early LC III phase. In its earliest form, the West shrine had two entrances, one at the east and one (later blocked) at the south, and a door communicating with the service chamber. There were two niches (also later blocked), one to either side of the door into the service chamber. It is suggested that these were for the display of ritual objects kept in the secondary room. Platform-altars were found in both shrines.

In middle LC III the layout of the sanctuary changed following a serious collapse. Much of the contents were destroyed and some of the architectural debris was used to form a blocking wall which divided the West shrine into two, only the north half now remaining in use (together with the East shrine).

Other LC III sites are less informative architecturally. At Kea, reoccupation after the LC II earthquake was quite extensive. The old buildings were repaired and re-used, though from ground level only, the basements being left full of debris.

The mid-thirteenth-century fortified settlements of Koukounaries and Ayios Andreas consisted of houses within restricted fortified areas. Ayios Andreas has quite regular blocks of buildings suggesting an orderly plan. At Koukounaries the complex is a single architectural unit or 'mansion', some 22m long and over 16.5m broad. The south side which faces the path of ascent is retained by a massive wall which may originally have been about 9m high (Fig. 50). The lowest rooms were cellars and have

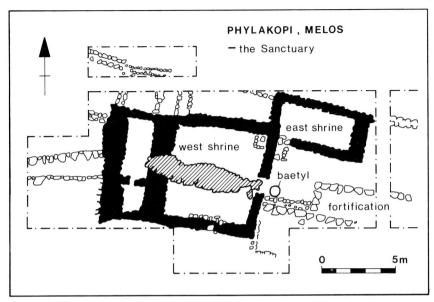

156. Phylakopi, Melos. Plan of the Mycenaean sanctuary. (After Renfrew 1981a, 8).

157. Phylakopi, Melos. The Mycenaean sanctuary from the west. (C. Renfrew).

produced large numbers of finds – storage vessels, domestic artefacts such as obsidian blades and terracotta spindlewhorls, and some weapons and luxury items. The rooms of the mansion are divided by two main passages (running west-east and north-south). One entrance may have been via a gate (and court) at the west of the fortification wall and another at the north. The thick central wall dividing the rooms in squares D 3 and 4 and the discovery of an ivory inlay from some fine piece of furniture (possibly a throne) have inspired the suggestion that there was a Mycenaean-style megaron on the first floor, though it must be said that this is not in any way conclusive.

The terrace/fortification wall, which consists of two faces of large roughly squared blocks with rubble infill and has insets in its outer face, resembles Mainland fortifications in those respects.

Such Mycenaean features make it possible that Koukounaries was the home of early refugees from the Mainland, since it was founded at the time when the contraction of Mycenaean civilisation begins to be evident.

There are traces of buildings, and a further fortification system, on part of the lower slopes of the hill. The area as a whole thus seems to have been quite extensively settled but the mansion would presumably have been the centre of administration – and the final place of refuge. In the end, it was attacked and burnt down in a massive conflagration. Human and animal remains show that defenders and their flocks were trapped in the destruction.

Fortifications[18]

These remain a feature of Cycladic towns in LC III, though there are some chronological uncertainties. The LC I system at Phylakopi presumably continued in use until substantial changes were made in the middle of the thirteenth century. These seem to have involved a more massive wall, of which a section was uncovered in the vicinity of the shrine in the recent excavations, and the addition of towers/bastions and casemates to the west sector (Fig. 49). If the whole of the west sector was actually constructed at this time, those elements were presumably added to it later in LC III.

It is not clear whether the Kea fortifications were actually in use in this period, but we have seen that in the mid-thirteenth century Koukounaries was protected by a massive Cyclopean wall (Fig. 50) which combined the functions of retaining the terrace on which the buildings stood and blocking the final part of the ascent to the site (a stepped approach through an easily protected defile). There was also a further selective defence system, down the slope and thus protecting an area considerably larger than the citadel itself – an arrangement which is unique in our present knowledge of Cycladic fortifications. About the same time, Ayios Andreas on Siphnos was provided with a double circuit which had gates and square projecting towers.

The wall at Phylakopi included both rough ashlar and rounded sea-shore boulders, the latter being much more evident in the recently discovered east stretch and contributing to the view that this part may be of a different date from that at the west. The best preserved section, at the west end of the site, is built of large roughly dressed stones (Fig. 49). The wall is double, with central crosswalls linking the inner and outer elements. The intervening spaces were mostly filled with rubble, giving a total wall thickness of about 6m, though some of the spaces were thought to have been used as rooms. The line of the wall is not straight but quite strongly indented to form projecting bastions. Some additions were made during the life of the system, in a less careful style of masonry. One of these was a projecting bastion in square B 5, which is not bonded in with the main wall. Another such (D 5-6) contains a staircase approached by a passage and door through the thickness of the wall and presumably leading to the rampart. There is an outwork in front of the main wall.

On Siphnos, the material is neatly laid flat slabs. On Paros, the wall has two faces of large roughly worked stones, with a rubble infill.

Burials[19]

Along with other elements of material culture, Mycenaean tomb-types and burial practices seem to have been adopted in the Cyclades in this period, although there is of course no means of telling whether Mycenaeans or islanders were buried in the tombs that are known. Most of these are chambers cut into the rock. In spite of the fact that this was a characteristically Mycenaean kind of tomb, it should not be forgotten that rock-cut chambers were used in the Cyclades as early as EC IIIB, although none are known from the intervening period. Most of the known tombs are from the Aplomata and nearby Kamini cemeteries on Naxos. Some of the chamber tombs at Phylakopi could belong to this period, although there is no good dating evidence. Another chamber tomb (early LC III) was found at Langadha on Melos. Otherwise whole vases from various islands are probably from burials, since pottery from settlements is usually broken – but the form of the tombs is unknown.

One of the most interesting of recent (1979) discoveries in the Cyclades was a real beehive or 'tholos' tomb at Ayia Thekla on Tenos. This reproduces the system used in the most elaborate of Late Bronze Age tombs on the Mainland, in which the chamber (cut into the hillside) is lined with stones and the upper part corbelled inwards until a small aperture is left at the apex, which is then closed with a capstone. The Ayia Thekla tholos, which contained many vases, was used in the LH IIIB period (early to middle LC III). It was of rather crude construction of unworked local stone.

One other tholos tomb was found early this century at Khosti, near the modern village of Komiaki on Naxos, although it cannot now be located. Two other 'domed' tombs ('Kuppelgräber') which were reported from Mykonos in the nineteenth century might have been tholoi but might

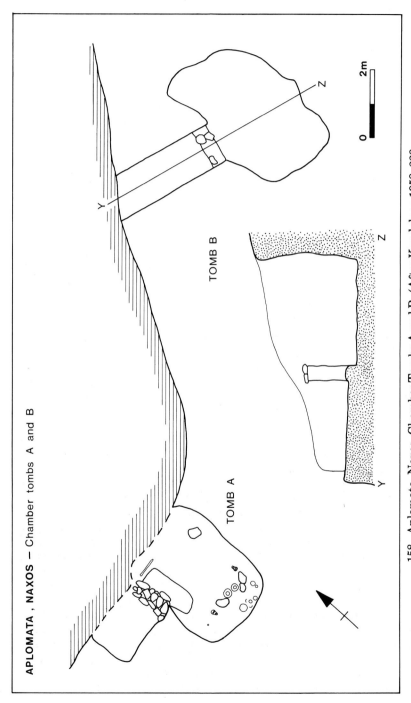

APLOMATA , NAXOS – Chamber tombs A and B

TOMB B

TOMB A

158. Aplomata, Naxos. Chamber Tombs A and B. (After Kondoleon 1958, 228; 1959, 180, 181).

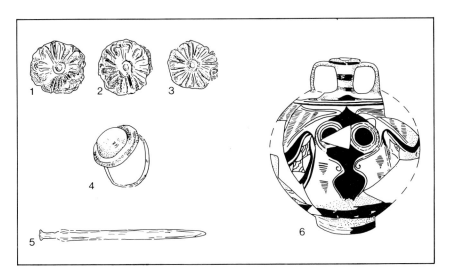

159. Gold dress ornaments (1-3), bronze ring (4), bronze sword (5) and Octopus stirrup jar (6, late LC III) from the tombs at Aplomata, Naxos. (After Kardara 1977, pls. 4a, 7e, 15a).

also have been straight forward rock-cut chambers. No trace of them survives.

For the sake of completeness, it should be mentioned that some shaft graves in the vicinity of Phylakopi may have belonged to this period, though there was no proper dating evidence.

It is noticeable that the cist tomb – the grave type with the longest continuous history in the Cyclades – is now no longer known, the latest examples being those from Aila on Naxos in LC I.

The Mycenaean cemeteries on Naxos, which must have belonged to the Grotta settlement, are situated on the hillside above the town. The three tombs found on the Aplomata ridge were rock-cut chambers approached by short passages (Fig. 158). Their entrances were blocked with stone fillings in the usual manner, which could be removed when new burials were to be inserted. Although one or two of the non-ceramic finds may be earlier than the twelfth century, all the pottery, and thus presumably most of the burials, belong to this period (LH IIIC). The finds from the tombs show the use of standard Mycenaean burial practices, according to which the dead person was laid to rest with due ceremony on the the floor of the tomb. When there was no room for a burial, earlier remains were put to one side. Thus skeletal remains and grave goods accumulated within a tomb.

The finds from the three excavated tombs on Aplomata show that, though pottery was the most common burial gift, the dead were interred wearing their fine clothes, jewellery and weapons, as appropriate, and with other objects (Fig. 159) as well. From Tomb B came 85 gold rosettes, with repoussée decoration (Fig. 153 nos. 1-3), which had probably been sewn on to a garment worn by one of the dead. Other finds from the three tombs included bronze weapons, gold rings, stone necklace beads, gold leaf lions (perhaps the ornate coverings for a harder material), a cylinder seal, some fragments of ivory, lead and of a silver vase. There were even some pieces of iron – a very rare material at that time. An area of burnt earth and fragments of charcoal adhering to some of the bones may be evidence of cremation. This was quite exceptional, though one or two instances are known from Aegean cemeteries (Eleona on Kos and Perati in East Attica) of the same period.

The excavator thought that Tomb A (gold lions and a dagger) was probably used for male burials and Tomb B (dress ornaments) for female, but this is not easily proved.

Among the vases were some imports, from Crete and East Attica, and some signs in the decoration of stylistic relationships with the eastern Mediterranean. Much of the pottery however is distinctly Naxian in style.

The Kamini tombs (only 0.5km from Aplomata) comprised three rock-cut chambers, another perhaps similar which has not been fully described and a child burial in a pit of which one side was walled. They contained about 150 vases, both simply and more elaborately decorated. Tomb A had at least two burials, one of which had been deposited late in the life of the tomb, after it had collapsed. There were traces of burning, though apparently not associated with the actual disposal of the dead. Tomb B had the remains of six burials collected together by the entrance and a seventh in the centre of the tomb at a higher level. Tomb G had one burial. In the right-hand wall of the dromos was a cutting closed by a small wall which contained a pot, perhaps originally associated with the burial of a child.

Apart from the vases, the finds included bronze weapons and jewellery, some gold and silver rings and beads and gold leaf (some in the form of bulls' heads; others with applied representations of children) as well as beads of semi-precious stones and some seals. Of particular interest are an iron knife or dagger and some long bronze dress pins of a kind known from the very end of the Bronze Age and the beginning of the Iron Age on the Mainland. Four vases decorated with scenes of dancers were found outside the tomb and have been plausibly associated with cemetery ritual. Burnt animal bones from the tomb with the pyre may also have been part of a ritual.

The finds in the Naxos tombs are particularly important, partly because of their richness and the suggestion (perhaps supported by the royal and ritual symbolism of the gold lion and bull motifs) that some may have contained the burial of refugee Mycenaean kings: partly because some of the Kamini material seems to belong to the final phase of LC III, and the placement of burials in already collapsed tombs surely suggests a situation where resources were lacking or where extreme haste was necessary.

160. Mycenaean ivory plaque of
warrior from Delos. (École Française
d'Athènes).

Religion

Evidence for religious practices not directly connected with burial comes
from Delos, Kea and, most fully, Phylakopi.

Delos

Delos is richer in finds than structures. Attempts have been made to
show that this island, which was a major Greek sanctuary in the Iron
Age, was of religious importance too in the Bronze Age. Four later shrines
are said to have developed on the sites of prehistoric burials but this is
highly speculative. The most important finds come from a deposit below
the important archaic temple of Artemis and represent either the
remains of earlier activity on the same site or a foundation votive deposit
for the Artemision, probably both. The finds included gold jewellery and
other objects (miniature birds, bees and animals, arrowheads, a
spindlewhorl, Mycenaean terracotta animal figurines and models and a

series of ivory plaques and cut-outs decorated with incised or relief decoration: Fig. 160). The latter are in a distinctively Mycenaean (possibly Cypro-Mycenaean) style and have characteristic scenes of warriors, animals (some in combat) and so on.

These are fine and precious objects indeed but the deposit as a whole is of a rather miscellaneous character, as the above mentioned items show, and would be quite appropriate to a votive deposit whose constituents came from worshippers with very different preoccupations (domestic, agricultural, military etc.). They may indeed represent ritual activity in the LC III period.

In common with other sites, Delos has also yielded several examples of typical Mycenaean terracotta figures (female figures, animals, models) which had ritual purpose but are commonly found in settlements as well as shrines. Nevertheless they demonstrate the adoption of specifically Mycenaean practices.

Delos has also produced the third example (the other two are from the shrine complex at Phylakopi) of bronze figures of Reshef – the 'Smiting God', whose home is in the Near East. Although it is possible that these figures were made in the Aegean, it seems much more likely that they were dedicated in Aegean shrines by sailors (either Greek or Near Eastern) who had brought them back from abroad.

Ayia Irini

Even after the LC II earthquake had devastated Ayia Irini, the Temple continued to be a focus of activity. The building was partially cleared and new platforms were constructed. One or two of the large terracotta figures were made in this period (in a different technique) and fragments of others were perhaps reused. But the majority lay buried in the earthquake debris and the ritual of the shrine must have taken on a very different aspect with their absence. It is possible that this would have happened in any case with the general dominance of Mycenaean influence and perhaps resident Mycenaeans and that the effect of the earthquake was almost incidental in this respect.

In the later part of LC III, the area in use gradually shrank until, by the final stage, although the original location and orientation were preserved, the shrine structure had been reduced to a small room built over the north-east corner of the former Temple. Apart from the disappearance of the terracotta figures, observances seem to have been conducted in a similar manner to previously. There are many drinking vessels and evidence of burnt sacrifice.

Phylakopi

The shrine at Phylakopi, whose physical layout has already been described, yielded more specific evidence of ritual activity which to some extent parallels that known from shrines on Mainland Greece (e.g.

162. Fragmentary Mycenaean terracotta 'psi' figurine from the sanctuary at Phylakopi. (C. Renfrew).

161. Mycenaean terracotta figure – the 'Lady of Phylakopi' – from the sanctuary. (C. Renfrew).

163. Fragmentary Mycenaean terracotta 'psi' figurine from the sanctuary at Phylakopi. (C. Renfrew).

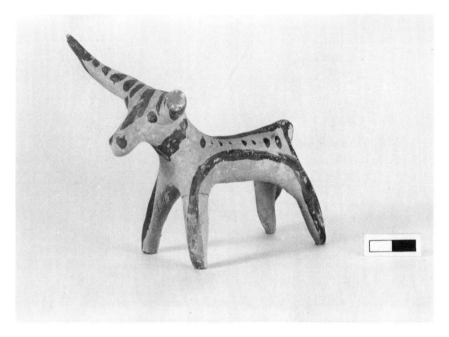

164. Myceanean terracotta figurine of animal from the sanctuary at Phylakopi.
(C. Renfrew).

Mycenae and Tiryns). Apart from the large (0.45m high) Lady of
Phylakopi (Fig. 161) found in the service room attached to the west
shrine, which finds counterparts at Mycenae, the shrine contained other
figures. Most of these are of known Mycenaean types. There are standard
human (Figs. 162, 163) and animal (Fig. 164) figures, some of the latter of
a type (wheel-made with hollow bodies and used as rhyta (hollow pouring
vessels)) sometimes thought to span the transition from Bronze to Iron
Age. A miniature gold leaf head (cf. the Naxos tombs), fragments of an
ostrich-egg vase and triton and tortoiseshells, not to mention the two
Reshef figures, add to the aura of ritual activity. One group of male
figurines (Figs. 165, 166) – thin, with squareish torsos and prominent
genitalia – have parallels only in Crete and might represent a local
element in whatever rites were practised in the shrine. They were found
fallen from one of the altars in the West shrine – on which they had
originally stood, mirroring a practice which we have already seen earlier
on Kea and which was standard in Mycenaean and Minoan shrines, of
setting figures on altars or benches (Fig. 167). Objects such as sealstones
presumably represent either offerings or the stamp of the goddess.
Pottery vessels, stands etc. were ritual paraphernalia.

Other items from the Phylakopi shrine (the baetyl in the court, the
carved column) are less easy to place in the context of what we know of
Mycenaean religion.

165. Terracotta male figurine from the sanctuary at Phylakopi. (C. Renfrew).

166. As Fig. 165, side view. (C. Renfrew).

167. Phylakopi, Melos. The West Shrine with platforms. (C. Renfrew).

The evidence from both Phylakopi and Kea suggests that obviously Cretan elements (the terracotta figures at Kea, the pillar rooms and a few other probably ritual objects at Phylakopi) which were evident in LC I-II have now disappeared. Taken together with the Mycenaean character of the artefacts, this seems yet another reflection of the dominance of Mycenaean attitudes. Further study may eventually allow us to postulate some distinctive local practices – or at least regional variations on a common Aegean religion – in Late Cycladic culture.[20]

Postscript: the end of the Bronze Age in the Cyclades

Both the chronology and the causes of the disappearance of Cycladic settlements in the eleventh century BC are obscure. At present it looks as if a cluster of inhabitants hung on at Ayia Irini rather longer than elsewhere, but it is hard to be sure, especially since a breakdown of intercommunications may have produced a situation where different sites came to use quite different kinds of objects (especially pottery), which are impossible to relate to each other archaeologically.

Since there is no evidence of destructions having terminated the existence of the settlements, we must assume that they ran down

168. Fragment of an Attic black-glazed cup of the fifth century BC, inscribed with a dedication to Dionysos, from the Temple at Ayia Irini, Kea. (University of Cincinnati).

gradually, in a worsening economic climate and, in most cases, finally faded out completely.

We know from later Greek tradition, dialect distribution, and the evidence of the first Iron Age pottery style (Protogeometric), which spread from Mainland Greece across the Aegean, that these Dark Ages[21] were a time of movement and migration, in which the Cycladic islanders must have been involved. The later stages of this migration period (ninth to eighth centuries BC) saw the establishment of new settlers and new settlements in some of the Cyclades: others may have arrived even earlier.

At Koukounaries a new town was built in the Geometric period over the ruined LC III mansion. Zagora (on Andros) and the little island of Donoussa (south east of Naxos) were settled now for the first time.

But do all the Iron Age settlements represent completely fresh starts? Is it possible that some inhabitants remained on the island sites, where there had been Bronze Age occupation, in the intervening period? On the face of it, it seems extremely unlikely that the islands would have been totally depopulated and the archaeological evidence, though scanty, tends to confirm that suspicion. Though it is virtually impossible to prove continuity of occupation at any specific site, there are occasional finds of both SubMycenaean and Protogeometric pottery in the Cyclades and these are the two ceramic stages which link the latest Mycenaean and the earliest Geometric pottery styles. Some of the wheel-made figurines and the pins from the Kamini tombs may fit into this intervening phase; conceivably also the male figures from the Phylakopi shrine with late parallels in Crete, though the pottery does not seem to support so late a date.

Such finds however are very few and it looks as if the survivors of the prosperous late LC III settlements eked out a precarious existence in flimsy shelters in or near their former homes. When new settlers came, the sites were rebuilt on new lines – or completely different locations were chosen. The remote and defensive situations of some of these (Zagora, Donoussa) show that times were hard.

At Grotta on Naxos, continuity of occupation has been claimed. The finds do not disprove it, but there was certainly architectural discontinuity between latest Mycenaean and Protogeometric times, since the Protogeometric structures located above the Mycenaean were quite differently aligned. At Koukounaries there are some Sub-Mycenaean and Protogeometric vases, but again the buildings of the Mycenaean and Geometric periods are differently aligned and widely separated in time. At Ayia Irini, offerings were made in the Temple shrine throughout the Dark Ages, perhaps continuously, until it became a shrine of Dionysos (Fig. 168) some time before 500 BC.

It is an analyst's convenience, though a depressing one, to say that, to all intents and purposes, life in the Cyclades came to an end in the early eleventh century BC and the Iron Age culture which later developed in the islands was a new and different phenomenon, with a negligible debt to the past.

Notes

Chapter 1

1. The geography and resources of the Cyclades, as well as their geology, climate etc., are conveniently summarised in Naval Intelligence Division 1944-5, I-III. The parts relevant to the Cyclades are I, 31-4 (bibliography, p. 34); III, 408-87 (bibliography, p. 487). The latter section includes entries on each island.
   Also useful are Cary 1949 (chs 1-3); Bintliff 1977 (Part 2, chs 6 and 7 are on Melos and Mykonos respectively); Renfrew and Wagstaff 1982 *passim*.
2. Population figures for the Cyclades have been conveniently collected by Kolodny (1974; see II, 794-5 (Table VII) for the Cyclades). The source for the 1981 figures is the *Pragmatikos Plithismos tis Elladhos kata tin apographi tis 5 Apriliou 1981* 1982 (Athens, National Statistical Service of Greece) 127.

Total figures:	1879	132,020
	1951	125,959
	1971	86,337
	1981	88,458

3. The Bronze Age agriculture of the Cyclades is discussed by J.M. Renfrew (1982), and in other articles in Renfrew and Wagstaff 1982. Papers relating mainly to the island of Thera may be found in Doumas (ed.) 1978 as follows: Davidson 1978 (soils); Rackham 1978 (flora and vegetation); Turner 1978 (vegetation). Discussion of the above papers is reported in Doumas (ed.) 1980, 285, 290-2, 293-4. This volume also includes a further paper: Diapoulis 1982 (plants).
4. Turner 1978; Wagstaff and Gamble 1982, 97-8; Meiggs 1982, ch. 4 for a helpful discussion of the uses of wood in the Bronze Age.
5. An important recent study of traditional crafts and practices in the Cyclades is Connell 1980. Du Boulay 1974, though primarily an anthropological work, is very illuminating on daily life in a peasant community. Agricultural methods are well illustrated in Theochares 1973, pls. 142-72 and Mouseio Benaki 1978. Aspects of household life in a Turkish village are treated by Weinstein 1973. A discussion of traditional land use on Melos is in Wagstaff and Augustson 1982.
6. Wagstaff and Gamble, 1982, 95-7; McCoy 1982.
7. See above, n. 5; and Chapter 8 (for evidence from Akrotiri).
8. Animal remains from Phylakopi and their significance are assessed by Gamble 1982. For faunal remains from Akrotiri, see Gamble 1978 (with Doumas 1982, 286-9). For Ayia Irini, see Coy 1973.
9. Gamble 1982, 168.
10. The role of fishing as an important element in the economy of Bronze Age

Melos is discussed by Bintliff 1977, 539-43 (criticised by Gamble (1979, 126-7; 1982, 171, n. 1)).

11. For general treatment of these resources, see works cited in n. 1. More detailed references may be found in subsequent chapters (especially Chapters 4 and 5), where architecture and artefacts are discussed in their historical contexts.

12. Shipping in the prehistoric Mediterranean is described by Casson (1971, 30-42), with useful comments on seasons, winds, sailing tactics and voyage lengths (270-99). Specific descriptions of Cycladic coasts and waters are given in Admiralty (Hydrographic Department) 1918, IV, 172-226. The Thera ship fresco is relevant to the seasonal nature of Bronze Age navigation: Morgan Brown 1978, 641.

13. Marinatos 1968-76, VI, pl. 9.

14. Melos: Davidson, Renfrew and Tasker 1976. For sea-level changes in the Bronze Age Aegean, see Rapp and Kraft 1978 (with Doumas 1980 (ed.) 272-3); Davidson and Tasker 1982.

15. Davis 1979.

16. Ovenden 1966

Chapter 2

1. For the basic evidence on which the sequence is founded, see below, nn. 4, 6, 11, 12, 16, 18, 21, 23-7. The archaeological material, including the pottery, is discussed in subsequent chapters.

2. For a full recent survey of the Neolithic and Early Bronze Age with a list of radiocarbon dates see Coleman (forthcoming). For a survey of radiocarbon evidence for the absolute chronology of the Cycladic Bronze Age, see Betancourt and Lawn 1984. Evidence and interconnections for the Aegean Bronze Age as a whole are surveyed by Cadogan (1978).

3. The new system is explained in Renfrew 1972, 53-5, and applied throughout that volume. Some weaknesses in the method of cultural identification were pointed out by Coleman (1974, 340), and fuller presentation of his and Renfrew's opposing points of view may be found in Coleman 1979a, 1979b and Renfrew 1979.

For some brief but pertinent remarks on problems of Cycladic and Aegean terminology in general, see Caskey 1978.

For the views of the present writer in favour of retaining the established system, see Barber and Macgillivray 1980, especially 142-4; 154-7; Barber 1983, 80-1 (n. 27 for other supporters of this viewpoint).

For the division of Early Cycladic material into groups, see Doumas 1977a, 11-27. (Readers should note that the groups are there assigned to the culture system, but the same writer (1982, 6, n. 12) now regards a historical framework as preferable).

4. The Neolithic period in the Cyclades has been most conveniently summarised by Coleman (n. 2 above and 1974). See also Renfrew 1972, 66, 75-6, 507-9 and Fig. Appx. I.1 (site list and map); Cherry 1979, 25-37; Cherry and Torrence 1982.

The two excavated sites have been published – Saliagos: Evans and Renfrew 1968; Kephala: Coleman 1977a. For a new view of the relationships of the Saliagos material, see Hadjianastasiou (forthcoming).

5. For a discussion of Early Cycladic-related material at Kephala, see Coleman

1977a, 104-7; 109-10 (radiocarbon dates) and Coleman (forthcoming).

6. See again n. 1. EC I material is summarised in Coleman (forthcoming); Barber and Macgillivray 1980, 144-8; and there are other brief but useful observations in Coleman 1974, 341, and Caskey 1971c, 797. The period is treated in more detail in Renfrew 1972, 152-69 (under the title 'Grotta-Pelos culture') and in Doumas 1977a, 15-20 and tables on pp. 25, 26 (the Lakkoudes, Pelos, Plastiras and Kampos groups).

7. Early Cycladic material from Phylakopi was published in the original report (Atkinson *et al.* 1904, 82-7; 239-48). See also Barber and Macgillivray 1980 *passim*. More recent finds (1974-7 excavations) are mentioned in Catling 1976, 25; Renfrew 1978, 405 (table II) with a more extended discussion in Evans and Renfrew 1984 (a preliminary presentation of material from the 1974-7 excavations).

8. See n. 6 above.

9. The Kampos group was originally defined by E.-M. Bossert (1965). It has been now much expanded and has perhaps ceased to be a coherent unit (Zapheiropoulou 1984; Renfrew 1984, 50; Coleman (forthcoming)).

10. See Chapter 5 (ii) below, for further discussion of the pottery types of the different Early Cycladic phases.

11. For EC II, see Barber and Macgillivray 1980, 148-50; Caskey 1971c, 795-7 (though the Chalandriani acropolis referred to (=Kastri) should be dated to EC IIIA rather than EC II. The cemetery is mainly EC II – Coleman 1974, 341; Coleman (forthcoming). EC II appears as the 'Keros-Syros culture' in Renfrew 1972, 170-85 and Doumas 1977a, 20-2 (Syros group only: the Kastri and Amorgos groups are essentially EC IIIA and EC IIIB respectively). Material from Ayia Irini is in Caskey 1972, 362-9; see also Coleman 1974, 343.

12. EC IIIA is defined and discussed in Barber and Macgillivray 1980, 150-1. As the 'Kastri' group of the Keros-Syros culture, it is treated in Renfrew 1972, 533-4 and Doumas 1977a, 22-3. See also Coleman 1974, 343. A key deposit of this phase from Kea is published in Wilson and Eliot 1984 (with references to Caskey 1972, 370-5) and material from Delos (Mount Kynthos) in Macgillivray 1980 (Group B). For possibly Anatolian metal at Kastri, see Gale and Stos Gale 1984, 268-9. For new EC IIIA material from the Cave of Zas on Naxos, I am most grateful to the excavator, K. Zachos, for information.

Terminology. The subdivision of EC III into A and B and the choice of these terms has been the subject of disagreement (see Rutter 1983, Barber 1983, Macgillivray 1983). This disagreement is linked to that over the existence or otherwise of a hiatus in the Cycladic sequence, which is discussed in the main text of this chapter.

The subdivision into A and B was proposed for two reasons. The first was that the archaeological character of the Anatolian-related material is highly distinctive and, together with several other features, represents a period of dramatic historical change in the Cyclades. Secondly, this stage is shown by the Kea stratigraphy to postdate EC II and, by pottery analysis and finds from other sites (see main text), to precede that originally called EC III (now EC IIIB). The term EC III seemed appropriate to mark the inauguration of a new phase in Cycladic history. By dividing A and B, the term EC III could still be used of the previously designated material which has, in any case, some stylistic connections with that of EC IIIA.

Critics of this approach prefer to call the new material EC IIB in recognition of the fact that it is first found in association with EC II pottery and because they regard it as contemporary with EH II on the Greek mainland (a view not accepted in the first camp). For similar reasons, the same scholars prefer to rename EC IIIB as Middle Cycladic, thus leaving a completely artificial EC III period, which has no material characteristics. For this proposal by Rutter, and criticism by Barber and Macgillivray, see those authors 1983, also Barber 1984c. For implied redefinition of EC IIIB as Middle Cycladic, see also Overbeck 1979, 114.

13. See n. 12 above.

14. For a full discussion of intrusive features in the context of invasions, see Hood 1986; also Gale and Gale 1984, 268-71.

15. That there is disagreement about the relative chronology here will be evident from n. 12 above. This stems from different views of the nature of the Early Helladic pottery sequence which are covered in the works cited there.

16. For definition and discussion of EC IIIB, see Barber and Macgillivray 1980, 151-3; also Caskey 1971c, 794-5. As the 'Phylakopi I culture', it is discussed in Renfrew 1972, 186-95, and Doumas 1977a, 23-4. Some material also appears in the 'Amorgos Group' (Renfrew 1972, 534-5; Doumas 1977a, 23-6) whose status needs reinvestigation.

For a pottery-based assessment of the position of EC IIIB within the Early Cycladic sequence, see Barber 1984c.

17. For relationships between Phylakopi and Ayia Irini, see Overbeck 1979, 114-17; Barber 1981b, 175-6; 1983, 78-9.

18. The Middle Cycladic period and its subdivision are set out in Barber and Macgillivray 1980, 153-4, and see further Overbeck 1979, with Barber 1983. The period as a whole is also discussed by Barber 1978a and Caskey 1973a. An earlier survey is included in Scholes 1956, 36-9. Some comments on the Middle Cycladic period at Akrotiri may be found in Doumas 1978b and 1983a, 27-8, and Marthari 1980. Important evidence for the ceramic and architectural sequence at Akrotiri at the end of the Middle Bronze Age is presented by Marthari (1984) and Palyvou (1984). Davis (1985) presents the finds from the later Middle Bronze Age at Ayia Irini (Period V).

19. Barber 1978, 377; 1983; Overbeck 1979, 117. But finds from Ftellos, Thera (n. 20) look to be characteristic of just such a phase!

20. Marthari 1983. For Middle Cycladic burials, see Chapter 6.

21. The Late Cycladic period as a whole was first reviewed by Scholes 1956, though an earlier survey by Furumark (1950) – the Cyclades discussed pp. 192-201 – in the wider context of Aegean prehistory in the Late Bronze Age is still very useful. A more recent survey, from which the subdivisions adopted in this chapter are taken, is by Barber (1981), where fuller details of the sequence, a site list and further references may be found. For modifications of the LC III framework see Barber and Macgillivray 1984, 301 (table). Cummer and Schofield 1984, is now of fundamental importance.

For LC I, see Barber 1981a, 2-6; Cummer and Schofield *passim* (p. 32 for destruction levels within LC I). Many useful works on various aspects of the earlier Late Cycladic period are cited in the notes to Chapter 7. Aspects of the sequence are treated in Davis and Cherry 1984; Schofield 1984; Renfrew 1978b.

22. Palyvou 1984.

23. Barber 1981a, 6-8; see also Schofield 1984; Cummer and Schofield 1984, 2.

24. Barber 1981a, 8-15; Cummer and Schofield 1984 *passim*; and see below, Chapter 9. For the 'Late Phase', see Kardara 1977 (Aplomata tombs); Mountjoy 1985 (Phylakopi shrine); Schilardi 1984 and Koehl 1984 (Koukounaries).

25. This subdivision was not employed in Barber 1981a but now seems necessary to accommodate the latest material in the sequence (Macgillivray and Barber 1984, 300 and 301 (table)).

Chapter 3

1. The only work specifically concerned with the history of archaeological research in the Cyclades is Doumas 1977c. See also Doumas 1977a, 27-8, for work in Early Cycladic cemeteries.
For full details of works mentioned in this chapter, see Bibliography; for sites and related publications, see subsequent chapters.

2. See Chapter 8.

3. Sir Arthur Evans collated the Cycladic material in the Ashmolean Museum, Oxford, with his finds from Crete, producing a parallel Cycladic sequence. See also Harland 1924 and the Cycladic entries in Fimmen 1924, 13-15.

4. See Chapters 4 and 9.

5. See Bibliography (abbreviations), *AR* (English), *BCH* (French); also (Greek) *Ergon, AD, PAE. AR* is obtainable from The Secretary, Hellenic Society, 31-34 Gordon Square, London WC1.

Chapter 4

1. Factors governing site location have been fully assessed by Bintliff 1977. Of the Cyclades, he considered individually Melos (Part 2, ch. 6) and Mykonos (Part 2, ch. 7). His conclusion that proximity to food resources (agriculture and fishing) in the interests of basic self-sufficiency was of absolutely overriding importance in the choice of sites has been criticised by C. Gamble (1979, 126-7; see also 1982, 171, n. 1), who suggests that the position of each site was determined not so much by its own need for self-sufficiency in food as by its role within a broader regional organisation of sites such as must have developed in the more complex social environment of the Bronze Age. As evidence for this from Melos, he points out that Phylakopi does not, on the basis of excavation finds, appear to have exploited its favourable fishing location and that the same site was far from conveniently placed *vis-à-vis* the best agricultural land on the island. Other factors therefore must have weighed heavily in the choice of location.
The location of Early Cycladic settlements is also discussed by C. Doumas (1972).

2. For cisterns: at Ayios Andreas, Philippaki 1977, 360; at Phylakopi (rock-cut chamber, more probably a tomb), Atkinson *et al.* 1904, 236. Waterspout: Marinatos 1968-76, III, 17, pl. 15-2. Clay pipes: ibid. III, 52, fig. 29. Terracotta runnel: Atkinson *et al.* 1904, 61, fig. 57, 275 (index: drainage and water conduits). The use of pithoi for water collection and storage was suggested by Caskey 1971, 365, because of the frequent discovery of such vessels in the houses of the settlement at Ayia Irini.

3. Tunny fishing: Bintliff 1977, 539-42; Gamble (see n. 1 above).

4. For references, see n. 16 below.

5. There is no work solely devoted to this topic but it is covered in the works cited in relation to the discussion of settlements (n. 7).

6. This analysis may be found in Hall *et al.* 1973, 248.

7. For Early Cycladic sites, see Doumas 1972. There are no synthetic discussions of Middle or Late Cycladic settlements. The most useful works (also with some reference to Early Cycladic material) are Atkinson *et al.* 1904, ch. II; Caskey 1971; Rubensohn 1917. For Middle/Late Cycladic Akrotiri, Palyvou 1984;

for the main town at Akrotiri, Doumas 1974; 1983a, ch. 4; Shaw 1978. Also useful in this context is Shaw's survey (1971) of Minoan architecture (materials and techniques).

For information on the character of Cycladic villages of more recent times, see Doumanis and Oliver 1974, 53-97; Wagstaff and Cherry 1982, 146-55.

8. Hood 1986.

9. See n. 16 below.

10. Renfrew 1978b, 411-12 and pl. D (p. 417).

11. Caskey 1971, 384-6 and refs.

12. Atkinson *et al.* 1904, 55-8, and see n. 10.

13. Renfrew l978a; 1981a.

14. Gallet de Santerre 1958, 83-4.

15. Balos: Fouqué 1879, 118-23; Ftellos: Doumas 1973; Therasia: Fouqué 1879, 94-6; Karvounolakkoi: Zapheiropoulos 1965, 505-6.

16. Panormos: Doumas 1964, 411-12; Kastri: Bossert 1967; Mount Kynthos: Plassart 1928, ch. 1; Macgillivray 1980, 4-8; Phylakopi: Atkinson *et al.* 1904, 30-5; Renfrew 1978b, 407-8; Ayia Irini: Caskey 1971, 363-5, 367-8, 373-7. Ayios Andreas: Philippaki 1973; Koukounaries: Schilardi 1984 and refs.

17. Surface evidence for Cycladic settlement in the Neolithic and Early Bronze Age was collected by Renfrew (1972, 507-25), who also discussed the problems of estimating the extent and intensity of settlement (ibid. 225-64, the whole Aegean area). The results of an intensive survey of parts of Melos and their significance for interpretation of the existing body of information for Cycladic Bronze Age settlement, with a review of Renfrew's earlier discussion, may be found in Cherry 1979, 37-43; Wagstaff and Cherry 1982, 136-40.

For Early Cycladic settlement, see further Barber and Macgillivray 1980, 145, 149, 150, 152, and Barber 1978a, 374 and figs. 1, 2 (where, for Lefkandi I, read EC IIIA and for Phylakopi I, EC IIIB); for the Middle Cycladic, ibid., 374 and fig. 3; for the Late Cycladic, Barber 1981a, 15-20. For some recent site discoveries see Cherry 1982b (Melos), Marangou 1984 (Amorgos). An earlier but still valuable survey and list of Middle and Late Cycladic sites is by K. Scholes (1956, 10-13).

Settlement counts made for this text have been drawn up from published evidence according to the following assumptions:

(1) A settlement and a neigbouring cemetery which are clearly related count as one site.
(2) A cemetery is taken to imply the existence of a neighbouring settlement and *vice versa*.
(3) Sites which are clearly of specialised character (i.e. not settlements or cemeteries but, e.g., obsidian working areas) are *not* counted.
(4) The existence of unlocated finds from an island are counted as representing sites only if there is no previously known site on the island of the appropriate period from which such finds could have come. However many finds of this kind there may be, they are counted only once for each period represented.
(5) Unlocated finds which are referred to specific sites by report only are treated either as representing a settlement at the site in question or as being unlocated finds or are ignored, according to an arbitrary assessment of the reliability of the information.

18. The many difficulties involved in establishing absolute population figures have been discussed by Renfrew 1972, ch. 14, and Cherry 1979, 37-43. Both have

suggested specific totals. Cherry, mainly on the basis of cemetery size and likely burial rate, allied with an assessment of likely population growth rate, estimated the Early Cycladic population of Melos as 80 (EC I), 400 (late EC II) and 740 for Middle Cycladic Phylakopi, also a population for the Cyclades as a whole in late EC II of 6,600. Renfrew's figures, based mainly on possible average size of settlement divided by estimated amount of floor space required by each inhabitant times possible number of settlements, are considerably higher (34,400 in comparison with the 6,600 for the Cyclades in EC II).

19. Davis 1979, 149.

Chapter 5

1. The most comprehensive study is that of Doumas (1977a), on which the account given here is closely based. A more summary version is Doumas 1977b.

2. See Chapter 3 for the history of exploration.

3. Tsountas 1898; 1899.

4. See n. 1.

5. For the dating of Early Cycladic cemeteries, see Barber and Macgillivray 1980, 147 (table II), and text *passim*; for Middle and Late Cycladic cists, see Chapters 6 and 7 below.

6. Discussed in Doumas 1977a, ch. 4. Some further observations are made by Höckmann (1977a) in a speculative discussion of Early Cycladic religion.

The functions of the marble figures are also relevant, see (v) below.

7. Doumas 1977a, 62 and references; Atkinson *et al.* 1904, 84.

8. See Wheeler 1974, especially 422-3.

9. Coleman 1977a, 48; Wheeler 1974.

10. This summary is based on Barber and Macgillivray 1980, where further references relating to the development of shapes and decorative motifs may be found.

The following works also contain information about Early Cycladic pottery. Since they sometimes use terms different from those employed in this book (see Chapter 2, pp. 24-5), captions for the illustrations to suit my own usage are added:

Doumas 1977a, 15-27 (figs. 3-7: EC I [6 and 7 are Kampos group]; figs. 8-10, 12: EC II; fig. 11: EC IIIA; fig. 13: EC IIIB). The drawings are schematic but a wide range of material is shown and in chronological groups.

Coleman 1977b. A clear and helpful discussion, with useful photographs, which are however confined to objects in the exhibition concerned.

Renfrew 1972, 152-95, 526-38 (figs. 10.1-4: EC I; figs. 11.1, 20.4, no. 5: EC II; figs. 11.2, 20.4, nos. 1-4: EC IIIA; figs. 12.1-2: EC IIIB).

Caskey 1972 (figs. 3-4: EC II; fig. 5: EC II-IIIA; figs. 6-7: EC IIIA). The EC IIIA material is now more fully published in Wilson and Eliot 1984.

Bossert 1967. Another important EC IIIA group.

Macgillivray (1980) discusses further the ceramic identity of EC IIIA. For the relationship of EC IIIA pottery to EC IIIB, see Barber 1984.

A useful source of illustrations is Zervos 1957 and the primary publications by Tsountas (1898; 1899) of his late nineteenth-century work in the Cyclades are valuable.

Decoration: Early Cycladic decorative motifs are considered by Otto (1977).

11. Some examples of the uses of pottery and other vessels in a primitive community can be found in Weinstein 1973.

12. For frying-pan types, Renfrew 1972, 420-1, 527-8 and index; Coleman 1977b, 113-14 (n. 23, for use as mirrors); 1985. For possible mirror use (via Anatolian parallels), Mellink 1956.

13. Caskey 1972, 365-6.

14. For the Anatolian connections of the pottery, Macgillivray 1980, 25; Popham and Sackett 1968, 8; French 1967; and 1966 for other Anatolian-related pottery from the Cyclades.

15. See Chapter 2, n. 17.

16. The only serious discussion of marble vases is Getz-Preziosi 1977a, on which this account is largely based.

17. My attention has been drawn to an interesting marble bell cup from the destruction level of the House of Tiles at Lerna (Caskey 1956, 164, fig. 4 and pl. 47) which might be Cycladic.

18. For the processes of manufacture of Minoan stone vases, which are relevant, see Warren 1969, ch. 4; 1978; Caskey 1962, 272-3 and pl. 98 g, h.

19. Aspects of Aegean metallurgy have been discussed by a number of writers:

Muhly 1973 (sources of and trade in copper and tin); Branigan 1974 (Aegean metallurgy in the Early and Middle Bronze Age); 1977; Sapouna-Sakellarakis 1977 (Early Cycladic jewellery, including metal pieces); Renfrew 1967 and 1972 (ch. 16) (Early Cycladic metallurgy in its Aegean context); Gale and Stos Gale 1984 (with further references) (Cycladic Bronze Age metallurgy).

Useful information on technical processes of mining and artefact production can be found in Hodges 1976.

20. Branigan 1974, 125-7 (tables 13-15).

21. Barber and Macgillivray 1980, 154, and n. 136, for further references. The question needs further investigation.

22. The various classes are reviewed briefly by Branigan (1977) and in more detail by Branigan (1974). For jewellery see Sapouna-Sakellarakis 1977; Higgins 1967, ch. 6; Hood 1978, chs. 7-9 (jewellery and other metal objects).

23. For the identity of local schools, see Branigan 1974, 123-7.

24. Branigan 1968, 198-9.

25. Gale 1978, 541.

26. Branigan 1974, ch. 2; Muhly 1973; Gale 1978; 1980; Gale and Stos Gale 1984; Gale *et al.* 1983

27. Gale 1980, 188-9; Wagner and Weisberger 1979.

28. For a full discussion, Muhly 1973, chs. 4 and 5.

29. Branigan 1974, 64. Muhly 1973, 288, sensibly observes that eastern features in Early Minoan metallurgy suggest that the source of tin for Crete at that period was the East Mediterranean.

30. If copper was actually smelted at Kastri, as opposed to being worked into artefacts, the site may well have been exceptional. Its fortifications and remote position show that it was a fastness and it belongs to a period when it might well have been unsafe to carry out smelting work unprotected, outside the settlement.

For the suggestion of Anatolian settlers at Kastri, see Schachermeyr 1976, 189; now reinforced by Gale and Stos Gale 1984, 268-70.

For new information about smelting from Kythnos, see Hadjianastasiou and Macgillivray (forthcoming).

31. The primary discussion of Melian obsidian is that by R.C. Bosanquet 1904. A thorough report on recent obsidian work at Phylakopi and its wider implications is Torrence 1982. Also useful for the character and chronology of artefacts are Torrence 1979 and Cherry and Torrence 1982; 1984.

32. For possible sources in the Aegean, south-east Europe and Anatolia, see Renfrew *et al.* 1965.

33. Reports on the excavations at Koukounaries regularly mention quantities of obsidian objects, e.g. Orlandos 1977, 146, 148.

34. Bosanquet 1904, 221-4.

35. See n. 31.

36. See Torrence 1979, 77-9.

37. In fact, the earliest occurrences are probably eleventh millennium BC (Perlès 1979).

38. Torrence 1982.

39. See above Chapter 5 (ii).

40. Rubensohn 1917, 67.

41. Cycladic marble figures have been discussed in scholarly publications since the nineteenth century. The first detailed classification was by Renfrew 1969 (criticised by Caskey (1971b, 125-6)). Most aspects of the study of the figurines are treated in Doumas 1968, 1983b. Introductory articles by various authors may be found in Thimme 1977. A colloquium on Cycladic sculpture (Fitton 1984) includes articles on a number of aspects.

For specific references to literature on classification, style, the identification of individual hands, techniques of manufacture and possible functions of the figures, see notes below.

42. These are discussed *inter alia* in an article otherwise devoted to an unsuccessful attempt to identify the provenance of marble objects by scientific analysis (Renfrew 1968).

43. Doumas 1977a, 15.

44. Chapter 2.

45. Caskey 1971b, nos. 30-36, see p. 124 and fig. 5; 1974, nos. 41, 42.

46. In Renfrew's classification (1969), the features of the individual variants of the schematic class are analysed. Thimme (1977, 415 and fig. 184 (p. 416)) adopts a rather different basic division into 'schematic' and 'canonical' (see below). His former class consists of (a) a schematic group whose members, though simple and stylised, have one or two important features similar to those of the canonical figures (arms, head, legs) and (b) an abstract-schematic group, whose members have no arms, head or legs.

47. Renfrew's individual types are named after sites with which they are associated. Thimme uses a division into 'canonical' (the most common type – standing female, with arms folded, right below left), 'precanonical' (lacking some of the canonical features but recognisable as a fore-runner) and 'post-canonical' (supposedly late examples, when the strict canon had been abandoned).

48. Getz-Preziosi 1979.

49. Dr. P. Getz-Preziosi has analysed the methods of Early Cycladic sculptors and this account is closely based on her work (as reported in Getz-Preziosi 1977b). A detailed study (*Sculptors of the Cyclades*) is soon to be published.

50. Getz-Preziosi 1977b, 82-91; 1984; and see above, n. 49

51. Experimental work is reported by E. Oustinoff (1984).

52. Discussed by Doumas (1968, 88-94); and in papers by Barber (1984) and Renfrew (1984) at the British Museum colloquium. The subject has also been considered by Höckmann (1977a) and Thimme (1965).

53. Renfrew 1984a, 27-8.

54. The external relations and relative chronology of the Cyclades in the Early Bronze Age have been reviewed in detail by Renfrew (1972), chs. 10-13.

Summaries are Coleman 1974 and Barber and Macgillivray 1980 (relative chronology). An earlier assessment was made by Weinberg (1965, 301ff). (new edition by Coleman forthcoming). Articles in Thimme 1977a (Sakellarakis 1977a, Weinberg 1977) are relevant but those on the relationships of the Cyclades to the Eastern and Western Mediterranean (Höckmann 1977b, 1977c) are highly speculative.

55. See Chapter 2.

56. Ayia Fotia: see below, n. 59. Palaia Kokkinia: Theochares 1951; 1955. Pyrgos: see Renfrew 1972, 201.

57. Iassos: Pecorella 1984. See also Renfrew 1972, 133-4; Wheeler 1974.

58. Caskey 1971a, 368-72.

59. Mainland. Ayios Kosmas: Mylonas 1959. Marathon (Tsepi): Marinatos 1970a, 1-9; 1970b.

Crete. Doumas 1976a; 1979; Sakellarakis (1977b) considers the evidence from the various sites.

Archanes: Sakellarakis 1977b and references.

Ayia Fotia: the most accessible brief account is Davaras 1976, 128-9. See also Davaras 1971 and n. d., with note to fig. 2-11, for further references.

60. At Archanes, there was also a weaving area apparently on the upper floor of a mortuary building. See Chapter 8.

61. Sakellarakis 1977a; Doumas 1976a; 1979.

62. Macgillivray 1983, esp. p. 82.

63. Gale and Stos-Gale 1984, 269.

64. Barber 1984c, 90-1.

65. Rutter 1983; 1984; Barber 1983; Macgillivray 1983.

66. Barber 1981b, 175-6 and 1983, 78-9.

67. See Barber 1981b, 174-5.

68. Buck 1964, 301-2.

69. Topp and Plantalomor 1983.

70. Scholes 1956, 14.

Chapter 6

1. Summaries of Cycladic culture in the Middle Bronze Age may be found in Barber 1978a, Overbeck 1979, Caskey 1973a. Some references to the Middle Cycladic architecture of Akrotiri are in Palyvou 1984 and Marthari 1984; comments on Middle Cycladic Akrotiri in Doumas 1983a, 27-8; 1978b, 778-80.

Forthcoming reports of recent excavations at Ayia Irini (*Keos* series – see already Davis 1985) and Phylakopi will add considerably to our understanding of this period, and further work in the Middle Cycladic levels at Akrotiri is eagerly awaited.

2. Barber 1983, with further references.

3. Marthari 1983.

4. For details and illustrations, see Chapter 4.

5. For the date of the wall, see Chapter 4.

6. Wagstaff and Augustson 1982, 139; Gamble 1982, 168.

7. Middle Cycladic pottery is discussed in all the references given in n. 1 above. See also Scholes 1956, 13-24 (an early synopsis); J.C. Overbeck 1984 (summary of Middle Cycladic pottery from Ayia Irini), Marthari 1980 (Mainland pottery in late Middle Cycladic Akrotiri), Marthari 1983 (possible early Middle Cycladic

deposits from Ftellos, Thera), Furumark 1941, 220-2 (important for the distinction between the earlier and later Curvilinear styles and their Minoan relationships: it should be noted that the later Curvilinear style was called 'Naturalistic' by Scholes and this term is used in the text here), Atkinson *et al.* 1904, ch. 4, sections 9 (= Cycladic White), 10 (= Black-and-Red style, mostly on Cycladic White fabric), 13 (= Later Local – mainly Late Cycladic). Dark Burnished pottery was not recognised as a major Middle Cycladic fabric in the original publication of Phylakopi and was mentioned only in passing (153-4). This omission was partially rectified in the report of the 1911 season (Dawkins and Droop 1911, 19-21). See also Barber (forthcoming).

8. The only useful discussion of Middle Cycladic burials so far published is that of G.F. Overbeck (1984), with appropriate references to Caskey 1971a. It should be noted that the same graves are differently numbered in these two publications, the system of Overbeck being that which will be used in the final report. For pottery associated with the Kea tombs, see Caskey 1972, 383-6, where other finds are also briefly reported. Recently discovered cists tombs on Thera (Marthari 1983, 96 and n. 15) will be of great interest when more fully published. For tombs at Aila, Naxos, see Papathanasopoulos 1961-2, 129-32.

For Middle Cycladic elements in the Kea Temple and possible sacrificial hearths, see Caskey 1971a, 385; 1966, 369.

9. Some useful observations on Cycladic contacts with Crete and the Mainland respectively in the Middle Cycladic period may be found in Barber 1984b; Macgillivray 1984a and Dickinson 1977, 36-7. A summary of connections between Phylakopi and Middle Minoan Crete is in Renfrew 1972, 198-9; between Kea and Middle Helladic Greece in Overbeck 1982b.

10. Shelford *et al.* 1982, 191, but the relative extent of use of obsidian in the Middle and Late Bronze Age in the Aegean is not yet adequately documented. See Chapter 9; Renfrew *et al.* 1965, 240.

11. For analytical work, see Jones 1978 and 1985; Davis and Williams 1981; Williams 1978. For attributions on the basis of observation only, see Barber 1984b, 181-2; 1978b, II, 234-5; Macgillivray 1984a, 156.

Chapter 7

1. For an outline of the whole of the Late Cycladic period and its characteristics, see Barber 1981a (LC I-II, pp. 2-8), also Scholes 1956. An earlier discussion by Furumark (1950), although heavily dependent on the finds from Phylakopi, is still valuable. Davis (1979) and Schofield (1982) review the relationship between the Western Cyclades and Crete. Davis (1980) concentrates on Ayia Irini, and Cummer and Schofield (1984) give a valuable synopsis of the finds from House A at the same site. Renfrew (1978b) considers recent early Late Cycladic finds from Phylakopi. Discoveries on Thera are reported in Marinatos 1968-76; the most useful and recent survey of finds is Doumas 1983a.

Questions relating to the Minoan thalassocracy and Cretan influence on Cycladic culture in the Late Cycladic period are dealt with in most of the papers in Hägg and Marinatos 1984, some of which are cited individually below. See also Doumas 1982.

For Akrotiri, see Chapter 8 and notes.

2. Phylakopi: Atkinson *et al.* 1904, 50-8; Renfrew 1978b; 1982, fig. 4.3 (latest plan of site, including shrine). Ayia Irini: Caskey 1971; Cummer and Schofield

1984, chs. 1-6 (House A). Akrotiri: Doumas 1974; 1983a, 45-55; Palyvou 1984; Marthari 1984; Shaw 1978 (Minoan features of architecture).

3. For details and illustrations of architectural features, see Chapter 4; for frescoes, see below.

4. Only Mallia has been seriously considered as a fortified site. The Cretan palaces themselves however could be regarded as fortified strongholds, even though no obviously military architectural features have been noted.

Pottery

5. For early Late Cycladic pottery in general, see Furumark 1950, 192-201, and Scholes 1956, 24-9.

Akrotiri: Marinatos 1968-76, I-VII *passim*; Doumas 1976c; 1983, 108-13 (a useful and up-to-date summary); Marthari 1980 (for the Mainland and Mainland-related material).

Ayia Irini: Caskey 1972, 391-7; Cummer and Schofield 1984, 45-8, and illustrated catalogue.

Phylakopi: Atkinson *et al.* 1904, ch. IV, section 13; Dawkins and Droop 1911, 9-15; Davis, Cherry and Macfarlane (forthcoming).

6. This still seems fundamentally true (as Furumark 1950, 195) but Cycladic characteristics now appear more prominent, especially on Thera (Doumas 1983, 112). See also comments in Cummer and Schofield 1984, 145.

7. Cummer and Schofield 1984, 145.

8. Ayia Irini: Cummer and Schofield 1984, 144-5; Schofield 1982, 14.

Akrotiri: Marthari 1980, 208

Phylakopi: Dickinson 1977, 102, with n. 3 (ch. VII (1) p. 125); and personal communication from Dr. E.B. French.

9. For Cypriot sherds on Melos and Thera (Therasia), see Popham 1963, 93 n. 16 and references. For the Syrian amphora from Akrotiri, see Marinatos 1968-76, VII, 15, 30, pl. 49b. For the Syro-Palestinian vessels, see Warren 1979a, 106-7.

10. Mainland: Davis 1979, 153-5; Barber 1978b, II, 227-32 and see Schofield 1982, 13.

Crete (very limited in quantity): Cadogan 1978a, 76, fig. 19 (Myrtos-Pyrgos); Shaw 1977, 238, pl. 52a (d) (Kommos); Barber 1978b, 232-3

11. Schofield 1982, 12-13; Barber 1978b, II, 234-5; 1984c, 90-1. The obviously Theran sherd from Melos is very prominent among the Melian material: Atkinson *et al.* 1904, fig. 92.

Frescoes

12. Cycladic frescoes have been published and discussed as follows:

Generally, by Hood (1978), 48-77, where Crete and the Cyclades are treated together.

An important consideration of the relationship between Cretan, Mainland and Cycladic frescoes is Cameron 1978.

Akrotiri: the primary publication and the best and widest range of illustrations are in Marinatos 1968-76, I-VII, especially IV-VII (vol. VI has a separate folder of plates). See also Doumas 1983a, 56-108, with plates III-XV (colour), figs. 26-32 (black and white); also figs. 9-12, 20-1. Marinatos 1984b has many good illustrations, some previously unpublished, in a discussion centred on the religious significance of the frescoes. The interpretation of the frescoes has been widely discussed (see nn. 14, 16, 17 below).

Ayia Irini: Coleman (Abramowitz) 1973 and Abramowitz 1980. Phylakopi: Atkinson *et al.* 1904, ch. 3. There are more fragments from the recent excavations, as yet unpublished.

13. For comments on technique, see Asimenos 1978, Philippakis 1978 (pigments), also Hood 1978, 83-7.

14. Among the considerable literature on the subject may be mentioned: Marinatos 1974; Morgan Brown 1978 and forthcoming; Negbi 1978; Warren 1979; Sakellariou 1980; and important comments in Immerwahr 1977 and Doumas 1983a, 85-106.

15. Doumas 1983a, 55-6.

16. Morgan Brown 1978, Sakellariou 1980, 149-52.

17. See especially Cameron 1978 (and discussion of this paper in Doumas (ed.) 1980, 315-18).

18. Marinatos 1968-76, VI, 54.

19. See Cameron 1978 and n. 17 above; for Cycladic features on Kea and respects in which the Kean and Theran paintings differ, see Coleman 1980.

20. Marinatos 1983; 1984a, b.

Burials

21. Aila: Papathanassopoulos 1961-2.

Kea: G.F. Overbeck, 1984, with references to Caskey 1971.

Phylakopi: Evans 1921-35, IV, 445 – a tantalising reference to a Melian tomb, presumably at Phylakopi, with LM IB (= LC II) pottery. The tomb seems likely to have been a chamber, possibly a cist.

Finds 'in the neighbourhood of the tombs' at Phylakopi, and the chambers themselves, included a small quantity of 'imported Mycenaean' (Atkinson *et al.* 1904, 234-7).

Religion

22. The architecture of the Ayia Irini Temple is discussed in Caskey 1971. For the terracotta figures see Caskey 1986; also Caskey 1981 (with suggestions on the nature of the cult); Eisner 1972.

For the identification of shrines at Akrotiri, see Marinatos 1984a, b; also Chapter 8 below.

For pillar rooms at Phylakopi, see Atkinson *et al.* 1904, 17-18 and Renfrew 1978b, 411.

23. Comparisons of Cretan and Theran practices are conveniently set out in N. Marinatos 1984a.

For the shrine in House A at Ayia Irini, see N. Marinatos 1984a, 176 (comment by E. Schofield) and Cummer and Schofield 1984, 39.

24. See Caskey 1971b; 1974; n. 23 above (for House A shrine).

Other finds

25. A comprehensive listing of finds in the various categories is provided by Barber 1978b (Appendix II).

26. Warren 1969 contains references to local and imported vases from Phylakopi and Ayia Irini; 1979a to material from Akrotiri. The Kea finds are not yet fully published, though pieces are mentioned in interim reports on the excavations and in Cummer and Schofield 1984, 38-9 etc. (see p. 171 and index).

For an example of manufacturing technique on Akrotiri, see Warren 1978; for stone vase cores from Kea, see Caskey 1962, 272-3, pl. 98g, h.

27. Gale and Stos-Gale 1981; 1984.

28. Petruso 1978; 1979.

29. See Chapter 6 n. 10.

30. Akrotiri: Doumas 1983a, 120-1.

Ayia Irini: Caskey 1970; Bikaki 1984 (potters' marks) 42-3.

Phylakopi: Renfrew 1978, 412, 418-19; Renfrew and Brice 1977.

31. The most frequently quoted reference is Thucydides 1.4. For others, and an assessment of the reliability of the tradition, see Huxley 1968. See also n. 1 above.

32. Davis 1979; Schofield 1982.

33. After settlement of the islands was centralised in the Middle Bronze Age, the number of cattle rose, probably because many more draught animals were needed in order to work lands relatively far from the main settlement. The abandonment of more distant agricultural land by the newly concentrated population and the increased availability of transport may have led to the use of those ares for the rearing of sheep.

Davis 1979, 132-3; Renfrew and Wagstaff 1982, 170.

34. Davis 1979, 146-7, and references.

35. Attempts to construct models of colonialism and to illustrate the effects on material culture of different kinds of historically documented colonialisation are made by Branigan 1984 and Wiener 1984. See further Hägg and Marinatos 1984 *passim*.

36. For interpretations of the significance of Minoan influence on material culture, see *inter alia* Cadogan 1984, Davis 1984.

37. Hood 1984.

38. Wagstaff and Cherry 1982, 259.

39. Warren 1984.

40. For pottery, frescoes and religion, see above; for minor objects, see Davis 1980, 258.

41. Barber 1984 on the relationship between Thera and Melos.

Chapter 8

1. Basic information is derived from Marinatos 1968-76, I-VII, and associated excavation reports in the *Ergon* and *Praktika (PAE)* of the Greek Archaeological Society. Doumas 1983a is an excellent, readable survey of all aspects of Bronze Age Akrotiri.

For the rebuilding of the town at the beginning of LC I, see Palyvou 1984 and Marthari 1984. Doumas 1974 is also important for the architecture. For an interesting and well illustrated (though controversial) analysis of the frescoes with particular reference to religion and social structure see Marinatos 1984b.

For further discussion of architectural details, see Chapter 4; for individual elements of material culture, Chapter 7; for the history of excavations on Thera, Chapter 3.

2. A broad and helpful (though now somewhat dated) analysis of the Thera volcanic sequence and related archaeological problems is Page 1970, whose summary of the effects of the Krakatoa eruption and explosion is particularly useful. A more popular study is Luce 1969.

Many aspects of Theran vulcanology and archaeology are discussed in conference papers given to the Thera congresses (Kaloyeropoulou 1971; Doumas (ed.) 1978a; 1980).

The sequence adopted here is derived from Pichler and Friedrich 1980 (in Doumas ed.). The primary research into the area of ash fall is reported in Ninkovitch and Heezen 1965.

For an analysis of the nature of the destructions at the sites in Crete and an LM IA horizon of destructions possibly associated with the volcanic activity, see Hood 1978b. For sites with LM II occupation, see Popham 1980.

Chapter 9

1. The only general summary of this period is Barber 1981a (esp. 8-15), which includes a list of Late Cycladic sites. A later version of the chronological table (p. 21) may be found in Barber and Macgillivray 1984, 301.

The most important publications of LC III sites and finds are those of Ayia Irini, House A (Cummer and Schofield 1984) and the Temple (Caskey 1984); recent excavations at Phylakopi, especially the shrine (Renfrew 1978a; 1981a; Mountjoy 1985); Koukounaries on Paros (Schilardi 1984) and the Aplomata tombs on Naxos (Kardara 1977).

2. The extent of occupation at Ayia Irini in this period is not entirely clear, but Cummer and Schofield (1984, 144 and n. 15), suggest that it may have been substantial.

3. There is some difficulty in assessing the course of events between the III-ii destruction and the building of the megaron (Barber 1981a, 7). The former is dated by the occurrence of LM IB pottery; the latter by Mycenaean (= Late Helladic) IIIA: 1. This appears to leave a gap in LH IIB/LM II. It does not seem that the whole of the site was destroyed in the III-ii catastrophe but, if the town was attacked by Mycenaeans whose aim was simply to subdue it for a while as part of their advance into the South Aegean, while the consolidation of their authority and control was left till later (when it was symbolised by the construction of the megaron), it is possible that the prosperity of the town was very much reduced in the intervening period and there was little external contact and correspondingly few imports. There are however some signs of LM II and, more evident, LH IIB influence (Furumark 1950, 194-5; Dickinson 1977, 125 n. 3 (ch. VII-1) and references); but it is not clear to exactly what point in the sequence they should be attributed. If it is to III-ii, the date for the destruction stated above would have to be lowered. Perhaps it is most likely that the material belongs between the destruction and the construction of the megaron. This is not unlikely in the historical context, and strata representing this intervening phase may eventually be detected.

4. E.B. French, unpublished paper delivered to the Workshop on Cycladic chronology, London, June 1983; Scholes 1956, 31-4; Cummer and Schofield (n. 2 above).

5. See Barber 1981a, 19 (table 1).

6. For useful comments on the relative chronology of the various events, see Schofield 1984.

7. See Barber 1981a, 10 and references.

8. Renfrew 1978a, 11; Sherratt 1980, 191 (and the article generally for regional

variation); and unpublished paper to Workshop on Cycladic chronology, London, June 1983.

9. Phylakopi fortifications: Atkinson *et al.* 1904, 30-4 Renfrew 1982, 41; 1978b, 407-8 (for the shrine, see below n. 17).

Ayios Andreas: Philippaki 1973 (Greek, with English summary) and subsequent reports (Greek) in the *Ergon* and *Praktika* of the Athens Archaeological Society (English summaries in *Archaeological Reports*).

Koukounaries: Schilardi 1979; 1984; other reports, as for Ayios Andreas. A useful article on the pottery is Koehl 1984.

Ayios Spyridon: Cherry 1982b, 306.

To Froudhi tou Kalamitsou: see Barber 1981a, 20 and references.

Grotta: Lambrinoudakis 1979, 252 and pl. 155.

10. A survey (somewhat over-analytical) of the situation on the Mainland at this period may be found in Hooker 1976, ch. 7.

11. Aplomata: Kardara 1977.

Kamini: Orlandos 1960, 189-92.

See also Desborough 1964, 150-2.

12. Kardara 1977.

13. For an outline description of the Mainland sequence and further references, see Barber 1981a, 12, n. 117. For tabular indications of relationships between Cycladic and Mainland phases, see Barber and Macgillivray 1984, 301 (table); Koehl 1984, 221 (table 1).

For pottery of the final phase of LC III, see Caskey 1984; Popham and Milburn 1971, 348.

14. See however Koehl 1984; Mountjoy 1984; Caskey 1984; Schilardi 1984; Renfrew (forthcoming).

15. Cummer and Schofield 1984, 146.

16. Koehl 1984; Kardara 1977, especially ch. 2. See also Desborough 1964, esp. 20-1. (The connections described are still valid, though the sequence of styles is now outdated, see n. 13 above.)

17. For Grotta, see Kondoleon 1961, reports in *PAE* intermittently since 1949. Recent work is by V. Lambrinoudakis. Also Scholes 1956, 32ff.; Desborough 1964, 149-52.

For Phylakopi (City III), see Atkinson *et al.* 1904, 50-69 (55-8 for the megaron). For the shrine, see Renfrew 1978a; 1981a; forthcoming; Mountjoy 1984.

For the Kea shrine, see Caskey 1981; 1984 (with references to earlier reports).

For Koukounaries, see Schilardi 1979; 1984; Koehl 1984.

For Ayios Andreas, see Philippaki 1973 (and subsequent reports in *PAE*).

For Delos, see Gallet de Santerre and Tréheux 1947-8; Gallet de Santerre 1958, esp. ch. 4. For the ivories, see Poursat 1973, 19.

For fortifications, see n. 9 above.

18. See n. 9 above.

19. Aplomata and Kamini: n. 11 above

Khosti: Stephanos 1908.

Langadha: Papadopoulou 1965, 510-13

Ayia Thekla: Despinis 1979.

Mykonos: *AM* 23 (1898) 362; Hogarth and Bosanquet 1899, 321

Phylakopi: Atkinson *et al.* 1904, 234-7.

20. These views are based on those expressed in Renfrew 1981b.

21. This period and its problems are comprehensively discussed in Desborough 1972 (site index for Cyclades pp. 370-1); also 1964, 147-52.

Bibliography

The bibliography gives full details of those works cited by author's name and date of publication in the notes. It contains all works which I wished to include published up to the end of 1984. A few selective entries only have been incorporated to items which have appeared subsequently.

Readers who wish to pursue the subject further, but without searching for specialist publications, may consult the following:

Thimme 1977
Zervos 1957
Caskey 1971c; 1973a
Hood 1978
Vermeule 1964
Doumas 1983a; 1983b
Archaeological Reports (*AR*, see Chapter 3, n.5).

Abbreviations

AA	*Archäologischer Anzeiger*
AAA	*Athens Annals of Archaeology*
ADelt	*Archaiologikon Deltion*
AE	*Archaiologike Ephemeris*
AJA	*American Journal of Archaeology*
AM	*Mitteilungen des deutschen archäologischen Instituts: Athenische Abteilung*
Ann	*Annuario della Scuola Archeologica Italiana di Atene*
AR	*Archaeological Reports*
AS	*Anatolian Studies*
BCH	*Bulletin de Correspondence Hellénique*
BICS	*Bulletin of the Institute of Classical Studies,*
BSA	*Annual of the British School at Athens*
Ergon	*To ergon tes Archaiologikes Etaireias*
ILN	*Illustrated London News*
JAS	*Journal of Archaeological Science*
JdI	*Jahrbuch des deutschen archäologischen Instituts*
JFA	*Journal of Field Archaeology*
KrChron	*Kretika Chronika*
PAE	*Praktika tes en Athenais Archaiologikes Etaireias*

Abramowitz, K. (1980) 'Frescoes from Ayia Irini, Keos. Parts II-IV' in *Hesperia* 49, 57-85

Admiralty (Hydrographic Department) (1918) *The Mediterranean pilot* IV, London

Asimenos, K. (1978) 'Technological observations on the Thera wall-paintings' in Doumas (ed.) 571-8

Atkinson, T.D. *et al.* (1904) *Excavations at Phylakopi in Melos* (Society for the Promotion of Hellenic Studies Supplementary Paper 4), London

Barber, R.L.N. (1974) 'Phylakopi 1911 and the history of the later Cycladic Bronze Age' in *BSA* 69, 1-53

(1978a) 'The Cyclades in the Middle Bronze Age' in Doumas (ed.) 367-79

(1978b) 'The Cyclades in the Middle and Late Bronze Age', St. Andrews (unpublished Ph.D. thesis)

(1981a) 'The Late Cycladic period: a review' in *BSA* 76, 1-21

(1981b) 'A tomb at Ayios Loukas, Syros: some thoughts on Early-Middle Cycladic chronology' in *Journal of Mediterranean Anthropology and Archaeology* I, 167-79

(1983) 'The definition of the Middle Cycladic period' in *AJA* 87, 76-9

(1984a) 'Early Cycladic marble figures: some thoughts on function' in Fitton (ed.) 10-14

(1984b) 'The status of Phylakopi in Creto-Cycladic relations' in Hägg and Marinatos (eds.)

(1984c) 'The pottery of Phylakopi, First City, phase ii (I-ii) in Macgillivray and Barber (eds.) 88-94

(forthcoming) 'The Middle Cycladic pottery' in C. Renfrew (ed.) *Stratigraphic excavations at Phylakopi in Melos*

Barber, R.L.N. and Macgillivray, J.A. (1980) 'The Early Cycladic period: matters of definition and terminology' in *AJA* 84, 141-57

(1984) 'The prehistoric Cyclades: a summary' in Macgillivray and Barber (eds.) 296-302

Bent, J.T. (1884) 'Researches among the Cyclades' in *JHS* 5, 42-59

(1885), *The Cyclades*, London

Betancourt, P. and Lawn, B. (1984) 'The Cyclades and radiocarbon chronology' in Macgillivray and Barber (eds.) 277-95

Bikaki, A.H. (1984) *Ayia Irini: the potters' marks (Keos IV)*, Mainz on Rhein

Bintliff, J.L. (1977) *Natural environment and human settlement in prehistoric Greece*, Oxford

Blegen, C.W. and Rawson, M. (1967) *The palace of Nestor at Pylos in western Messenia*, Vol. 1, part 1, Princeton.

Bosanquet, R.C. (1904) 'The obsidian trade' in Atkinson *et al.*, 216-33

Bosanquet, R.C. and Welch, F.B. (1904) 'The minor antiquities' in Atkinson *et al.*, 190-215

Bossert, E.-M. (1954) 'Zur Datierung der Gräber von Arkesine auf Amorgos' in *Festschrift für Peter Goessler* (Tübinger Beitrage zur Vor- und Frühgeschichte), (Stuttgart), 23-34

(1960) 'Die gestempelten Verzierungen auf frühbronze-zeitlichen Gefässen der Agäis' in *JdI* 75, 1-16

(1965) 'Ein Beiträg zu den frühkykladischen Fundgruppen' in *Anadolu Arastimalari* 2, 85

(1967) 'Kastri auf Syros' in *ADelt* 22, Meletai, 53-76

Branigan, K. (1968) 'A traditional phase in Minoan metallurgy' in *BSA* 63, 185-203

(1971) 'Cycladic figurines and their derivatives in Crete' in *BSA* 66, 57-78

(1974) *Aegean metalwork of the Early and Middle Bronze Age*, Oxford

(1977) 'Metal objects and metal technology of the Cycladic culture' in Thimme (ed.) 117-22

(1981) 'Minoan colonialism' in *BSA* 76, 23-33

(1984) 'Minoan community colonies in the Aegean' in Hägg and Marinatos (eds.) 49-53

Brock, J.K. and Mackworth Young, G. (1949) 'Excavations in Siphnos' in *BSA* 44, 1-92

Buck, R.J. 'Middle Helladic matt-painted pottery' in *Hesperia* 33, 231-313

Cadogan, G.A. (1978a) 'Pyrgos, Crete, 1970-7' in *AR* 1977-8, 70-84

(1978b) 'Dating the Aegean Bronze Age without radiocarbon' in *Archaeometry* 20, 201-14

(1984) 'A Minoan thalassocracy' in Hägg and Marinatos (eds.) 13-15

Cameron, M.A.S. (1978) 'Theoretical interrelations among Theran, Cretan and mainland frescoes' in Doumas (ed.) 579-92

Cary, M. (1949) *The geographic background of Greek and Roman history*, Oxford

Caskey, J.L. (1956) 'Excavations at Lerna, 1955' in *Hesperia* 25, 147-73

(1962) 'Excavations in Keos, 1960-1' in *Hesperia* 31, 263-83

(1964) 'Chalandriani in Syros' in *Essays in memory of Karl Lehmann* (Marsyas Supplement 1), (Locust Valley), 63-9

(1966) 'Excavations in Keos, 1964-5' in *Hesperia* 35, 363-76

(1969) 'Crises in the Minoan-Mycenaean world' in *Proceedings of the American Philosophical Society* 113, 433-49

(1970) 'Inscriptions and potters' marks from Ayia Irini in Keos' in *Kadmos* 9, 107-17

(1971a) 'Investigations in Keos. Part 1: excavations and explorations, 1966-70' in *Hesperia* 40, 359-96

(1971b) 'Marble figurines from Ayia Irini in Keos' in *Hesperia* 40, 113-26

(1971c) 'Greece, Crete and the Aegean islands in the Early Bronze Age' in *Cambridge Ancient History*, revised (3rd) edition, Vol. 1, Part 2, Chapter 26a, Cambridge

(1972) 'Investigations in Keos. Part 2: a conspectus of the pottery' in *Hesperia* 41, 357-401

(1973a) 'Greece and the Aegean islands in the Middle Bronze Age' in *Cambridge Ancient History*, revised (3rd) edition, Vol. 2, Part 1, Chapter 4, Cambridge

(1973b) 'Ayia Irini in Keos, 1972' in *ADelt* 28, Chronika, 547-50

(1974) 'Addendum to the marble figurines from Ayia Irini' in *Hesperia* 43, 77-9

(1978) 'Aegean terminologies' in *Historia* 27, 488-91

(1979) 'Ayia Irini, Keos: the successive periods of occupation' in *AJA* 83, 412

Caskey, M.E. (1981) 'Ayia Irini, Kea: the terracotta statues and the cult in the Temple' in Hägg and Marinatos (eds.) 127-35

(1984) 'The Temple at Ayia Irini, Kea: evidence for the LH IIIC phases' in Macgillivray and Barber (eds.)

(1986) *Keos II, Part I. The Temple at Ayia Irini: the statues*, Mainz

Casson, L. (1971) *Ships and seamanship in the ancient world*, Princeton, N.J.

Catling, H.W. (1976) 'Archaeology in Greece' in *AR* 1975-6, 3-33

Cherry, J.F. (1979) 'Four problems in Cycladic prehistory' in Davis and Cherry (eds.) 22-47

(1982a) 'A preliminary definition of site distribution on Melos' in Renfrew and Wagstaff (eds.) 10-23

(1982b) 'Register of archaeological sites on Melos' in Renfrew and Wagstaff (eds.) 291-309

Cherry, J.F. and Davis, J.L. (1982) 'The Cyclades and the Greek mainland in LC I: the evidence of the pottery' in *AJA* 86, 333-41

Cherry, J.F. and Torrence, R. (1982) 'The earliest prehistory of Melos' in Renfrew and Wagstaff (eds.) 24-34

(1984) 'The typology and chronology of chipped stone assemblages in the prehistoric Cyclades' in Macgillivray and Barber (eds.) 12-25

Coldstream, J.N. (1969) 'The Thera eruption: some thoughts on the survivors' in *BICS* 16, 150-2

Coleman, J.E. (1974) 'The chronology and interconnections of the Cycladic islands in the Neolithic period and the Early Bronze Age' in *AJA* 78, 333-444

(1977a) *Keos I: Kephala, a Late Neolithic settlement and cemetery*, Princeton, N.J.

(1977b) 'Early Cycladic clay vessels' in Thimme (ed.) 109-17

(1979a) 'Chronological and cultural divisions of the Early Cycladic period: a critical appraisal' in Davis and Cherry (eds.) 48-50

(1979b) 'Remarks on Terminology and beyond' in Davis and Cherry (eds.) 64-5

(1985) ' "Frying pans" of the Early Bronze Age Aegean' in *AJA* 89, 191-219

(forthcoming) 'The relative chronology of the Aegean in the Stone and Early Bronze Ages' in R.W. Ehrich (ed.) *Chronologies in Old World Archaeology* (3rd ed.), Chicago

Coleman (Abramowitz), K. (1973) 'Frescoes from Ayia Irini, Keos. Part I' in *Hesperia* 42, 284-300

Connell, C. (1980) *In the bee-loud glade*, Nafplion

Coy, J.P. (1973) 'Bronze Age domestic animals from Keos, Greece' in Matolcsi, J. (ed.) *Domestikationsforschung und Geschichte der Haustiere, Internationales Symposium in Budapest 1971*, Budapest, 239-43

Cummer, W.W. and Schofield, E. (1984) *Keos III: Ayia Irini, house A*, Mainz

Davaras, C. (1971) 'Protominoikon nekrotapheion Ayias Foteias Siteias' in *AAA* 4, 392-7

(1976) *Guide to Cretan antiquities*, New Jersey

(n.d.) *Mouseion Ayiou Nikolaou*, Athens

Davidson, D.A. (1978) 'Aegean soils during the second millennium B.C. with reference to Thera' in Doumas (ed.) 725-39

Davidson, D.A., Renfrew, A.C., Tasker, C. (1976) 'Erosion and prehistory in Melos: a preliminary note' in *JAS* 3, 219-27

Davidson, D.A. and Tasker, C. (1982) 'Geomorphological evolution during the late holocene' in Renfrew and Wagstaff (eds.) 82-94

Davis, J.-L. (1979) 'Minos and Dexithea: Crete and the Cyclades in the Late Bronze Age' in Davis and Cherry (eds.) 143-57

(1980) 'Minoans and Minoanisation at Ayia Irini, Keos' in Doumas (ed.) 257-60

(1982) 'The earliest Minoans in the southeast Aegean: a reconsideration of the evidence' in *AS* 32, 33-41

(1984) 'Cultural innovation and the Minoan thalassocracy at Ayia Irini, Keos' in Hägg and Marinatos (eds.) 159-66

(1986) *Keos V: Ayia Irini: Period V*, Mainz

Davis, J.L. and Cherry, J.F. (eds.) (1979) *Papers in Cycladic prehistory*

(Monograph 14, Institute of Archaeology, University of California), Los Angeles

(1984) 'Phylakopi in Late Cycladic I: a pottery seriation study' in Macgillivray and Barber (eds.) 148-61

Davis, J.L., Cherry, J.F. and Macfarlane, C. (forthcoming) in C. Renfrew (ed.) *Stratigraphic excavations at Phylakopi in Melos*

Davis, J.L. and Williams, D.L. (1981) 'Petrological examination of later Middle Bronze Age pottery from Ayia Irini, Keos' in *Hesperia* 50, 291-300

Dawkins, R.M. and Droop, J.P. (1911) 'The excavations at Phylakopi in Melos' in *BSA* 17, 1-22

Desborough, V.R. d'A. (1964) *The last Mycenaeans and their successors: an archaeological survey c. 1200 - c. 1000 B.C.*, Oxford

(1972) *The Greek dark ages*, London

Despinis, G. (1979) 'Anaskaphe Tenou' in *PAE* 228-35

Diapoulis, C. (1982) 'Prehistoric plants of the islands in the Aegean sea' in Doumas (ed.) 129-40

Dickinson, O.T.P.K. (1977) *The origins of Mycenaean civilisation* (Studies in Mediterranean Archaeology 49), Göteborg

Doumanis, O.B. and Oliver, P. (eds.) (1974) *Oikismoi stin Elladha (Shelter in Greece)*, Athens

Doumas, C. (1963) 'Naxos' in *ADelt* 18, Chronika, 275

(1964) 'Archaiotetes kai mnemeia Kykladon, 1963' in *ADelt* 19, Chronika, 409-12 (Keros, Naxos)

(1968) *The N.P. Goulandris collection of Early Cycladic art*, Athens

(1972) 'Notes on Early Cycladic architecture' in *AA* 87, 151-70

(1973) 'Ftellos' in *AE* 161-6

(1974) 'Peri tes Minoikes architektonikes en Thera' in *AE*, 199-213

(1976a) 'Proistorikoi Kykladites sten Krete' in *AAA* 9, 69-80

(1976b) 'Protokykladike kerameike apo ta Christiana Theras' in *AE*, 1-11

(1976c) 'Anaskaphe Theras' in *PAE* 309-29

(1977a) *Early Bronze Age burial habits in the Cyclades* (Studies in Mediterranean Archaeology 48), Göteborg

(1977b) 'Early Cycladic architecture' in Thimme (ed.) 31-3

(1977c) 'An historical survey of Early Cycladic research' in Thimme (ed.) 185-91

(1978a) (ed.) *Thera and the Aegean world I*, London

(1978b) 'The stratigraphy of Akrotiri' in Doumas (ed.), 777-82

(1979) 'Proistorikoi Kykladites sten Krete II' in *AAA* 12, 104-9

(1980) (ed.) *Thera and the Aegean world II*, London

(1982) 'The Minoan thalassocracy and the Cyclades' in *AA* 5-14

(1983a) *Thera: Pompeii of the ancient Aegean*, London

(1983b) *Cycladic art: the N.P. Goulandris collection*, London

Eisner, R. (1972) 'The Temple at Ayia Irini: mythology and archaeology' in *Greek, Roman and Byzantine Studies* 13, 123-33

Evans, A.J. (1921-35) *The palace of Minos at Knossos* I-IV and index, London

Evans, J.D. (1972) 'The Early Minoan occupation of Knossos' in *AS* 22, 115-28

Evans, J.D. and Renfrew, C. (1968) *Excavations at Saliagos near Antiparos* (British School at Athens Supplementary Volume 5), London

Evans, R.K. and Renfrew, C. (1984) 'The earlier Bronze Age at Phylakopi' in Macgillivray and Barber (eds.) 63-9

Filippakis, S.E. (1978) 'Analysis of pigments from Thera' in Doumas (ed.)

599-604

Fimmen, D. (1924) *Die Kretische-Mykenische Kultur*, Leipzig-Berlin

Fitton, J.L. (ed.) (1984) *Cycladica*, Studies in memory of N. P. Goulandris, London

Fotou, V. (1983) 'Les sites de l'époque Néolithique et de l'Âge du Bronze à Naxos' in Centre Nationale de la Recherche Scientifique (CNRS), *Les Cyclades. Matériaux pour une étude de géographie historique*, Paris

French, D.H. (1966) 'Anatolian pottery in the Aegean area' in *AS* 16, 49-53
  (1967) 'Anatolian pottery in the Aegean area' in *AS* 17, 36

French, E. (1969) 'The first phase of LH IIIC' in *AA* 84, 133-6

French, E.B. and Wardle, K.A. (1987) (eds.) *Problems in Greek prehistory*, Bristol

Furumark, A. (1941) *The Mycenaean pottery: analysis and classification*, Stockholm
  (1950) 'The settlement at Ialysos and Aegean history c.1550 – c.1400 B.C.' in *Opuscula Archaeologica* 6, 150-271

Gale, N.H. (1978) 'Lead isotopes and Aegean metallurgy' in Doumas (ed.) 529-45
  (1980) 'Some aspects of lead and silver mining in the Aegean' in Doumas (ed.) 160-95

Gale, N.H. and Stos-Gale, Z.A. (1984) 'Cycladic metallurgy' in Macgillivray and Barber (eds.) 255-76

Gale, N.H., Papastamataki, A., Stos-Gale, Z.A. and Leonis, K. (1983) 'Copper sources and copper metallurgy in the Aegean Bronze Age' in *Proceedings of the 1982 British Museum symposium on early furnace technology*, London

Gale, N.H. and Stos-Gale, Z.A. (1981) 'Cycladic lead and silver metallurgy' in *BSA* 76, 169-224
  (1982) 'Bronze Age copper sources in the Mediterranean: a new approach' in *Science* 216, 11-19

Gallet de Santerre, H. and Tréheux, J. (1947-8) 'Rapport sur le dépôt Égéen et Géométrique de l'Artémision sur Délos' in *BCH* 71-2, 148-254

Gallet de Santerre, H. (1958) *Délos primitive et archaïque*, Paris

Gamble, C. (1978) 'The Bronze Age animal economy from Akrotiri: a preliminary analysis' in Doumas (ed.) 745-53
  (1979) 'Surplus and self-sufficiency in the Cycladic subsistence economy' in Davis and Cherry (eds.) 122-34
  (1982) 'Animal husbandry, population and urbanisation' in Renfrew and Wagstaff 161-71

Getz-Preziosi, P. (1977a) 'Early Cycladic stone vases' in Thimme (ed.) 95-108
  (1977b) 'Cycladic sculptors and their methods' in Thimme (ed.) 71-91
  (1979) 'The hunter/warrior figurine in Early Cycladic sculpture' in Davis and Cherry (eds.) 87-96
  (1984) 'Five sculptors in the Goulandris collection' in Fitton (ed.) 48-74

Hadjianastasiou, O. (forthcoming) 'A Late Neolithic settlement at Grotta, Naxos' in French and Wardle (eds.) (1987)

Hadjianastasiou, O. and Macgillivray, J.A. (forthcoming) 'An Early Bronze Age copper smelting site on the Aegean island of Kythnos' in J. Ellis Jones (ed.) *Ancient metallurgy and mining: acta of the British School at Athens centenary conference at Bangor, April 1986*, Bangor

Hägg, R. and Marinatos, N. (eds.) (1981) *Sanctuaries and cults in the Aegean Bronze Age* (Skrifter utgivna av Svenska institutet i Athen 28), Stockholm

Hägg, R. and Marinatos, N. (eds.) (1984) *The Minoan thalassocracy: myth and reality* (Skrifter utgivna av Svenska institutet i Athen 32), Stockholm

Hall, G., McBride, S. and Riddell, A. (1973) 'Architectural study (of Asvan)' in *AS* 23 245-69

Harland, J.P. (1924) 'Aegean (Bronze Age) chronology and terminology' in *AJA* 28, 69-72

Higgins, R.A. (1967) *Minoan and Mycenaean art*, London

Höckmann, O. (1977a) 'Cycladic religion' in Thimme (ed.) 37-52

(1977b) 'The Cyclades and their eastern neighbours' in Thimme (ed.) 155-63

(1977c) 'The Cyclades and the western Mediterranean' in Thimme (ed.) 163-72

(1978) 'Theran floral style in relation to that of Crete' in Doumas (ed.), 605-16

Hodges, H. (1976) *Artifacts*, London

Hogarth, D.G. and Bosanquet, R.C. (1899) 'Archaeology in Greece 1898-9' in *JHS* 19, 319-29

Hood, M.S.F. (1971) *The Minoans*, London

(1973) 'The eruption of Thera and its effects in Crete in Late Minoan I' in *Pepragmena G diethnous Kretologikou synedriou*, Vol. A (Athens), 111-18

(1978a) *The arts in prehistoric Greece*, Harmondsworth

(1978b) 'Traces of the eruption outside Thera' in Doumas (ed.) 680-98

(1984) 'A Minoan empire in the Aegean in the 16th. and 15th. centuries B.C.?' in Hägg and Marinatos (eds.) 33-7

(1986) 'Evidence for invasions' in Cadogan, G.A. (ed.) *The end of the Early Bronze Age in the Aegean* (Cincinnati Classical Studies 6) Cincinnati 31-68

Hooker, J.T. (1976) *Mycenaean Greece*, London

Huxley, G.L. (1968) *Minoans in Greek sources*, Belfast

Iakovides, Sp. (1969-70) *Perati: to nekrotapheion I-III*, Athens

Immerwahr, S.A. (1977) 'Mycenaeans at Thera: some reflections on the paintings from the West House' in Kinzl, K.H. (ed.) *Greece and the Eastern Mediterranean in Ancient History and Prehistory*, Berlin, 173-91

Jacobsen, T.W. (1981) 'The beginning of settled village life in Greece' in *Hesperia* 50, 303-19

Johnston, P.F. (1982) 'Bronze Age Cycladic ships' in *Temple University Aegean Symposium* 7 (Philadelphia), 1-8

Jones, R.E. (1978) 'Composition and provenance studies of Cycladic pottery with particular reference to Thera' in Doumas (ed.) 471-82

(1985) *Greek and Cypriot pottery: a review of scientific studies*, Athens

Kaloyeropoulou, A. (1971) *Acta of the first international scientific congress of the volcano of Thera*, Athens

Kardara, C. (1977) *Aplomata Naxou: kineta euremata taphon A kai B*, Athens

Koehl, R.B. (1984) 'Observations on a deposit of LC IIIC pottery from the Koukounaries akropolis on Paros' in Macgillivray and Barber (eds.) 207-24

Kolodny, E.Y. (1974) *La population des îles de la Grèce I-III*, Aix en Provence

Kondoleon, N.M. (1958) 'Anaskaphai Naxou' in *PAE* 228-9

(1959) 'Anaskaphai Naxou' in *PAE* 180-7

(1961) 'Mykenaike Naxos' in *Epeteris Etaireias Kykladikon Meleton* I 600-8 (Athens 1961-)

Lambrinoudakis, B.K. (1970) 'Anaskaphes Naxou' in *PAE* 249-54

Levi, D. (1955-6) 'Atti della scuola' in *Ann* 33-4, 292-303

Luce, J.V. (1969) *The end of Atlantis*, London

(1976) 'Thera and the devastation of Minoan Crete: a new interpretation of the evidence' in *AJA* 80, 9-16

(1978)'The chronology of the LM I destruction horizon in Thera and Crete' in Doumas (ed.) 785-96

McCoy, F.W. (1982) 'Climatic change in the Mediterranean during the past 240,000 years' in Doumas (ed.) 79-100

Macgillivray, J.A. (1980) 'Mount Kynthos in Delos: the Early Cycladic settlement' in *BCH* 104, 3-45

    (1981) 'Early Cycladic potters' marks from Mount Kynthos in Delos' in *BCH* 105, 615-21

    (1983) 'On the relative chronologies of Early Cycladic IIIA and Early Helladic III' in *AJA* 87, 81-3

    (1984a) 'Cycladic jars from Middle Minoan III contexts at Knossos' in Hägg and Marinatos (eds.), 153-8

    (1984b) 'The relative chronology of Early Cycladic III' in Macgillivray and Barber (eds.) 70-7

Macgillivray, J.A. and Barber, R.L.N. (eds.) (1984) *The prehistoric Cyclades*, Edinburgh

Maffre J.-J. (1972) 'Collection de l'École Française d'Athènes: III. Céramique' in *BCH* 96, 21-72

Marangou, L. (1984) 'Evidence for the Early Cycladic period on Amorgos' in Fitton (ed.) 99-115

Marinatos, N. (1983) 'The West House at Akrotiri as a cult center' in *AM* 98, 1-19

    (1984a) 'Minoan threskeiocracy on Thera' in Hägg and Marinatos (eds.) 167-78

    (1984b) *Art and religion in Thera*, Athens

Marinatos, S. (1968-76) *Excavations at Thera I-VII*, Athens

    (1970a) 'Anaskaphai Marathonos' in *PAE*, 5-28

    (1970b) 'Further discoveries at Marathon' in *AAA* 3, 349-66

    (1974) 'Das Schiffsfresko von Akrotiri' in Gray, D. 'Seewesen' (*Archaeologica Homerica* i G) 140-51

Marthari, M. (1980) 'Akrotiri, kerameike mesoelladikes paradoses sto stroma tes hephaisteiakes katastrophes' in *AE* 182-211

    (1983) 'Anaskaphe sto Ftello Theras (Periodos 1980)' in *AAA* 15, 86-101

    (1984) 'The destruction of the town at Akrotiri, Thera, at the beginning of LC I: definition and chronology' in Macgillivray and Barber (eds.) 119-33

Mee, C. (1982) *Rhodes in the Bronze Age*, Warminster

Meiggs, R. (1982) *Trees and timber in the ancient Mediterranean world*, Oxford

Mellink, M.J. (1956) 'The royal tombs at Alaca Huyuk and the Aegean world' in H. Goldman (ed.) *The Aegean and the Near East* (Locust valley) 39-58

Morgan, L. (1983) 'Theme in the West House paintings at Thera' in *AE* 85-105

    (1985) 'Idea, idiom and iconography' in P. Darque, J.-C. Poursat (eds.) *L'Iconographie Minoenne: table ronde de l'École Française d'Athènes, 21-2 Avril 1983* (Bulletin de Correspondence Hellénique Supplement 11), 5-19

Morgan Brown, L. (1978) 'The ship procession in the miniature fresco' in Doumas (ed.) 629-44

Mountjoy, P.A. (1984) 'The Mycenaean III pottery from Phylakopi' in Macgillivray and Barber (eds.) 225-40

    (1985) 'The pottery' in Renfrew 151-208

Mouseio Benaki (1978) *Paradosiakes kalliergies*, Athens. (Benaki Museum, *Traditional methods of cultivation in rural Greece*. In Greek, with substantial English summary).

Muhly, J.D. (1973) *Copper and tin: the distribution of mineral resources and the nature of the metals trade in the Bronze Age*, New Haven. (Transactions of the Connecticut Academy of Arts and Sciences, Vol. 43), with Supplement in Vol. 46 (1976) 77-136

Mylonas, G.E. (1959) *Aghios Kosmas: an Early Bronze Age settlement and cemetery in Attica*, Princeton

(1973) *O taphikos Kyklos B ton Mykenon*, Athens

Naval Intelligence Division (1944-5) *Greece* I-III, (Geographical Handbooks Series)

Negbi, O. (1978) 'The miniature fresco from Thera and the emergence of Mycenaean art' in Doumas (ed.) 645-56

Niemeier, W.D. (1980) 'Die Katastrophe von Thera und die spätminoische Chronologie' in *JdI* 95, 1-76

Ninkovitch, D. and Heezen, B. C. 'Santorini tephra' in *Colston Research Society Papers* (Bristol) 17, 413-52

Orlandos, A.K. (1960) *To ergon tes Archaiologikes Etaireias kata to 1960*, Athens

(1972) *To ergon tes Archaiologikes Etaireias kata to 1972*, Athens

(1975) *To ergon tes Archaiologikes Etaireias kata to 1975*, Athens

Otto, B. (1977) 'The ornamental motifs of the Cycladic Neolithic and Early Bronze Ages' in Thimme (ed.) 129-41

Oustinoff, E. (1984) 'The manufacture of Cycladic figurines: a practical approach' in Fitton (ed.) 38-48

Ovenden, M.W. (1966) 'The origin of the constellations' in *The Philosophical Journal* 3, no. 1 (Jan.) 1-18

Overbeck, G.F. (1984) 'The development of grave types at Ayia Irini, Kea' in Macgillivray and Barber (eds.)

Overbeck, J.C. (1982a) *The Bronze Age pottery from the kastro of Paros* (Privately circulated text of paper read to the Archaeological Institute of America on 29 December 1982)

(1982b) 'The hub of commerce: Keos and Middle Helladic Greece' in *Temple University Aegean Symposium* 7 (Philadelphia) 38-49

(1984) 'Stratigraphy and ceramic sequence in Middle Cycladic Ayia Irini, Kea' in Macgillivray and Barber (eds.) 108-13

Overbeck, J.C. and G.F. (1979) 'Consistency and diversity in the Middle Cycladic era' in Davis and Cherry (eds.), 106-12

Page, D.L. (1970) *The Santorini volcano and the destruction of Minoan Crete* (Society for the Promotion of Hellenic Studies Supplementary Paper 12), London

Palyvou, C. (1984) 'The destruction of the town at Akrotiri, Thera, at the beginning of LC I: rebuilding activities' in Macgillivray and Barber (eds.) 134-47

Papadopoulou, Ph. (1965) 'Kyklades (Melos, Kimolos, Naxos)' in *ADelt* 20, 508-22

Papathanasopoulos, G.A. (1961-2) 'Kykladika Naxou' in *ADelt* 17, Meletai, 104-51

Papavasileiou, G.A. (1910) *Peri ton en Euboia archaion taphon*, Athens

Pecorella, P.E. (1984) *La cultura preistorica di Iasos in Caria* (Archeologica 51, Missione Archeologica Italiana di Iasos I), Rome

Perlès, C. (1973) 'The chipped stone' in Jacobsen, T.W. *et al.* 'Excavations in the Franchthi cave, 1969-71: part 1' in *Hesperia* 42, 72-82

(1979) 'Des navigateurs méditerranéens il y a 10,000 ans' in *La Recherche* 10, 82-3

Petruso, K. M. (1978) 'Lead weights from Akrotiri: preliminary observations' in Doumas (ed.) 547-53

(1979) 'Reflections on Cycladic and Minoan metrology and trade' in Davis and Cherry (eds.)

Philippaki, B. (1973) 'E akropolis tou Ayiou Andreou Siphnou' in *AAA* 6, 93-103

(1977) 'Anaskaphe Ayiou Andreou Siphnou' in *PAE* 357-60

Pichler, H. and Friedrich, W.L. (1980) 'The mechanism of the Minoan eruption of Santorini' in Doumas (ed.) 15-30

Plassart, A. (1928) *Les sanctuaires et les cultes du Mont Cynthe* (Explorations Archéologiques de Délos 11), Paris

Popham, M.R. (1963) 'Two Cypriot sherds from Crete' in *BSA* 58, 89-93

(1967) 'Late Minoan pottery: a summary' in *BSA* 62, 337-51

(1980) 'Cretan sites occupied between c. 1450 and 1400 B.C.' in *BSA* 75 163-7

Popham, M. and Milburn, E. (1971) 'The Late Helladic IIIC pottery of Xeropolis (Lefkandi): a summary' in *BSA* 66, 333-52

Popham, M. and Sackett, L.H. (eds.) (1968) *Excavations at Lefkandi, Euboea 1964-66. A preliminary report*, London

Poursat, J.-C. 'Ivoires de l'Artémision: Chypre et Délos' in *BCH* Supplement 1, 415-25

Rackham, O. (1978) 'The flora and vegetation of Thera and Crete before and after the great eruption' in Doumas (ed.) 755-64

Rapp, G. and Kraft, J.C. (1978) 'Aegean sea level changes in the Bronze Age' in Doumas (ed.) 183-94

Renaudin, L. (1922) 'Vases préhelléniques de Thera à l'École Française d'Athènes' in *BCH* 46, 113-59

Renfrew, C. (1964) 'Crete and the Cyclades before Rhadamanthus' in *KrChron* 18, 107-41

(1967) 'Cycladic metallurgy and the Aegean Early Bronze Age' in *AJA* 71, 1-20

(1969) 'The development and chronology of the Early Cycladic figurines' in *AJA* 73, 1-32

(1972) *The emergence of civilisation: the Cyclades and the Aegean in the third millennium B.C.*, London

(1978a) 'The Mycenaean sanctuary at Phylakopi' in *Antiquity* 52, 7-15

(1978b) 'Phylakopi and the Late Bronze I period in the Cyclades' in Doumas (ed.) 403-21

(1979) 'Terminology and beyond' in Davis and Cherry (eds.) 51-63

(1981a) 'The sanctuary at Phylakopi' in Hägg and Marinatos (eds.) 67-80

(1981b) 'Questions of Minoan and Mycenaean cult' in Hägg and Marinatos (eds.) 27-33

(1982) 'Bronze Age Melos' in Renfrew and Wagstaff (eds.) 35-44

(1984) 'Speculations on the use of Early Cycladic sculpture' in Fitton (ed.) 24-30

(1984) 'From Pelos to Syros: Kapros Grave D and the Kampos group' in Macgillivray and Barber (eds.) 41-54

(1985) *The archaeology of cult. The sanctuary at Phylakopi* (British School at Athens Supplementary Volume 18) London

Renfrew, C., Cann, J.R. and Dixon, J.E. (1965) 'Obsidian in the Aegean' in *BSA* 60, 225-47

Renfrew, C. and Peacey, J.S. (1968) 'Aegean marble; a petrological study' in *BSA* 63, 45-66

Renfrew, C. and Brice, W. (1977) 'A Linear A tablet fragment from Phylakopi in

Melos' in *Kadmos* 16, 111-19

Renfrew, C. and Wagstaff, M. (1982) *An island polity: the archaeology of exploitation in Melos*, Cambridge

Renfrew, J.M. (1982) 'Early agriculture in Melos' in Renfrew and Wagstaff (eds.) 156-60

Ross, L. (1840-52) *Reisen auf dem griechischen Inseln des Ägäischen Meeres*, Stuttgart and Tübingen

Rubensohn, O. (1917) 'Die praehistorischen und frügeschichtlichen Funde auf dem Burghügel von Paros' in *AM* 17, 1-96

Rutter, J.B. (1983) 'Some observations on the Cyclades in the later third and early second millennium' in *AJA* 87, 69-76

   (1984) 'The Early Cycladic III gap' in Macgillivray and Barber (eds.) 95-107

Sakellarakis, J. (1972) 'Anaskaphe Archanon' in *PAE*, 310-53

   (1975) 'Anaskaphe Archanon' in *PAE*, 255-321

   (1977a) 'The Cyclades and Crete' in Thimme (ed.) 145-54

   (1977b) 'Ta kykladika stoicheia ton Archanon' in *AAA* 10, 93-115 (with English summary)

Sakellariou, A. (1980) 'The West House miniature frescoes' in Doumas (ed.) 147-53

Sampson, A. (1983) 'O protoelladikos oikismos kai to nekrotapheio tes Manikas Chalkidos' in *Archaiologia* 6 (Feb.), 69-76

Sapouna-Sakellarakis, E. (1977) 'Cycladic jewellery' in Thimme (ed.) 123-9

Schachermeyer, F. (1976) *Die Agäische Frühzeit I*, Vienna

Schilardi D.U. (1979) 'The destruction of the Mycenaean citadel at Koukounaries on Paros' in Davis and Cherry (eds.) 158-79

   (1984) 'The LH IIIC period at the Koukounaries acropolis on Paros' in Macgillivray and Barber (eds.) 184-206

Schofield, E. (1979) 'Kea and its Aegean connections in the Late Bronze Age' in *BICS* 26, 132

   (1982) 'The western Cyclades and Crete: a "special relationship"' in *Oxford Journal of Archaeology* 1, 9-25

   (1984) 'Destruction deposits of the earlier Late Bronze Age from Ayia Irini, Kea' in Macgillivray and Barber (eds.) 179-83

Scholes, K. (1956) 'The Cyclades in the Later Bronze Age: a synopsis' in *BSA* 51, 9-40

Shaw, J.W. (1971) 'Minoan architecture: materials and techniques' in *Ann* 49, 5-256

   (1978) 'Consideration of the site of Akrotiri as a Minoan settlement' in Doumas (ed.) 429-36

Shaw, J.W. *et al.* (1977) 'Excavations at Kommos (Crete) during 1976' in *Hesperia* 46, 199-240

Shelford, P. *et al.* (1982) 'The sources and characterisation of Melian obsidian' in Renfrew and Wagstaff 182-92

Sherratt, E.S. (1980) 'Regional variation in the pottery of Late Helladic IIIB' in *BSA* 75, 175-202

Stephanos, M.C. (1905) 'Les tombeaux prémycéniens de Naxos' in *Comptes rendus du congrès international d'archéologie* (Athens), 216-25

   (1908) 'Anaskaphikai ergasiai en Naxo' in *PAE* 114-17

Theochares, D.R. (1951a) 'Anaskaphai en Palaia Kokkinia, Peiraios' in *PAE*, 93-127

   (1955) 'Neoi Kykladikoi taphoi en Attike' in *Neon Athenaion* 1, 283-92

(Athens 1955-)

(1973) *Neolithic Greece*, Athens

Thimme, J., (1965) 'Die religiose Bedeutung der Kykladenidole' in *Antike Kunst* 8, 72-86

(1977) (ed.) *Art and culture of the Cyclades*, Karlsruhe

Topp, C. and Plantalomor, L. (1983) 'The Cycladic beaked jug supposedly found in Minorca' in *Bulletin of the Institute of Archaeology, University of London* 20, 155-67

Torrence, R. (1979) 'A technological approach to Cycladic blade industries' in Davis and Cherry (eds.) 66-86

(1982) 'The obsidian quarries and their use' in Renfrew and Wagstaff (eds.) 193-221

(in prep.) *The chipped stone from Ayia Irini* (Keos series)

Tsountas, Ch. (1898) 'Kykladika' in *AE*, 137-212

(1899) 'Kykladika II' in *AE*, 73-134

Turner, J. (1978) 'The vegetation of Greece during prehistoric times – the palynological evidence' in Doumas (ed.) 765-73

Varoucha, E.A. (1925-6) 'Kykladikoi taphoi tes Parou' in *AE*, 98-114

Vermeule, E.T. (1964) *Greece in the Bronze Age*, Chicago

Wagner, G.A. and Weisberger, G. (1979) 'The ancient silver mines at Ayios Sostis on Siphnos' in *Archaeophysika* 10, 209-22

Wagner, G.A., Gentner, N., Gropengeisser, M. and Gale N.H. (1980) 'Early Bronze Age lead-silver mining and metallurgy in the Aegean: the ancient workings on Siphnos' in P.T. Craddock (ed.) *Scientific studies in early mining and extractive metallurgy* (British Museum Occasional paper 20), London, 63-86

Wagstaff, J.M. and Augustson, S. (1982) 'Traditional land use' in Renfrew and Wagstaff (eds.) 106-33

Wagstaff, J.M. and Cherry, J.F. (1982a) 'Settlement and population change'in Renfrew and Wagstaff (eds.) 136-55

(1982b) 'Settlement and resources' in Renfrew and Wagstaff (eds.) 246-63

Wagstaff, J.M. and Gamble, C. (1982) 'Island resources and their limitations' in Renfrew and Wagstaff (eds.) 95-105

Warren, P.M. (1969) *Minoan stone vases* (Cambridge Classical Studies), Cambridge

(1978) 'The unfinished red marble jar at Akrotiri, Thera' in Doumas (ed.) 555-68

(1979a) 'The stone vessels from the Bronze Age settlement at Akrotiri, Thera' in *AE* 82-113

(1979b) 'The miniature fresco from the West House at Akrotiri, Thera, and its Aegean setting' in *JHS* 99, 115-29

(1980) 'Problems of chronology in Crete and the Aegean in the third and earlier second millennium B.C.' in *AJA* 84, 487-99

(1981a) 'Knossos and its foreign relations in the Early Bronze Age' in *Pepragmena tou D diethnous Kretologikou synedriou (Herakleion. 29 Augoustou-3 Septembriou 1976) A2*, 628-37 (Athens)

(1984) 'The place of Crete in the thalassocracy of Minos' in Hägg and Marinatos (eds.) 39-44

Weinberg, S.S. (1965) 'The relative chronology of the Aegean in the Stone and Early Bronze Ages' in R.W. Ehrich (ed.) *Chronologies in Old World Archaeology* 285-320, Chicago

(1977) 'The Cyclades and mainland Greece' in Thimme (ed.), 142-44

Weinstein, M. (1973) 'Household structures and activities (in Asvan)' in *AS* 23, 271-6

Wheeler, T.S. (1974) 'Early Bronze Age burial customs in western Anatolia' in *AJA* 78, 415-25

Wiener, M.H. (1984) 'Crete and the Cyclades in LM I: the tale of the conical cups' in Hägg and Marinatos (eds.) 17-26

Williams, D.F. (1978) 'A petrological examination of pottery from Thera' in Doumas (ed.) 507-14

Wilson, D.E. and Eliot, M. 'Ayia Irini III: the last phase of occupation at the EBA settlement' in Macgillivray and Barber (eds.) 78-87

Wolters, P. (1891) 'Marmorkopf aus Amorgos' in *AM* 16, 46-58

Xanthoudides, St. (1918) 'Megas protominoikos taphos Pyrgou' in *ADelt* 4, Chronika, 136-70

Zapheiropoulos, N.S. (1965) 'Archaiotetes kai mnemeia Kykladon (Naxos, Delos, Keos, Paros, Tenos)' in *ADelt* 20, 505-8

Zapheiropoulou, Ph. (1984) 'The chronology of the Kampos group' in Macgillivray and Barber (eds.) 31-40

Zervos, C. (1957) *L'art des Cyclades du début à la fin de l'âge du bronze*, Paris

Zschietzschmann, W. (1935) 'Kykladenpfannen' in *AA*, 652-68

Index

Abbreviations:
LN	Late Neolithic	LH	Late Helladic
EC	Early Cycladic	LM	Late Minoan
MC	Middle Cycladic	EBA	Early Bronze Age
LC	Late Cycladic		

References in *italic* type are to figure numbers. All other references are to page numbers. In some of the longer entries, more important page references appear in **bold** type.